AFTER NEWSPEAK

AFTER NEWSPEAK

*Language Culture and Politics
in Russia from Gorbachev to Putin*

MICHAEL S. GORHAM

CORNELL UNIVERSITY PRESS
ITHACA AND LONDON

First published 2014 by Cornell University Press
First printing, Cornell Paperbacks, 2014
Printed in the United States of America

Library of Congress Cataloging-in-Publication Data

Gorham, Michael S., author.
   After Newspeak : language, culture and politics in Russia from Gorbachev to Putin / Michael S. Gorham.
      pages cm
   Includes bibliographical references and index.
   ISBN 978-0-8014-5262-8 (cloth : alk. paper)
   ISBN 978-0-8014-7926-7 (pbk. : alk. paper)
   1. Language policy—Russia (Federation) I. Title.
   P119.32.R8G667   2014
   306.44'947—dc23   2013038096

Cornell University Press strives to use environmentally responsible suppliers and materials to the fullest extent possible in the publishing of its books. Such materials include vegetable-based, low-VOC inks and acid-free papers that are recycled, totally chlorine-free, or partly composed of nonwood fibers. For further information, visit our website at www.cornellpress.cornell.edu.

Cloth printing   10   9   8   7   6   5   4   3   2   1
Paperback printing   10   9   8   7   6   5   4   3   2   1

For Natalie Peter Gorham (1935–2005)

CONTENTS

PREFACE

If members of the sixth convocation of Russia's lower house of parliament, the State Duma, were at all chastened by the wave of protests that followed their contested election in December 2011, one could hardly tell, judging by the raft of new legislation they proposed in the first year of their new term. Draft laws restricting the consumption of tobacco and alcohol, prohibiting the defamation of the Russian Orthodox Church, banning the propagandizing of homosexual activity, applying the Soviet-era label of "foreign agent" to NGOs that received funds from outside of Russia, authorizing the creation of "black lists" of Internet sites promoting drugs, suicide, and child pornography, and banning Americans from adopting Russian orphans—to list just a few—all came before the legislative body and were approved with minimal debate. As a result of the extraordinary productivity, critics nicknamed the Duma "the out-of-control printer" (*vzbesivshiisia printer*).

Tucked among the proposals were draft amendments to an existing law "On the State Language," which, if approved, would impose fines for the use of foreign words in official settings where adequate Russian equivalents were available. The author and chief public promoter of the amendments was Vladimir Zhirinovskii, the flamboyant, gilded-tongued leader of Russia's Liberal Democratic Party (neither liberal nor democratic in its policy leanings). Known for his own salty speech turns (and a one-time defender of Russian obscenities), Zhirinovskii defended the provisions by claiming, "We've been inundated, tortured by these Americanisms. We'll introduce a bill and provide a list of words that must not be used when there are normal Russian words" (Romashkova 2013). In keeping with a long line of Russian linguistic purists and patriots, he went on to offer a glossary of target loan words, accompanied by their more organic Russian equivalent. If Zhirinovskii had his way, officials would no longer be able to use *boifrend* (boyfriend)*, menedzher* (manager), or even the more broadly accepted *kul'tura* (culture) and *mashina* (car), and would need to retrain their tongues to produce more Slavic-sounding equivalents, respectively: *polumuzh, upravliaiushchii, dukhotvorstvo,* and *dvigalo* ("Vladimir Zhirinovskii...." 2013; "V Gosdumu vnesli...." 2013).

It is easy to smirk at these half-baked expressions of linguistic patriotism, but they come about with such great historical regularity—particularly in the cultural history of the Russian language—that their persistent presence raises a number of questions that lie at the core of this book. Why do matters of language norms become such potent markers of symbolic authority, particularly during times of radical political and social change? Who are the main power brokers in debates over linguistic change, and what real impact do they have on common attitudes toward proper and improper forms of writing and speech? Is there any logic or likely evolution to popular attitudes toward language? To what degree are these phenomena linked to a specific national tradition? And, if there are such nationally specific links, what can trends in attitudes toward language tell us about the shifting attitudes toward broader issues, such as what it means to be "Russian" in the first place?

After Newspeak offers a cultural history of the Russian language from Gorbachev and glasnost to Putin and the emergence of Web 2.0 technologies. Beginning with the premise that language both shapes and is shaped by periods of radical change, I document the role and fate of the Russian language in the collapse of the Soviet Union and the decades of reform and national reconstruction that followed. Using tools from cultural studies, sociolinguistics, and new media studies, I map out the shifting contours of Russian language culture over twenty-five years of transition and investigate, more broadly, the fundamental role that language—and discourse on language—play in charting new models of authority and national identity. Be it in the mass publication of dictionaries of profanity, the burgeoning industry of linguistic self-help, the colorful speech turns of authoritative heads of state, the populist turns of blogging bureaucrats, or programs promoting the propagation of Russian in the so-called near abroad, language and politics are inextricably intertwined. Throughout the book I consider three central forces underlying this awkward relationship: language ideologies, linguistic economies, and communication technologies. In doing so, *After Newspeak* reveals a mix of global, postcommunist, and specifically Russian trends that have emerged in the aftermath of the Soviet Union's demise.

ACKNOWLEDGMENTS

While the bulk of this book was written on American soil, much of the creative and scholarly impetus for it came from Europe, where historically more attention has been devoted to matters of language in political and cultural contexts. Norway, in particular, has served as my scholarly home away from home for the research, primarily thanks to the generous support of the Norwegian Research Council for two working groups that met during most of the book's conception and realization—"Landslide of the Norm: Linguistic Liberalization and Literary Development in Russia in the 1920s and 1990s" (2005–2008), and "The Future of Russian: Language Culture in the Era of New Technology" (2008–2012). I am therefore most indebted to the mastermind of these projects, Professor Ingunn Lunde of the University of Bergen, without whose foresight, leadership, and friendship over the past nine years this book would simply not have been possible. I am also grateful to international scholars who were regular co-participants in these endeavors—Aleksandrs Berdicevskis, Karin Grelz, Gasan Gusejnov, Daniela Hristova, Elena Markasova, Martin Paulsen,

Tine Roesen, Ellen Rutten, Lara Ryazanova-Clarke, Irina Sandomir-skaja, Henrike Schmidt, Dirk Uffelmann, Susanna Witt, Alexei Yurchak, Ljudmila Zubova, and Vera Zvereva—as well as those who made cameo, but memorable, contributions: Natalia Fateeva, Eugene Gorny, Stephen Hutchings, Ilya Kukulin, Roman Leibov, and Daniel Weiss. I would also like to thank colleagues at home and abroad who provided additional time and audiences for sections of this book through special invitations, readings, or publications: Per-Arne Bodin, Craig Brandist, Helena Goscilo, Stefan Hedlund, Catriona Kelly, Elena Namli, Catharine Nepomnyashchy, Lara Ryazanova-Clarke, Aleksei Shmelev, Elena Shmeleva, Vlad Strukov, Dirk Uffelmann, Curt Woolhiser, and Vera Zvereva.

Colleagues at the University of Florida have likewise provided note-worthy support over the years, particularly Alena Aissing for her outstanding (and too-often-underappreciated) work as Slavic bibliographer behind the scenes. And I am extremely thankful to Helena Goscilo and Eliot Borenstein for their careful readings of the manuscript in its final stages of production, as well as to John Ackerman, Karen Laun, Susan Barnett, and Mary Petrusewicz at Cornell University Press for their expert efforts in shepherding it through to publication.

This book incorporates material that appeared in "Natsiia ili Sniker-izatsiia?: Identity and Perversion in the Language Debates of Late- and Post-Soviet Russia," *Russian Review* 59 (October 2000): 614–29; "Vladimir Putin and the Rise of the New Russian Vulgate," *Groniek: Historisch Tijdschrift* (Netherlands) 39, no. 172 (2006): 297–307; "'Let's Speak Russian!': Monitoring and Norm Negotiation in the Electronic Media," in *From Poets to Padonki: Linguistic Authority and Norm Negotiation in Modern Russian Culture,* Slavica Bergensia 9, ed. Ingunn Lunde and Martin Paulsen (Bergen, Norway: Slavica Bergensia, 2009), 315–35; "Linguistic Ideologies, Economies, and Technologies in the Language Culture of Contemporary Russia (1987–2008)," *Journal of Slavic Linguistics* 17, nos. 1–2 (2009): 163–92; "Language Ideology and the Evolution of Kul'tura iazyka ('Speech Culture') in Soviet Russia," in *Politics and the Theory of Language in the USSR, 1917–1938,* ed. C. Brandist and Katya Chown (London: Anthem Press, 2010), 137–49; "Virtual Rusophonia: Language Policy as 'Soft Power' in the New Media Age," *Digital Icons: Studies in Russian, Eurasian, and Central European New Media* 5 (2011): 23–48; and "Language Culture and Identity in Post-Soviet Russia: Economies of *Mat,*" in *Soviet and Post-Soviet Identities,* ed. Mark Bassin and Catriona Kelly (Cambridge, UK: Cambridge University Press, 2012), 237–53, all included here with permission.

Finally, I give heartfelt thanks to my father, Bill Gorham, who has been a quiet role model in so many ways; to my children, Anna and Jakob, the source of endless opportunities for playful and loving distraction; and to Veronika Thiebach, whose companionship means the world to me every day. I dedicate this work to the memory of my mother, Nat Gorham, whose spark lives on in all of us.

NOTE ON TRANSLITERATION
AND TRANSLATIONS

Throughout this book I have used the Library of Congress system of transliteration for rendering Cyrillic text in the Latin alphabet, with the exception of proper names and concepts that have become widely recognized through alternative spellings in the West (e.g., Dmitry Medvedev, Aleksei Navalny, glasnost). All translations from the original Russian into English are my own, unless otherwise specified.

AFTER NEWSPEAK

INTRODUCTION

Ideologies, Economies, and Technologies of Language

> Не пройми копьем — пройми языком!
> [Pierce not with the sword, pierce with the tongue!]
>
> —RUSSIAN PROVERB
>
> Осла узнаешь по ушам, а дурака—по словам.
> [You can tell an ass by his ears and a fool by his words.]
>
> —RUSSIAN PROVERB

Political Correctness—Russian Style

Along with *kreativ* (creative [n.]), it was the curious term *politkonkretnost'* ("polit-concreteness") that received the dubious award of "antiword of the year" *(antislovo goda)* from a panel of linguists and literary critics appointed to name both the word and antiword of the year for 2007 (Epshtein 2008). (The honor of "word of the year" went to *glamur* [glamour].) Although a close structural cousin to *politkorrektnost',* a derivative of the English "political correctness," the term carries a subtly different meaning (and can be translated literally as "political concreteness"), more akin to what some believe to have been the very first manifestations of "political correctness," now long forgotten, in Mao's "correct thinking" and the Leninist "correct line-ism" (Suhr and Johnson 2003, 8–9; Hughes 2010, 60–63). In Mikhail Epshtein's words,

Politikonkretnost' is when, in politics, everything is determined in advance, such as duma elections or the election of the next president. Putin comes out in support of "United Russia," they get a majority, nominate a successor, and everyone votes for him. It can be added that recently the word *konkretnyi* has acquired broad popularity in such slang expressions as *konkretnyi patsan* (real [i.e., genuine] lad) [and] *konkretnyi muzhik* (real bloke).

Who are these politically concrete? Those who have declared and positioned themselves within the framework of the dominant politics. The chair of the election commission, who suggests that "the president cannot be incorrect" (a formula of papal infallibility). Cultural and sports leaders begging the president (out of personal love for him) to violate the constitution. Pedagogues and caregivers organizing a movement of young "bear cubs" (*mishki*) for the sake of victory for the "all-bear" cause. You sense the difference: in the West—political correctness, in Russia—political concreteness. (Epshtein 2008)

On a certain level, the English and Russian terms do share a common orientation—one critical of a certain political or social agenda and cognizant of the powerful role of language in establishing and imposing that agenda. An interesting corollary here is that both terms seem to be deployed chiefly by *opponents* of the phenomenon they are using it to describe. While in the earliest days of its use, the label "politically correct" was worn with a sense of pride by those who viewed it as a mark of open-minded, liberal distinction, the term, over time, has taken on a more critical, or at least ironic, coloring. Few self-respecting individuals nowadays would label themselves "PC" without at least a tinge of irony, just as few in the Russian context would willingly don the mantel of "*politkonkretnost'*" (Hughes 2010, 63–65).[1] But the *objects* of criticism are quite different: in one case, Left intellectuals who are themselves largely marginalized in American culture; in the other, establishment players who belong, or aspire to belong, to dominant power structures. One sees political correctness as an illness of an outgroup and threat to established belief systems, the other views *politkonkretnost'* as a malady of party insiders keen on reinforcing the status quo and thereby buttressing their own claim to its authority. One challenges the status quo, the other seeks to reinforce it. And yet the

---

1. In fact, Hughes argues that "uses of the abbreviation PC, which come later, are critical from the beginning" (2010, 64).

two do share one assumption central to my work: that language not only reflects but itself shapes perception, identity, reality; that how we name things and call people helps define not only their image and status in society, but our own as well. In their very differences, the two terms also reflect a second important assumption—that language, culture, and politics are closely intertwined and mutually dependent on one another for meaning.

What does the case of *politkonkretnost'*, as both term and phenomenon, tell us about the state of the linguistic and political culture in Russia today? Presuming that this term has actually "gone native" (a point to which I will return later), it reflects, by virtue of the transformation through translation outlined above, quite a different political culture and different dynamic of power relationships. In the American case, the rise of PC signals the growing influence of the Left and the discursive empowerment of marginal groups; in the Russian case, the emergence of *politkonkretnost'* suggests that, by the end of Putin's second presidential term, toeing the party line once again had come to hold political sway. One word (or nearly one word); two very different semantic functions and sociopolitical implications.

My basic premise about the mutual dependence of language, on the one hand, and culture, power, authority, and identity, on the other, has become something of a truism in contemporary scholarship. Burke (1987, 14) remarks that "language is constitutive of society (or culture) as well as being created by society;...it plays a central part in the social construction of reality." Cameron (1995) devotes an entire book to an examination of what she calls the "slippage" between discourse on language and talk about social values. And Gal and Woolard (1995, 129) write that "bounded and naturalized representations" of "cultural categories of communication, such as named languages, dialects, standards, speech communities and genres..." are "enacted and reproduced in familiar linguistic practices: Translation, the writing of grammars and dictionaries, the policing of correctness in national standards, the creation of linguistic and folklore collections or academies. The work of linguistic representation produces not only individualized 'speakers' and 'hearers' as the agents of communication, but also larger, imagined and emergent social groupings, including our focus here, 'publics.' Such representational processes are crucial aspects of power, figuring among the means for establishing inequality, imposing social hierarchy, and mobilizing political action." Closer to the Russian context, Ries (1997, 3) begins her study of Gorbachev-era oral narratives of suffering by claiming that "the discursive world does not merely reflect the world of more obvious social action, but also helps to construct it;...in talk, various conceptual patterns and value systems are encapsulated in narrative, even mythic form, comprising models for life as much as models of it."[2] Complementing Ries's work is Zvereva's (2012) study of "Net conversations" and the role that the Internet and social media play in offering Russian-language speakers new and innovative platforms for self-expression and communication.

The interrelationship has become commonly recognized in identity studies as well. Hall (1996, 4) has written that "precisely because identities are constructed within, not outside, discourse, we need to understand them as produced in specific historical and institutional sites within specific discursive formations and practices, by specific enunciative strategies." Joseph (2006) shows quite clearly how, despite the common assumption through history of language as an essential component of national identity, national languages (and "standard languages") are as imagined a construct as national identity itself.[3]

Assuming this to be the case, we must take quite seriously the notion that discussions about language—particularly during times of radical change—tend to be laden with implications—sometimes quite direct—for broader issues of national identity. The political correctness movement in American language culture is a good example of the link among issues of language, politics, and identity, as well as the ability of speakers to serve as agents of linguistic (and political, and social) change (Cameron 1990). As much as those on the political right like to mock it, it has in many ways changed not only the way Americans speak, but also social and political perceptions, attitudes, and policies toward the minority groups their verbal innovation seeks to remake.

The link between language change and politics is particularly acute during times of radical social change. In the context of his discussion of

---

2. This idea is not just recent, of course; examples of it in Russian thought date back at least to Pavel Florenskii, who wrote, "We treasure language as something objective, imposed on us by the conditions of life,... but we also recreate it when we speak—all the while continuing to believe in its objectivity" (quoted in Seifrid 2005, 99).

3. For an excellent discussion of the history of *literaturnyi iazyk* and the standard language debates in Russia, see Paulsen (2009, 66–91).

politics and language in the French revolution, Baker (1990, 6) notes the heightened impact of language's constitutive force: "Human agents find their being within language; they are, to that extent, constrained by it. Yet they are constantly working with it and on it, playing at its margins, exploiting its possibilities, and extending the play of its potential meanings, as they pursue their purposes and projects. Although this play of discursive possibility may not be infinite, in any given linguistic context, it is always open to individual and collective actors. By the same token, it is not necessarily controllable by such actors." In his own discussion of language and revolutionary politics in England, Crowley (1996, 183) writes that "national identity is not something which is fixed forever, an eternal set of values, but rather something which is often proposed at particular times of crisis as a way of negating difficulties. Which is to say that national identity is not something waiting to be discovered, but something which is forged. It is a weapon in particular types of discursive struggle, and though it is often represented monologically, it is in fact the site of great contestation" (see also Grillo 1989; Gustafson 1992; Gorham 2003).

With the idea that language at once helps shape and is shaped by culture and society as my underlying premise, the goals of this book are twofold: first, to offer, through a series of keyword analyses and case studies, a socially and politically contextualized history of contemporary Russian language culture, and, second, to examine the late- and post-Soviet political culture through the lens of language in order to offer an account of the major discursive trends and dominants. In this introduction, I outline more precisely the methodological tools and framework best suited for executing such a study.

Language Culture

I use the notion of "language culture" as one of my primary methodological frames for examining the broad range of linguistic attitudes and practices that enjoy more or less legitimacy, authority, and power, and thus have helped shape public writing and speech in late- and post-Soviet Russia. By no means a static concept, language culture is influenced by a mix of institutional, ideological, economic, and technological factors that are both complex and fluid.[4] When we study language culture we are looking at more than just the history of a literary language or the evolving guide-posts for proper language usage—although those are certainly worthy and intriguing focuses. We are also looking at linguistic attitudes and practices of the broadest range of language users, from the standard bearers of the cultural "elite" to the profanity-laden vernacular of the "streets," in all their stability or disorder, in all their institutional permutations. And we are looking at these attitudes and practices as reflections of and influences on broader cultural, social, political, and economic trends.

For example, many qualified language specialists in Russia, when asked to comment on the current state of the language—where the underlying assumption is that there is a major problem that demands attention—will begin their observations with an antiprescriptive statement essentially de-bunking purist laments over the "degradation of Russian," and argue in-stead that it is not the language, but rather the "low speech culture of its users" that is the root of the problem (Chudinov 2001; cf. Shmelev 2005). As the Russian linguist Maksim Krongauz (2007) put it, alluding to the title of his 2008 book, "It is not the language, but rather the speakers of the Russian language, who are on the verge of a nervous breakdown." While on the surface true enough, this response oversimplifies the matter by ignoring language's fundamental role in shaping social practices and thus serving, for better or worse, as a catalyst for social change. "Language culture," by virtue of its attention not only to the language production of speakers and writers at all levels of the social spectrum but also to their attitudes about the appropriate form and function of language, allows us to acknowledge this truism (about the problem resting with users, not the language), while still recognizing that there are many ways in which shifts in language use and attitudes toward language do matter. They matter not only for what they tell us about the language and its users per se but also for what they tell us about perceptions (some changing, some more stable)

---

4. My focus is primarily the language of the public sphere in Habermas's meaning of "a realm of our social life in which something approaching public opinion can be formed" (1974, 49), nowadays constituted primarily by newspapers, journals, radio, television, and the internet (cf. Anderson 1983). By "culture" I follow Sewell's definition of "the sphere devoted specifically to the production, circulation, and use of meanings. The cultural sphere may in turn be broken down into the subspheres of which it is composed: say, of art, music, theater, fashion, literature, re-ligion, media, and education. The study of culture, if culture is defined in this way, is the study of the activities that take place within these institutionally defined spheres and of the meanings pro-duced in them" (1999, 41)

of broader issues of identity and authority, and perhaps even their ability, through newly configured methods of articulation, to influence these perceptions themselves. As Williams ([1976] 1983, 22) put it, "some important social and historical processes occur *within* language, in ways which indicate how integral the problems of meanings and of relationships really are" (cf. Hunt 1984, 19–51). And it is at this level that language, and discussions about language, provides an instructive view of broader issues of power, authority, and national identity, particularly during times of radical change. In this regard, I am adopting a methodological approach described by Fairclough (2003, 23–24) as a "moderate form of 'social constructivism' [which] recognizes that discourses *may* construct and reconstruct social practices, social structures and social life, but which also recognizes that there are no guarantees of such constructive effects—the sedimentation of institutions and the habituses of people may make them resistant."[5]

Through the prism of "language culture" we can more readily acknowledge the fact that, despite the antiprescriptive stances traditionally assumed by many linguists and despite the derogatory if not mocking attitude of linguistic purists toward the phenomenon, PC has had a marked impact on language use and production in the United States, and language culture can help us to better understand the forces underlying that influence. Through the prism of language culture we can better understand why this same term—PC—in a similar meaning has not gained traction in post-Soviet Russia and has, instead, taken on both a form and meaning of its own that stand in marked contrast to the source term.[6] Through the prism of language culture, we can better recognize that, even though much of the "problem" lies with users and not language, the issue of usage is not a minor one and has significant ramifications for shaping public opinion and various levels of identity alike. Both terms—"political correctness" and *politkonkretnost'*—describe a particular sociopolitical reality or conflict and imply a particular ideological position with regard to that reality. Each also demonstrates the privileged role of linguists and intellectuals in general in defining or at least influencing the terms of engagement.

---

5. Emphasis mine. Much of this language, of course, goes back to Foucault's (1972) notion of "discursive formation," which he uses as a less charged and problematic heuristic than "ideology."

6. For an excellent discussion of the ambiguities of American political correctness when translated into Russian, see Guseinov 2012, 21–25.

Language Ideologies

How do we go about studying language culture and documenting the contours, trends, and shifts that give it shape? I would like to argue that the specific shape and tone of a language culture will change over time and depend largely on three types of forces—ideological, economic, and technological—for their specific configuration. First, let me discuss the notion of "language ideologies" or "linguistic ideologies" and their link to language culture.

I use the term "ideology" in this context to refer to what Postman (1992, 123) calls "a set of assumptions of which we are barely conscious but which nonetheless directs our efforts to give shape and coherence to the world." In the context of "language ideology," Woolard (1998, 10) tells us, "ideology" serves as a reminder that "the cultural conceptions we study are partial, interest-laden, contestable, and contested [and this] demands that we ask how seemingly essential and natural meanings of and about language are socially produced as effective and powerful." "Language ideologies," according to Gal and Woolard (1995, 130) in another discussion of the term, "are cultural conceptions of the nature, form and purpose of language, and of communicative behavior as an enactment of a collective order." Or, as Woolard puts it elsewhere (1998, 3–4), language ideologies are "representations, whether explicit or implicit, that construe the intersection of language and human beings in a social world," and "the cultural system of ideas about social and linguistic relationships." They consist of both deep-seated and overarching attitudes toward language and its appropriate forms and functions in society—attitudes that are reflected in some of the oldest institutions and traditions of a society and therefore can transmit a strong sense of authority, stability—even immutability.

Where do they come from? As is the case with most national language ideologies, those attitudes that enjoy sustained authority in the Russian language culture come from a variety of sources. Some of the more influential and productive of these would certainly include folklore in all its varieties, aphorisms or chapters from literary history that have come down through the ages as canonical statements about language and its appropriate form or function, the canonical history of the Russian literary language (given the role of such narratives in shaping present perceptions of events past), views on language from Russian theologians and representatives of the Orthodox Church, views on language in the Russian philosophical tradition, and everyday language mythology and folk linguistics. Attitudes may or may not have an identifiable historical or literary source, but may nevertheless be a part of common parlance or attitudes—such as "speaking without notes" (*govorit' bez bumazhki*), a compliment paid to both Gorbachev and Putin for their ability to speak without prepared, printed remarks. One could quite easily fill a book, if not volumes, with examples of the various sources, voices, trends, and temperaments of Russian language ideologies. Let me offer some examples from these areas just listed to give a sense of what I have in mind when I speak of them, and to get at least a glimpse of some of the dominant themes that might emerge from a more sustained study.

Russian Folklore

What is striking when one looks at the body of aphorisms, proverbs, and sayings relating to language is the palpable ambivalence and even negative attitudes they reflect toward spoken language in particular.[7] For all the positive allusions to language as a powerful weapon, as a vehicle for popular wisdom *(e.g., vox populi, vox dei),* or as a source of wealth and nourishment (see appendix, sections 1–3), one finds at least twice and closer to three times as many negative ones—particularly with regard to oral discourse (see appendix, sections 4–6). These include aphorisms about the danger, weakness, or immorality of loose, empty, improper, excessive, or boastful language, as well as sayings that convey the same negative attributes as they somehow celebrate verbal moderation, paucity, or restraint. And in the balancing act between action and words, the scales far more often tip in favor of the former (appendix, section 7).[8]

Russian Literature

In contrast to a marked ambivalence toward oral, everyday forms of discourse in Russian proverbs, canonical sayings from the Russian literary

---

7. The degree to which this is uniquely Russian is difficult to determine; while the frequency of suspicion may be more reflective of Russian language ideology, similar ambivalence toward the spoken word may be found in English in sayings such as "Actions speak louder than words" and "Empty vessels make the most noise."

8. While not all of the language-related proverbs are reproduced here, I have tried, in my selection, to make the list proportionally representative.

tradition most often depict language as a source of strength and national pride, particularly in times of trouble (see Ryazanova-Clarke 2006, 46–52). The most cited passage from this discourse on language as personal and national bulwark is Ivan Turgenev's 1882 rumination:

> In days of doubt, in days of burdensome reflections on the fate of my mother-land, you alone are my support and buttress, o great, mighty, just, and free Russian language (*velikii, moguchii, pravdivyi i svobodnyi russkii iazyk*)! Were it not for you, how would I not fall into desperation at the sight of all that is taking place at home. But it is impossible to believe that such a language was not given to a great people.... (Turgenev [1882] 1988, 174)[9]

One finds a similarly patriotic linguistic ideology, albeit of a more popu-list sort, in the famous passage from Nikolai Gogol's *Dead Souls*—a pas-sage that reflects the underlying tension between oral and written modes of communication as well as the author's own attempt at differentiating national linguistic ideologies: "The Russian people express themselves strongly!... The word of the Briton is evocative of knowledge of the ways of the heart and wise perception of life; the ephemeral word of the French-man sparkles and flies apart like a light dandy; the German intricately concocts his own smartly spare word, not accessible to all; but there is no word that is so dashing, spritely, that so expresses itself from the heart, that so boils and trembles, as the nimbly uttered Russian word" (Gogol' [1842] 1951, 108–9).

The Turgenev and Gogol' statements nicely reflect two strains of Rus-sian language ideology—one sacred and patriotic, the other more profane and popular—that appear in other institutions and are central to their generation, perpetuation, and codification. They also refer to two differ-ent understandings of the word "language"—language as canonized insti-tution (and lofty marker of national identity, in Saussurian [1993] terms, *langue*), and its imperfect manifestations when produced by the tongues of commoners (Saussure's *parole*)—the very object of aphoristic suspicion noted above.

---

9. Notable exceptions to this dominant trend include Fedor T'utchev's famous poem about the spoken thought being a lie ("*Mysl' izrechennaia est' lozh'*" [from "Silentium!" (1829)]).

History of Russian Literary Language

We see a different but parallel bifurcation in the discourse of the history of the Russian language, where linguists describe how the high Church Slavonic was introduced to bring sacred writing to the inhabitants of pagan Rus', who spoke a language (commonly referred to as East Slavonic or "Rusian" [Franklin 2002, 83–89]) so distinct from that of the Church as to constitute what Uspenskii (1994) argues was a completely separate language, and others such as Franklin (2002) more cautiously describe as a separate register. Peter the Great reformulated the distinction between "high" and "low" in his call for simple language and attacks against the "incomprehensible" language of the Church (here, the balance of power shifting toward the oral), and Mikhail Lomonosov offered yet another interpretation in his tripartite stylistic delineation of Russian at the end of the eighteenth century. In the debates between the "archaists" and "innovators" several decades later, Admiral Shishkov maintained a romantic view of language as "the spirit of the people" (*dukh naroda*) and fought for the preservation of Church Slavonic, whereas Nikolai Karamzin's ideal for the literary language was based on the spoken language of polite society. And, Soviet mythmaking aside, Aleksandr Pushkin lays claim as the founder or father of modern Russian language largely by virtue of his ability to synthesize these two traditional but long contentious ideologies of language (Zhivov 1996, 71–156).

Religious Perspectives

Religious and theological views on language-related issues, as might be suspected, placed heavy emphasis on the sanctity of the divine *logos,* with frequent references to the opening lines of the Gospel of John ("In the beginning there was the Word, and the Word was of God, and the Word was God"). Indeed it was largely due to its origins as a sacred language (and only that) that Church Slavonic stood out (in contrast to Latin) in this regard: "The Slavonic language," wrote the seventeenth-century monk Ioann Vishenskii, "through simple, diligent reading...leads to God....It was established, raised up and is protected...and the devil hates Slavonic" (quoted in Koniaev 2007). Here, too, when the focus shifts to the oral language, the tone of the discourse becomes more cautionary. Pick up one of the several contemporary Church-published books devoted to language (two of them bearing the ominous title taken from another popular aphorism, "My language is my enemy" *[Iazyk moi—vrag moi]*) and you will find sermons on a variety of verbal sins, ranging from "idle talk" (*prazdnoslovie*) and "verbosity" (*mnogoslovie*) to "blasphemy" (*bogokhul'stvo*) and "foul language" (*skvernoslovie*)—the last one being declared one of the biggest sins among the Russian people, made doubly dangerous by its widespread presence in public ("One might think that the air here in Russia is already infected with the cancer of shameful speech" [*iazva sramosloviia*]) (*Iazyk moi—vrag moi* 1998, 74). A similar volume reprints a sixth-century Byzantine exhortation by John Climacus on good and evil in their linguistic manifestations of "silence" *(molchanie)* and "wordiness" (*mnogoglagolanie*), respectively, a discourse reflective of the apophatic tradition in Russian culture that underscores the inexpressibility of the sacred:

> Wordiness is a sign of unreason, a door to slander, a guide to ridicule, a servant of falsehood, the extermination of loving emotion, an appeal for despondency, a precursor of sleep, the dissipation of attention, the extermination of loving preservation, a cooling of holy warmth, an obfuscation of prayer.
>
> Prudent silence is the mother of prayer, an appeal from mental captivity, a repository of the divine flame, a guardian of thought, a spy of enemies, a school for lamentation, a friend of tears, a laborer for the memory of death, a portrait artist for eternal suffering, a loving tester of the impending trial, a facilitator of redemptive grief, an enemy of impudence, the silence of spouses, an opponent of pedantry, the communion of reason, the creator of dreams, the imperceptible assumption, the secret ascension. (quoted in *Iazyk moi—vrag moi* 2000, 16)

Essence or Instrument?

Overall, one finds in the vast ideological store available to Russians two distinct perceptions of Russian: one as a tool, the other as an essence.[10] The essentialist view treats language as more of an abstract ideal (*langue*) that reflects innate features of "Russianness," whereas the instrumental view

---

10. In his essay "Identity in Language?" (2004), Boris Gasparov similarly distinguishes between "nominalist" and "realist" approaches to the issue of identity and language.

regards it more as a more concrete tool or weapon (*parole*) that can either be used adeptly by the tongue of the speaker ("Pierce not with the sword, pierce with the tongue!") or inadequately, if not dangerously ("You can tell an ass by his ears, a fool by his words"). The former is most commonly associated with the sacred canon of divine texts (literary or religious), and as such situated above, though not immune to, the corrupting influence of everyday discourse. The latter is most linked to language in its more direct and immediate instantiation—be it the revolutionary tongues of orators, prosecutors, and political leaders, or the imperfect, impure, corruptible speech of the tongue-tied masses. The tension between these two languages is built into the history of Russian (Church Slavonic vs. Rusian) and manifests itself throughout history—particularly during periods of radical change, such as that comprising the central focus of this book. And while one may detect manifestations of each at any given time, one can also witness in the course of language cultural history a general shifting in the overall authority—both symbolic and real—of each, depending on the broader level of stability in the culture and society in question. Revolutionary times ascribe greater import to language's instrumental capacity to break down and transform reality, whereas periods of restoration place more value in language's immutable, institutional function as a marker of identity and therefore stabilizing force, and regard with suspicion more discrete manifestations of verbal imperfection, resistance, or excess.

Given the breadth of attitudes they reflect toward the nature and function of language, one rightly wonders whether and why language ideologies are either useful or meaningful. There is no question, as the brief summary I have offered here attests, that we can and must only speak of language ideolog*ies* in the plural, that there is not, nor can there be, any single dominant immutable language ideology that dictates how Russians feel toward or use language. Instead, we have a weave of attitudes, sometimes competing, sometimes complementary, which at different times enjoy different levels of linguistic capital and authority. Moreover, different language ideologies can enjoy different levels of authority within different institutions (e.g., the Church, the Academy, the mass media, glossy youth magazines, the Internet), depending on what might be identified as institution-specific inclinations. And it is precisely for these reasons that other levels of analysis (namely, economic and technological) must be considered in any discussion of language culture. What can be said is that these extant language ideologies, by virtue of their active circulation in public discourse, provide a considerable degree of authority and legitimacy for a given attitude toward language. One merely need mention the phrase *velikii i moguchii* ("the great and mighty"—from the Turgenev passage quoted above) in a context remotely linked to language to garner nods of recognition, albeit in some cases nods of ironic recognition. They form a potent tradition of language attitudes that can be invoked to buttress claims and positions more grounded in immediate (and perhaps fleeting) issues and concerns.

The role and importance of linguistic ideologies as one powerful and nationally specific source of authority in determining the contours of a language culture can be seen more clearly through a contrastive lens. The experience with American English, in particular, offers an interesting contrast to the Russian case, precisely for its privileging of oral, colloquial speech over a more dense, written style. This preference has at least some roots in early American efforts to set themselves apart from their British heritage linguistically by promoting an American vernacular and drawing the link, through the nineteenth century, between patriotism and popular speech. The lexicographer Noah Webster stood at the forefront of the plain speech movement, arguing that the English language had been corrupted by the British aristocracy and praising folk language as proper idiom because "the usages of the common people retains more of the genius of the original language" (Baron 1982, 124, 151, 138).[11] Ironically, it was the views of the Englishman George Orwell that so influenced American linguistic ideologies in the twentieth century, particularly his satirical mocking of "newspeak" and his mistrust of jargon that fogs truth. The term has come to be associated with the cliché-ridden, duplicitous language of the Soviet state, but Orwell was quite clear that it posed equal threat to his own native tongue and political culture. "In our time," he quipped in his 1946 essay "Politics and the English Language," "political speech and writing are largely the defense of the indefensible." And on the perniciousness of euphemism in political language: "A mass of Latin words falls upon the facts like soft snow, blurring the outline and covering up all the details. The great enemy of clear language is insincerity." Orwell's more general intolerance for convoluted writing and speech was compounded by the

---

11. Not unlike in the Russian experience, American attempts at language purification generally failed (Baron 1982, 240–41).

tradition of American anti-intellectualism that placed priority of clarity and directness over the more opaque writing that tends to be the hallmark of academic writing (see Miller 2000).

Indeed, it is largely this same antipathy toward opaqueness and verbal innovation that fuels conservative intolerance for political correctness. Which brings us to the impact of politics on language, and more precisely, the politics of stability versus change. Be it in the discourse of the American or Bolshevik revolution, the political correctness movement or the Petrine reforms, it is no surprise that, when it comes to bringing about change in the status quo, we find a clear preference for more instrumental metaphors of language. Language becomes first and foremost a tool or weapon for tearing down old canons and building new ones. "Norms" become the object of suspicion and attack, be they institutional, behavioral, or linguistic. Just as Daniel Webster used plain speech as a call to arms against British heritage, so too did Vladimir Maiakovskii and other Russian Futurists call for tossing the "classics" overboard from the ship of modernity.

Concurrently, voices resistant to change or demanding stability in the wake of tumultuous political transformations naturally fall back on more essentialist discourses when invoking language to support their cause. Russian Orthodox representatives declared blasphemous Peter's successful attempts to rid the Russian alphabet of "arcane" letters, vestiges of outdated medieval Church writings (Zhivov 1996). Russian émigrés bemoaned the coarsening of the Russian language in the wake of the Bolshevik revolution, deeming the widespread growth of crudeness and illiteracy emblematic of the greater violence brought on Russian culture and society (Gorham 2003). Violations of language norms become potent symbols of a culture and society gone sadly astray, and discourses of restoration and protection serve as surrogate arguments for preserving or regaining a national identity that has been unwisely and unjustly abandoned. Both language and national identity are couched in organic, genetic, and ethical terms that make their abandonment all the more tragic, if not criminal.

Economies of Language

This ever-shifting dynamic between views of language as a weapon or tool and language as an essential marker of national identity can be seen throughout the late- and post-Soviet Russian language culture. The shift in the relative weight or value of the competing discourses can be best understood in economic terms. Language ideologies, though diverse and ultimately mutable, are still relatively stable and deeply rooted, less susceptible to transformation as a result of certain historical, social, or political forces. In order to better understand the nature and dynamic of a language culture, we have to consider economies of language that give value, symbolic or more concrete, to different ways of speaking and writing and thus influence the degree of power and authority they enjoy at a given point in time. The value of a certain language ideology or style will vary depending on a variety of market forces—again, both symbolic and more concrete. While underlying language ideologies do influence the relative value of a particular discourse, economies of language are more directly linked and influenced by shifting trends in a specific political, economic, and cultural context.

On the symbolic level, it is not by accident that economic metaphors frequently figure in to discourse on language. Whether touting a language's "richness" and "wealth" or bemoaning its "cheapening" or "devaluation," language mavens and folk linguists alike often turn to monetary symbolism to make their point. Goux (1990) argues that monetary metaphors are so prevalent in discourse on language because money and language share fundamental affinities that make their relationship not just analogically close but also, as he calls it, "isomorphic." "The term," he writes, "representing a concept, and the *coin,* representing a value, are both universal equivalents, resulting from similar dialectical processes." The congruity lies in the fact that both are representative sign systems that are commonly acknowledged as "general equivalents" to that which they signify and thus serve as forms of "exchange," which accounts for their formidable power and authority. Money gets its value for being a substitution for material worth or commodities; language, through its role as substitute for meaning (Goux 1990, 96, 2–3; cf. Goux 1999).[12] In a similar vein, Osteen and Woodmansee (1999, 22) note that "all metaphors are in a sense economic, since the etymology of 'metaphor' contains within it the concept of transfer or exchange."

---

12. Goux underscores the place here of "substitution," for herein lies the radical nature of the exchange that both systems represent.

Bourdieu (1991) has also adopted economic metaphors to account for the manner in which language, like other cultural categories or discursive fields, functions as a domain for the struggle for, production of, and consecration of power and authority. Particularly useful is his discussion of the "Economy of Linguistic Exchanges" and the manner in which competing discourses obtain and perpetuate their control over "linguistic capital," which itself constitutes a form of cultural authority. Symbolic authority, Bourdieu argues, is not engrained in the language itself but rather bestowed on the speaker or writer by institutions with the power to bestow it by means of mechanisms of production and reproduction (of legitimate language). Crises in language cultures (and political cultures, for that matter) arise when the relative authority of competing institutions of linguistic production and reproduction are contested.

Taking the perestroika era as a case in point, we can find examples of linguistic devaluation (in the decline in authority of the language of the Soviet state) and capital accumulation (in the rise in influence of the language of democratic systems and market-style economies). The value of the spoken word and forums such as public meetings and rallies eclipsed the importance of more staged and scripted party events, pamphlets, and decrees. By the late 1980s the discourse of the market and of democracy had largely eclipsed the language of the single party-state in the public sphere. While the media had not yet been relieved of state oversight and ownership, a shift in the policies and values that governed state demands of mass media shifted dramatically, to the extent that the main message coming from the Politburo's media head, Aleksandr Iakovlev, was, quite literally, "Write anything—just don't lie" (Zhirnov 2000). By the end of the 1980s it had reached the point where, as one observer put it, "the experienced television viewer of the 'perestroika era' could without difficulty determine the position of the authors of a given political program based on the speech stereotypes they used, including even the intonational particularities of the announcers" (Naidich 1995, 7). And at this point in the history of contemporary language culture, it was the more open, fast-paced, democratic—some would say brash and even vulgar—language of glasnost and *svoboda slova* (freedom of speech) that held a majority stake in the market of linguistic capital.

It is one of the primary theses of this book, more generally, that instrumental attitudes toward language acquire greater cultural capital during times of radical social and political change, that this process naturally leads to more rapid transformations of the language culture, which are, in turn, perceived as linguistic degradation or contamination by those more inclined to an essentialist view. And just as social transformations often face restorationist resistance, so too does language culture in transformation encounter purist cries of protest. The ongoing negotiation for authority between these two forces eventually leads to a period of perceived stability in the language culture, where language becomes less of a flash point for debate, revolt, or resistance, and various perspectives can coexist in relative peace.

Technologies of Communication

The success or failure of a given discourse on language depends not only on underlying ideologies of language and trends in cultural value, but also on its ability to be heard. The discourses of socialism and nationalism did not lose their cultural capital entirely among the general population in the early 1990s; they were simply overwhelmed by the market- and democratic-oriented discourses that dominated the mass media. And here is where the importance of the technologies of communication comes in. Beyond ideologies and economies (though not unrelated to them), technologies of communication are the methods and media by which various institutions responsible for language production and control—academies and schools, church and state, representatives from "low" and "high" culture, to name some of the more important—produce models of language and opinions and guidance about proper language usage. As students of the media from McLuhan (1964) to Baudrillard (1994) have shown, the power of the media not just to manipulate reality and our perception of it, but to create it as well, must not be underestimated.

In the midst of the heady new openness of the glasnost era, with new premiums on critical, unscripted, and democratic forms of expression (including giving more people access to the public airways), the purist laments of nationalists and patriots went relatively unnoticed, relegated as they largely were to academic conferences and low print-run journals and books. Shmelev (2005) has gone so far as to argue that it is not even the language users who had changed, as was suggested earlier, as much as the technologies responsible for producing and controlling public discourse: "The level of the speech culture of politicians and journalists has remained the same as before—it is just that earlier we had fewer opportunities to form an adequate impression of them.... In the Brezhnev years, we did not hear the spontaneous speech of Soviet leaders; it is impossible to draw any conclusions about the level of their speech culture when you are watching them reading from a script (*po bumazhke*)." Krongauz (2003) also points to the influence of perestroika-era mass media, but places the focus more on the inundation of the media by a new cadre of "dilettantes, people who were not just illiterate, unable to write or speak correctly, but who were principally uninterested in learning how." As a result, the media went from being a "guardian of literary norms to a destroyer of them."

As with economies of language, technologies of communication are also prone to shifts over time, particularly over the past two decades with the growing influence of television and the new media. Even from the Gorbachev era, when the print media were arguably the driving force behind social and political change, we have witnessed a massive shift in the balance of power among the various media available. While fewer people are bothering to read "thick journals" and even the more serious daily and weekly newspapers, television and, increasingly, the Internet have become the media most capable of transmitting models of language to the broadest audiences. Access to and smart use of electronic and digital media have proven instrumental in determining the value of one or another ideology, be it linguistic or political.

Which brings us full circle back to *politkonkretnost'*. As it turns out, the emergence of the word into broader circulation is largely due to its being actively *promoted* by linguists and philologists. The "word of the year" and "antiword of the year" awards came out of the Center for the Creative Development of the Russian Language, with Mikhail Epshtein serving as its academic director (the same Epshtein who penned the widely circulated announcement of the 2007 awards). The jury responsible for selecting the winners included prominent linguists and literary scholars such as Epshtein, Krongauz, Natal'ia Fateeva of the Academy of Sciences Russian Language Institute, and St. Petersburg University's Liudmila Zubova. When I contacted the Center's executive director, Ol'ga Glazunova, for leads on the origins of the term, I learned essentially that in *politkonkretnost'* we have a magnificent case documenting the role that language specialists themselves play—not just in the reflection or description of language culture but also the shaping process itself. For in her reply to my inquiry, Glazunova wrote:

> The word *politkonkretnost'* came to me after the deafening victory of United Russia in the elections [of December 2007—MSG]. I cannot say that I was disillusioned by this victory; we in Russia have long lived by the saying, "One does not seek kindness from kindness." Nevertheless, such unity cannot help but put one on one's guard, and here, again, our Russian history is "guilty."
>
> It was only later that Mikhail Epshtein checked the Internet and established that practically no one had used it prior to me. And he publicized it far and wide.[13]

Responding to a similar request for information, Epshtein referred me to his own websites and to Yandex searches that, according to him, produced over five hundred hits for the term and its adjectival formant. Most of these hits, as it turns out, are actually re-postings of Ephstein's own article on the awards.[14]

There do seem to be examples of usage orally and perhaps in blogs that reflect the meaning spelled out by Epshtein in his article (despite Glazunova's claim of having come up with the word herself). But there is no question the word has received a greater boost in attention thanks to the PR generated by the award. And there is no question, given the political and social context both Epshtein and Glazunova provide, that there are basic political reasons for its introduction and promotion.

Is this a case of lexical conspiracy on the part of a group of politically marginal (albeit influential) language specialists? No—and that is just the point. Though it may not be as conscious a process all the time, this is largely how language "happens." Linguists have as much right to attempt to tweak discourse (with the concurrent hope of tweaking reality) as politicians or anyone else possessing some semblance of linguistic capital and access to technology that can bring about that change. And Epshtein and company are not unique among philologists—we see it more often in

---

13. Personal correspondence, 28 April 2008.

14. Based on checks in June 2008, July 2009, and August 2012, a time period during which no trend of increased dissemination is evident.

purist attempts such as Aleksandr Solzhenitsyn's *Russian Dictionary of Language Expansion (Russkii slovar' iazykovogo rasshireniia,* 1990) an effort to revive and/or ratify language viewed as quintessentially Russian but on the verge of extinction.[15] In a sense, particularly given Glazunova's conscious political contextualization ("we in Russia have long lived…," "here, again, our Russian history is 'guilty'"), the case of *politkonkretnost'* is simply a more innovative, reform-oriented enactment of the canonical strains of Turgenev (usually rhetorical ammunition reserved for purists): "In days of doubt, in days of burdensome reflections on the fate of my motherland, you alone are my support and buttress, o great, mighty, just, and free Russian language!"[16]

Overview of Chapters

Whether a word, speech style, or linguistic trend takes on a life of its own, whether it earns, as it is often put by observers of language change, the "right to citizenship," will depend largely on the factors outlined above: the existence of overarching language ideologies that help create echoes of traditional support and a degree of legitimacy for the word, style, or trend; the particularities of market forces in the linguistic economy that will either boost their symbolic value or doom them to the bone pile of failed neologisms or jargons; and the appropriate technologies needed to ensure wide dissemination and eventual codification. In the following chapters I explore them more closely through a series of case studies of keywords and trends that have shaped contemporary Russian language culture and

---

15. Indeed, language creation is one of the core missions of the Center, according to its website: "The activity of the Center is constructive in nature and governed by the principle that, while nothing can be forced upon or forbidden of language, it is possible to develop models and methods for its revitalization that will subsequently be, to one degree or another, accepted and used by society, by the linguistic environment" ("Tsentr tvorcheskogo razvitiia russkogo iazyka," *Iazykovod,* http://yazykovod.ru/index.php?option=com_content&task=blogcategory&id=6&Itemid=38 [accessed 9 July 2013]).

16. In fact, Epshtein has spearheaded a more sustained effort to "enrich" contemporary Russian, which he views as having gone through an extended period of depletion, through the creation of new and useful words based on historic Russian roots. Both the underlying philosophy and the execution of the project may be examined in greater detail at the project website, *Dar slova* (Gift of the word), http://www.emory.edu/INTELNET/dar0.html (accessed 15 August 2012).

politics. In doing so, *After Newspeak* offers a cultural history of the Russian language from Gorbachev and glasnost to Putin and the emergence of Web 2.0 technologies, devoting particular attention to the close relationship between the politics of language and the language of politics.

I begin, in chapter 1, with an examination of two seemingly contradictory legacies of Soviet-era language culture—the so-called speech culture movement born in the push for developing "civilized behavior" (*kul'turnost'*) among citizens under Stalin, and the cliché-ridden official language of the Soviet state. If the first celebrated the classics of nineteenth-century Russian literature as the primary model for writing and speech, the second held up the ideology-laden rhetoric of Marxist-Leninist doctrine as the standard language of political practice. While the wooden structures of the latter seem to fly in the face of the former's purity and grace, each, as I show, embraces a top-down model of rhetorical authority that positions everyday citizen speakers and writers as subjects beholden to languages of power whose legitimacy rests with elite state-run institutions—be it the Academy of Sciences or the Politburo. The differences are more a reflection of their specific views of language—as an essence of Russianness in the academic and pedagogical context, as in instrument of power in the political.

Chapter 2 begins with a conceptual history of the notion of "glasnost" (which as a public relations term dates back to the beginning of the nineteenth century), devoting particular attention to how the built-in ambiguity of the notion both ensured the success of the policy and served as a rhetorical flash point in the battle between reform-minded democrats and members of the Soviet bureaucracy, or apparatchiks. Analyzing Gorbachev's own writings and speeches, leading party doctrinal publications and transcripts, and the contemporary print media, I trace the emergence of competing metaphors of language and speech. I conclude with a case study of two key political events in 1988 and 1989—the Nineteenth Communist Party Congress and the First Congress of People's Deputies—documenting how the rhetorical strategies of the vocal liberal minority managed to overwhelm the tongue-tied conservative majority and reshape the terms of debate.

Chapter 3 picks up the story after the collapse of the Soviet Union and concurrent devaluation of glasnost as a viable policy. The rise to power of Boris Yeltsin marked the ascendancy, instead, of "freedom of speech" (*svoboda slova*) as a dominant language ideology in post-Soviet language culture, largely a result of loosening state control of the leading technologies of communication. But while the lifting of censorship and control over the media led to new, more democratic styles of speaking and writing, it also undercut the cultural authority traditionally enjoyed by the Academy, the schools, and other institutions of speech culture and proper usage. In the new market-driven media climate, the literary language ceded cultural capital to speech styles laden with slang, vulgarity, and loanwords (referred to in loaded linguistic terms as "barbarisms"). And as the political and economic climate grew more troubled over the course of the 1990s, so too did the perception that "freedom of speech" was perhaps not all that it was cooked up to be, amounting at best to little more than a license to swear in public and, at worst, a crisis state of "linguistic lawlessness."

Much of the backlash against perceived threats to the standard literary language assumed the form of a linguist purism that saw a direct correlation between the "contamination" of the language and the broader degeneration of Russian national identity itself. In chapter 4 I begin by describing the varieties of purist discourse that were audible in the debates over language in the 1990s and show how genetic, historical, and ecological metaphors of language in these writings combined to project a vision of language identity that was essentially and indelibly linked to more general notions of Russian national identity, "language identity" (*iazykovaia lichnost'*), or "mentality" (*mentalitet, mental'nost'*). While never truly absent from public discourse, the purist voice, articulated in its earliest form in dictionary projects by Aleksandr Solzhenitsyn and others, enjoyed a resurgence of cultural capital as the legitimacy of "free speech" grew increasingly suspect. I then examine a concurrent and arguably more influential trend of linguistic self-monitoring that takes on increasing prominence in mass media outlets over the latter part of the 1990s. From popular self-help manuals and newspaper columns to radio programs dedicated to monitoring usage, the media themselves devoted growing attention to issues of language moderation and normalization—be it through exposés of mangled language on the part of leading public figures or the generation of practical resources for everyday users.

If the late 1990s witnessed a shift toward a more moderate reconciliation between linguistic lawlessness and radical purism, language policy under Vladimir Putin can largely be understood as a further attempt to establish a modicum of order within a language culture in flux. But as I demonstrate in chapter 5, political initiatives to legislate language laws and allocate federal funding toward promoting language literacy produce limited results. Far more consequential for the contours of linguist authority would be the actual speaking style of Putin as president himself. Given that he is most renowned for sound bites about bumping off Chechens in the loo and castrating sympathizers of global terrorism, it may seem odd at first glance to credit him with bringing about a degree of normative stability to the language culture. But his strategic use of the "nimbly uttered Russian word," as Gogol put it, together with his adept manipulation of national media platforms, helped create the sense of national pride, unity, and strong central authority that made him such a popular figure during his first two terms as president. In addition to presenting a critical linguistic profile of Putin based on hundreds of interviews and press conferences during this period, I examine the rhetorical impact of his annual multimedia "Conversations with the President of the Russian Federation" as a means of articulating a coherent image of a strong and unified Russian nation. I then look at Putin's attempt to use Russian language and culture as a tool for creating a transnational "Rusophonia," creating the Russian World Foundation (*Fond Russkii Mir*) to foster a sense of global Russian patriotism among Russians and Russian-language speakers living abroad.

Finally, in chapter 6 I consider the impact of the rapid spread of the Internet and new media technologies on the language culture of Russia today. In stark opposition to efforts to use language and new media to create more of an international presence, trends in national language policy, if anything, point to the belated attempt to construct what some have called an "electronic" or "cyber curtain"—a net-based space featuring all-Cyrillic interfaces, swift and affordable access, state-operated mail services and search engines, and content that is likewise limited and controlled by the state. But as a medium that, by original design, was meant to break down national borders and foster free, democratic modes of communication, the Internet has served as a political game changer in ways that run quite counter to Putin's desire to control technologies of communication. While at the moment of writing the fate of this most recent reform effort is uncertain, there is little doubt that the norms and bounds of political expression are as ambiguous, dynamic, and consequential today as they were twenty-five years ago in the era of glasnost.

1

THE SOVIET LEGACY

From Political to Cultural Correctness

"The literary language is the highest form of the national language, a symbol
of national distinctiveness (*samobytnost'*), a vehicle and medium for culture
and civilization."

—LEV SKVORTSOV, "Foundations for the Normalization of the Russian
Language" (1969)

Кто с правилами дружен, тот твёрдо убеждён:
ФарфОр нам очень нужен, а фАрфор не нужЁн!
Нельзя сказать «алфАвит», а можно—«алфавИт».
Кто говорит «алфАвит», неверно говорит!

Не говори «катАлог», а только «каталОг».
А «твОрог»? Можно «твОрог», а можно и «творОг».
А если в магазин вдруг портфЕли завезли—
Только не в «магАзин»: не купишь «портфелИ»!
—ALEKSANDR LIVSHITS AND ALKSANDR LEVENBUK, *Radio Nanny*

One obvious reason for post-Soviet reticence toward Western notions of
political correctness is that the Soviet era featured a state-sponsored form
of PC that was both ubiquitous and hypertrophied. The well-documented
clichéd, wooden language of official speeches, documents, and newspapers
assumed such a degree of dominance that it came to symbolize, in the
Gorbachev-era revolts against that system, all that was wrong with it. Stale

passive constructions veiled authority while deflecting responsibility, convoluted deverbal noun constructions symbolized official inertia, and superlatives meant to spark pride and elation simply stupefied like a worn cant.

Less obvious was an additional source of linguistic correctness that emerged as a dominant, authoritative discourse on language in the Soviet era. As Soviet citizens and school children were provided with explicit models from the Marxist-Leninist annals for describing the world around them, they underwent a parallel process of linguistic shaping that had more to do with cultural correctness than political correctness. As influential in shaping speech practices and language culture of the Soviet era was the "speech culture" or *kul'tura rechi* movement that had its roots in linguistic theories of the early Soviet period and the more conservative attitudes toward language, writing, and speech espoused by such influential figures as Maxim Gorky (Gorham 2003, 103–19). Particularly on the frontlines of Russian language methodology and instruction and in contrast to other, more well-researched keywords of the time (such as "dialogicity" or *skaz*), speech culture came to enjoy enormous cultural and linguistic capital over the decades of Stalin's rule—despite its decidedly unproletarian, unrevolutionary, and un-Marxist orientation. And its capital has lasted well into the postcommunist era.

Lineage of Linguistic Engineering

From the post-Stalin era to the present day, the study of "speech culture" has largely occupied itself with tracking, documenting, and proscribing speech practices of the Russian speaking and writing population. Practitioners pride themselves in their role as negotiators of norms and arbiters of proper usage. Comparisons of prefaces to speech-culture manuals from the 1950s and 1990s reveal little substantive difference—despite the enormous political and social transformations that had taken place over the decades dividing them. "Speech culture," according to a 1956 textbook on the topic, is dedicated to the study of "those norms of the literary language, the stepping back from which leads to a worsening of speech" (Golovin 1956, 3–4). Forty-three years later the editors of a comparable textbook geared toward a university audience remark in their introduction that "one of the main tasks of speech culture is the protection of the literary language, its norms. It behooves us to note that such protection is a matter of national importance, inasmuch as the literary language is the very thing that, on the linguistic level, unites a nation" (Graudina and Shiraev 2000, 12).

The continuity of this norm-oriented understanding of *kul'tura rechi* might not be so remarkable if not for its stark contrast to the original spirit of the term as introduced by its Russian progenitor, Grigorii Vinokur. Particularly in his earlier writings, the term had far more radical, even revolutionary, implications. For the Vinokur of 1923, language was a "social fact"; language culture, a means of "overcoming language inertia." In his first published article on language culture, he wrote about language as something that was "constructed" and, in its stagnated state, a domain ripe for human organization and control: "In so much as it is a social process, the speech process is realized in the widest variety of environments of social order. We build our language, be it written or oral, in dependence on these environments. Our language must obviously be *constructed*. It is the object of cultural management (*preodolenie*), requiring a certain *organization from the outside*" (Vinokur 1923, 105 [emphasis original]). While he did show some concern for nurturing basic linguistic competence that presumed pre-existing norms, Vinokur devoted far greater attention to metaphors of "technology" and "organization" that led him ultimately to conclude that language could and should be "material for cultural construction" (1923, 110, 106).

Implicit or explicit throughout his early writings was a language ideology that ascribed to speakers both the power and the responsibility to construct and organize their speech, to engage in a process of "cultural negotiation." Rather than viewing language as a pre-existing set of rules and norms that must be obeyed for speakers to earn the badge of proper speech culture, he focused instead on linguistic self-consciousness and invention. Language was a technology that was rightly the object of human engineering, rather than an organic and essential precursor to human identity.

The contrast between the linguistic ideology underlying Vinokur's original discussions of language and that implicit in the speech culture movement dominant through the final decades of the Soviet era and beyond leads one to wonder what became of this more proactive, or constructive, strain of discourse on language. One certainly does see vestiges of it in the writings of some of the more frequently studied linguists. Valentin Voloshinov's main criticism of Saussure and others was directed precisely at the basic assumption that language consisted of objective, self-replicating norms and thus constituted an objectively identifiable "system" that existed apart from individual and collective users. He argued that this was neither what language was, nor how it was perceived by users—that such a norm-oriented view of language was based on a philological tradition that placed priority on dead, written texts. Language, he countered, could not be isolated from its social and ideological context, and it was not isolated by ordinary users. We choose the words and phrases we do, not out of some pressure from abstract norms, but rather in order to express ourselves in a concrete, dialogic context (Voloshinov [1929] 1993, 71–90). Norms hold some sway, he argued, but "they exist only in relationship to the subjective consciousness of the members of a given collective": "for the individual speaker, linguistic form is important not as a stable signal that is always one and the same, but rather as a constantly changing and flexible sign" (72, 74).

Curiously enough, in terms of language ideology, Nikolai Marr shared common space with Voloshinov to the extent that each viewed language as a constructed or created product of society prone to significant "re-creation" during times of "truly new social forms of life and everyday existence (*byt'*)" (Marr 1927, 19). In an article on writing and grammar reform, Marr argued that norms were outdated and reflected different class relations; and he called for a complete "speech revolution" using the "new language material." The main reason teachers and scholars were reluctant to abandon norms and grammar was that they recognized it would mean abdicating their power and authority in this area (Marr 1930, 46–47). Echoing the creative and constructive tenor of Vinokur's early writings, Marr emphasized the need for "language creation" (*iazykotvorchestvo*) and "creativity of speech" (*tvorchestvo rechi*), contrasting the primacy of spoken, colloquial language to "obsolete (*otzhivshie*) systems of speech" (Marr [1931] 1977, 32). Tellingly, he also acknowledged that the practical application of his theories must be deferred to a time when they would be better "understood and accepted," implying (correctly) that they were not yet understood or accepted—a gap between theory and practice that was to persist throughout the 1930s and 1940s, when his ideas were in ideological favor (Marr [1931] 1977, 34–35).[1] As late as 1949, one Marr sympathizer asked point

---

1. Vladimir Alpatov gives two reasons for the relative lack of impact of Marr's teachings— the sheer utopian nature of his prescriptions (such as doing away with grammar) and the predominantly negative nature of his proposals (Alpatov 1991, 106–8).

blank on the pages of *Russian Language in the School,* "How are they understanding and teaching language in school? The profound teaching of
N. Ia. Marr has not penetrated the schools because of the strength of resistance from formalists. Our textbooks in no way provide a correct understanding of language" (Petrova 1949, 52).

From a purely political standpoint, we are accustomed to viewing
Marr and Voloshinov through quite different lenses. And yet, when examined more closely, they, together with the early Vinokur, shared a language ideology that viewed the individual speaker as a creative force in
the process of language production. They also shared the more dubious
distinction, despite attempts to drape their work in Marxism (at least in
the cases of Voloshinov and Marr), of being patently ignored by language
practitioners—not only the professionals responsible for disseminating
language models, be it through grammars, guides, dictionaries, curricular
guidelines, or classroom instruction, but also the folk linguists, everyday
citizens engaged in language production in Stalinist Russia. Instead, the
linguistic ideology that came to dominate linguist practice of the Stalin
era turned out to be one that ignored Marxist ideology and relied instead
for its symbolic authority on the parallel discourses of culturedness, or
kul'turnost', and norms.

The Quiet Conservatism of the Practitioners

It is in the quiet conservatism of the practitioners—the mavens, the cod-
ifiers, and the pedagogues—where we witness the emergence of "speech
culture," or *kul'tura rechi,* as a dominant linguistic ideology. While some
mention of norms could be found in the writings of the philologist Aleksei
Shakhmatov (1864–1920), he and most prerevolutionary linguists viewed
the task of the linguist as one of describing "how people speak," not pre-
scribing "how they should speak" (Shvartskopf 1970). In this earlier period it was widely held that norms and language could not be managed
or manipulated by society, linguists, or individual speakers. One exception, however, came in the form of Vasilii Chernyshev's *Correctness and
Purity of Russian Speech (Pravil'nost' i chistota russkoi rechi)* (1911), a book
the Petersburg philologist intended as a practical guide to the "frequently
asked questions" of "how to speak better and more properly" (Chernyshev 1911, 3). Noting the frequency of "violations of unquestionable rules

of speech in books, newspapers, letters, and conversation…," Chernyshev identified four different source models for "literary language": "(1) generally accepted contemporary usage, (2) the works of representative/model Russian writers, (3) the best grammars and grammar research on the literary Russian language," and, finally, (4) the language of the people (*narodnyi iazyk*)" (1911, 3).

Lev Shcherba was among the first linguists in Soviet times to employ a more norm-oriented discourse—perhaps because he also worked in the trenches as a Petrograd school director and later became involved in curricular design. In a 1931 essay he acknowledged that more "catastrophic" events might spark significant change in a language, but attributed change under more normal circumstances to forces that lay beyond the individual speaker. Speakers, in his view, were passive objects of normative change from more abstracted "language material": "People usually say that change in a linguistic system occurs upon generational change. This is in part true, but the experience of our revolution has shown that a sharp change in the language material inevitably entails change in the speech norms even of the elderly. A massive number of words and phrases that several years ago would have seemed wild and unacceptable have now entered into everyday use" (Shcherba [1931] 1974, 29). Unlike many of his contemporaries, Shcherba embraced the notion of norms, albeit in a somewhat qualified manner ("I shall now touch on another issue of so-called norms in language. Our spoken language activity is in fact guilty of numerous deviations from the norm" [36]). That embrace became less guarded by 1939, when he unequivocally asserted that it was the "literary language," based on the literary classics, that served as the source for linguistic "norms" (Shcherba [1939] 1957, 113, 126).

Shcherba's equation of linguistic norms with the literary language proved the rule rather than the exception in Soviet language studies, where more generic notions of "standard language" were all but non-existent (Paulsen 2009, 66–80).[2] Linguistic authority, according to this narrative, rested in the lofty lair of the literary tradition as it developed from the time of Pushkin, a move that enhanced the value of essentialist notions of

---

2. Although Paulsen documents the nineteenth-century origins of the term, he argues that "literary language" achieved the status of a foundational principle in linguistics only in the twentieth, particularly with the writings of the Soviet linguist Viktor Vinogradov (Paulsen 2009, 66–75).

language as an innate marker of Russian national identity. This discourse on language as a marker of national identity and pride became more notable in metalinguistic commentary of the early 1940s, by which time even Shcherba would invoke organic and biological metaphors of language in lieu of those describing it as a tool, weapon, or technology: "And, truly, the word 'native' (*rodnoi*) is a magical word and touches on the most treasured side of our essence. With its intimate warmth it heats up everything it is placed next to as a modifier: 'native country,' 'native home,' 'birth mother,' 'native language'" (Shcherba [1939] 1957, 113).

Dictionaries by definition presume the existence of norms and the need for codification, but in his preface to the 1935 *Interpretive Dictionary of the Russian Language*, Dmitrii Ushakov distinguished his compendium apart from its predecessors precisely because of its "normative goal—of being a guide for the model literary language." In his own rendition of constructing publics, Ushakov claimed that the events of 1917 had increased the need for a dictionary that was "intended for a broad readership, indicate[d] the norms of usage for words, and [was] close to the here and now (*blizkii k sovremennosti*)" (Ushakov 1935, 1–2, 3). The speaking and writing public, according to his linguistic-ideological slant, consisted not of newly empowered proletarian or popular innovators, but rather of needy seekers of codified rules.

As the cofounder and first director of the Academy of Sciences Russian Language Institute (established in 1944), Sergei Obnorskii could claim a fair amount of authority when he weighed in on the issue of speech culture. In a pair of articles written in the 1940s, he presented a model of language as an inherited legacy with "inexhaustible inner strength and beauty," but also susceptible to "spoiling," and thus in need of "preservation" and "purification" (Obnorskii [1944] 1960; [1949] 1960). As with the later Shcherba, he viewed language as a source of national identity and patriotism, no doubt reflecting the war-time climate: "The Russian language is a great language of the great Russian people. Language enters as an essential component into the notion of nation. It serves as one of the primary weapons of culture, a basic factor in the spiritual development of a nation, its works, its national self-consciousness" (Obnorskii [1949] 1960, 272). It was on the basis of these spiritual, creative, and national underpinnings that the normalization of the contemporary literary language should be established. The speaking and writing public should, moreover, "in its work on its own speech and in common activities in the area of speech culture take its departure from the literary language established by Pushkin" (283).

More so than other specialists cited here, Obnorskii struck a resolutely purist tone. In his description of Maxim Gorky's exemplary contribution to Soviet linguistic culture, he offered a stunning display of Soviet newspeak to tell the story of the nationalization of language, invoking an army of metaphors and implied language-speaker relationships that underscored language's status as an organic entity, a national heritage, a treasure, and a boundary marker of national and civic identity:

> Такое положение не могло не привлечь общественного внимания к проблеме развития литературного языка. Известна дискуссия на эту тему начала 30-х годов, в которой руководящая роль принадлежала великому нашему деятелю и тонкому ценителю русского слова А. М. Горькому. На этой дискуссии было подчеркнуто, что русский литературный язык есть величайшее общественное достояние, что направление развития его далеко не безразлично для самой общественности. И действительно, итоги дискуссии были чрезвычайно важны для дальнейшего развития русского литературного языка.
>
> Активно было начато оздоровление языка. Так, при быстрых темпах строительства в начальный период революционной поры в язык в громадном количестве стали проникать сокращенные слова разных типов образования. Но это не полнокровная, не дающая нормального обогащения языка лексика, это слова условного, временного назначения.
>
> Понятно, что началось освобождение языка и от этих пластов лексики.
>
> Подобным образом определились грани допустимой для литературного пользования лексикой диалектного происхождения, просторечной и т. д. Наш литературный язык постепенно, в результате неуклонных забот о нем, выравнялся [*sic*] (в своей общей линии) и принял прежнее устойчивое положение языка, преемственно развивающегося на основе прочных традиций. (Obnorskii [1949] 1960, 284–85)

[Such a situation could not but have attracted public attention to the problem of the development of the literary language. The discussion of this theme in the beginning of the 1930s, in which our great public figure and subtle appreciator of the Russian word, A. M. Gorky, played a leading role, is well known. In this discussion it was emphasized that the Russian literary language is the greatest of public achievements [and] that the direction of its development is by no means a matter of indifference for the public itself. And, in fact, the conclusions of the discussion were enormously important for the subsequent development of the Russian literary language.

The revitalization of the language was actively initiated. In the context of fast tempos for construction in the beginning period of revolutionary times, truncated words of various types of formation had begun to infiltrate the language in huge numbers. But this was not a full-blooded lexicon that contributed to the normal enrichment of the language; these were words with a conditional, temporary function.

It is clear that the liberation of the language from these layers of vocabulary had begun.

In such a manner the acceptable limits for the literary use of vocabulary of dialectal origin, colloquial vocabulary, etc., were determined. As a result of the unwavering concern for it, our literary language gradually came into alignment (in its general line) and assumed its formerly stable status of a language developing successively on the basis of durable traditions.]

Even Vinokur in his later writing shifted his emphasis from the creative aspects of language production to the more organic role of literary language as a marker of national identity or a cue to membership: "To speak like [the founders of the Russian state and the classics of our literature and science] means to become a member of their cultural milieu, an equal participant in the Russian cultural-historical process, to earn the right to consider oneself as *belonging (schitat' sebia svoim)* in this spiritual atmosphere" (Vinokur [1945] 1967, 11). Vinokurov actually raised the stakes by drawing the link between linguistic norms, on the one hand, and civic and ethical norms, on the other ("the observance of linguistic norms grows in significance to the level of observing norms of civil and ethical content" [11]). The constructive or creative dimension is there, but as the de-emphasized member of the partnership, something of an afterthought introduced by Vinokur only in the closing pages of the article ("The master of language usage not only knows the norms of language well, but also influences and creates them himself")— and, even then, burdened with various limitations and qualifications ("not all people are equally gifted in this regard") (Vinokur [1945] 1967, 13, 10).

Speech Culture and Linguistic Civilization

Particularly because of their emphasis on "mastery" and the "masters of high literature," proponents of "speech culture" left themselves vulnerable to accusations of bourgeois philistinism leveled by neo-Marxist followers of Marr. Be that as it may, they also happened to echo rhetorically growing concerns, beginning in the mid-1930s, over the need for *kul'turnost'*, or "culturedness." Volkov (1999, 211) identifies 1935 as the point at which *kul'turnost'* eclipsed class-based models of behavior in an effort to bring about what he calls the "Stalinist civilizing process," characterizing *kul'turnost'* as an "inculcation of norms and types of discipline." Boym (1994, 104–5) likewise interprets *kul'turnost'* as a way of translating ideology into everyday life, a type of "civilizing process," and a means of justifying bourgeois practices and hierarchies. If *kul'turnost'* in everyday life and behavior became the key means of instilling order and discipline, then so much the better for *kul'tura rechi,* given language's central role in shaping identity.

Language, of course, is particularly susceptible to the discourse of *kul'turnost'*, given the common perception that it is somehow essential or innate to our national and personal identity. Boris Volin, a Bolshevik pedagogue and high-ranking official at Glavlit (the central Soviet censorship organ), illustrated this new weave of literacy, discipline, and culturedness in a 1935 speech dedicated to the stubborn problem of illiteracy in Soviet schools, where he expressed hope that recent directives from the Communist Party Central Committee with regard to "literacy, discipline, [and] the culture of the schools" would ensure that "the school issue [would] progress, literacy [would] strengthen, culture [would become] ingrained, and discipline [would be] provided" (Volin 1936, 17). What was ostensibly an article bemoaning the still-low levels of literacy in the country (itself a significant fact), turned into a call for more cleanliness, "culture," and discipline in the schools: "How," Volin asked, "is it possible to teach kids, raise them as literate, knowledgeable, cultured Soviet citizens if order and culture are absent from the schools themselves?" (14)

The head censor found plenty of support for this sentiment among Soviet school teachers, who had been asking this same question for decades and by the mid-1930s were fed up with relentless reforms from above and frustrated by deteriorating linguistic competence from below (Ewing

1994, 143–48; Kotriakhov and Holmes 1993, 62–64). Articles bearing titles such as "In the Battle for Pupils' Speech Culture" grew more common on the pages of trade journals and lamented that "the worst situation of all existed in the teaching of the Russian language" ("V bor'be za kul'turu" 1936, 31). Flying in the face of Marr's "New Teaching on Language," period pedagogues espoused a more pragmatic approach to language instruction, in which grammar (which Marr proposed exiling from the classroom) was once again let in the door (Tekuchev 1937). With this sort of focus of attention, one can understand the shift in discourse on language from "creativity" to "normalization." The shift in discourse on language reflected a greater shift toward some modicum of standard "decency" in a variety of spheres.

Whatever awkwardness there was in the underlying bourgeois ideology of the "speech culture" movement was relieved altogether by Joseph Stalin's foray into the realm of linguistics in *Marxism and Issues in Linguistics* (1950). Originally published as a part of an ongoing "discussion" on the pages of *Pravda,* these essays were all more or less intended to dethrone Marrism and its followers from Soviet linguistics. Didactic and repetitive in tone, they boiled down to a few main points: (1) a refutation of Marr's claim that language was a superstructure that changed with every change of the base, (2) a rejection of the idea (held by Marr and others) that language was class-based, and (3) a debunking of Marr's theory of language evolution and change, known as *stadial'nost'*. Each refutation effectively created a more conducive atmosphere for the flourishing of the "speech culture" movement, as each in its own way asserted that there were certain traditions in the history of the language that were less mutable, and that, as a consequence, there were "standards" and "norms" that governed it. "Language," Stalin declared, "is the product of a whole series of eras, over the course of which it has been formed, enriched, developed, and polished.... Everywhere and at all stages of its development as a means of communication among people in a society, language has been one and the same for society, equally serving the members of society without regard to social status" (Stalin 1950, 17–18, 25; cf. Yurchak 2006, 44–47).

In addition to providing political cover for the speech culture movement, Stalin's treatises gave immediate and absolute legitimacy to the more purist attitude toward language teaching and usage commonly espoused by the practitioners. All pretentions to a revolutionary language culture—be it avant-garde or proletarian—dissolved in the more immediate demands of a minimally articulate population. Special issues dedicated to various pedagogical topics "in the light of Stalin's teaching on language" spilled over with calls for cleaning up student speech: "Every teacher must rigorously monitor the oral speech of students, correct pupils' speech deficiencies in a timely manner, and aggressively press for an elevation in the culture of their speech" (Dobromyslov and Solov'ev 1951, 25). As the main poster child for norms, grammar instruction resumed a central role in language instruction, having "reestablished its rights," as one commentator put it. Grammatically conscious speech, as he explained it, "disciplined thought and regulated pupils' speech" (Dobromyslov 1951, 2, 10). Metaphors of norms, linguistic vigilance, and regulation were accompanied by descriptions of language itself as a "national heritage" (*narodnoe dostoianie*) that must be "enriched" and "preserved from spoiling and pollution" (Barkhudarov 1951, 10).

Institutionalization of *Kul'tura rechi*

This shift to a norm-oriented ideology found firmer institutional grounding in the Russian Language Institute, founded in 1952, with the distinguished lexicographer Sergei Ozhegov as its head. Under Ozhegov's editorship, the Institute soon began publishing *Issues in Speech Culture (Voprosy kul'tury rechi)*, dedicated to "the normalization of literary languages in the area of lexicon, stylistics, grammar, pronunciation, and terminology" (Ozhegov 1955a, 1:3). In his opening essay in the first volume, Ozhegov focused on norms. Careful to underscore the scholarly status of *kul'tura rechi,* he distanced the journal from what he called "purism," which he essentially understood as unscholarly attempts (by Russian émigrés during the revolution, for instance) to regulate language. At the same time he pointed to the plethora of usage-related letters sent to central newspapers by everyday language users as proof of the popular demand for specialized attention to speech culture. "It is not only writers, scholars, and public figures who contribute to the elevation of speech culture," he wrote, "everyone is taking active part—workers and teachers, those working in the theater and in agriculture, and representatives of the Soviet intelligentsia from the widest range of specialties. Their appearances on the pages of the newspapers and journals with expressions relating to specific issues of speech culture... usually contain a fair number of interesting assessments and suggestions" (Ozhegov 1955b, 12, 15). While careful to identify a linguistically engaged public, his nod of approval to grassroots folk linguistic practices stopped well short of recognizing the more creative, empowering notion of speech culture posited by Vinokur as recently as 1945.

Indeed, a closer look at the eight volumes of *Issues in Speech Culture* published over twelve years (1955–1968) shows a clearly demarcated relationship between an imagined public both in need of linguistic first aid and cognizant of that need, and a small but dedicated pool of specialists qualified to provide it. In his preface to the journal's inaugural issue, Ozhegov described "wide circles of Soviet society" linguistically self-reflexive and eager to improve their mastery of Russian (Ozhegov 1955a 1:3). The editors tailored the contents of the journal to fit this imagined target audience, keeping to a minimum longer pieces dense with linguistic jargon and highlighting shorter and more practically oriented rubrics such as "Brief Notes," "Debates and Discussions," and the "Russian Language Service" (*Sluzhba russkogo iazyka*). This last rubric featured one-page specialist responses to questions submitted by readers, a genre that would be replicated later with great success on the pages of the authoritative *Literary Gazette*.[3] Here readers could find brief elucidations of sticky issues in Russian usage, including the meaning and usage of relevant loanwords (*Van Klibern ili Ven Klaibern* [1963]; *bitnik* [1964]; *khobbi; personazh* [1966]);[4] correct usage and/or grammatical forms for commonly mistaken words (*poriadka desiati tysiach; oplatit'* [1963]; *odolzhit'* [1964]; *kolgotki* [1966]);[5] correct stress on words of similar origin (*iazykovoi* and *iazykovyi* [1955]; *valovoi vs. valovyi* [1965]);[6] insight into gender-marked inflection [*traktorist/traktoristka* [1963];[7] *uvazhaemyi tovarishch ili uvazhaemaia tovarishch?* [1965];[8] and the

---

3. Dagmar Christians documents efforts made by the editorial staff to underscore the great interest taken by readers as reflected by the scores of letters and comments sent to the paper, in part in response to the Russian Language Service set up in 1964 (Christians 1983, 32–38).

4. In order of appearance, "Van Cliburn," "beatnik," "hobby," and "character, persona."

5. In order of appearance, "on the order of ten thousand," "to pay," "to lend," "pantyhose."

6. The adjectives for "language" and "tongue," respectively; and alternative pronunciations for the economic term "gross" (*valovoi* being the more accepted).

7. "Tractor driver" (m.)—"tractor driver" (f.).

8. "Respected (m.) comrade or respected (f.) comrade?"

proper use of a variety of near synonyms (*nol'—nul'; nomer—numer* [1955]; *tomat—pomidor* [1959]; *tsifra vs. chislo* [1964]).[9]

Contributors to *Issues* consistently insisted that the population's usage problems be addressed by practitioners of language sciences, in part through the expert articulation of more concrete norms. While the "opinions, values, and desires of society" needed to be taken into consideration, Ozhegov wrote, it was the job of the specialists, based on sound scholarship, to determine norms (Ozhegov 1955b, 33). They underscored the urgency of the task by regularly pointing out the dearth of guides that were both comprehensive and accessible to the general reading public—despite "the huge interest in issues relating to speech culture" (Vorontsova and Sumkina 1955, 208–20). And while some dissenting voices occasionally labeled Academy linguists "norm-mongers" (*normirovshchiki*), "forbidders" (*zapretiteli*), and "unificationists" (*unifikatory*), and characterized their practices as linguistic oppression of the masses by a bourgeois elite (Iugov 1959), journal editors persistently staked out a middle ground between purism and excessive prescriptivism (Kostomarov 1966). In the opening article of the 1963 issue, the philologist Viktor Grigor'ev (1963) challenged language specialists to engage more actively in establishing and discussing language norms. By begging off "prescriptive" practices in the name of science, he argued, they were ceding their professional authority to "purists" and other types of language dilettantes who were more willing to stake their claims—however erroneous. Arguing that school teachers (who did not have the luxury of remaining aloof) were far more likely to heed the advice of specialists, Grigor'ev called for the creation of a "Russian language service" (*Sluzhba russkogo iazyka*) that would provide a rapid response mechanism for resolving practical speech culture issues among the population (Grigor'ev 1963; "Sluzhba iazyka" 1965). In similar centrist fashion, Lev Skvortsov wrote that "language policy in the area of youth jargon must be equally bereft of subjective-evaluative negation as it is of abstract 'scientific' justification of elements of youth slang regardless of their function, character, and fate" (Skvortsov 1964, 70). Youth slang was at the center of controversy in a chapter on the topic by Grigor'ev in I. S. Il'inskaia's oft-cited *Book about the Russian Language* (1969) as well. Discussing the general dismay over the linguistic behavior of the contemporary young "hipsters" (*stiliagi*) and

---

9. Variants of "zero, null," "number," "tomato," and "digit, date," respectively.

"scumbags" (*podonki*), Grigor'ev suggested that targeting language would be misguided: "It is senseless to denounce jargon in cases where jargon typifies scumbags: you have to fight the scumbags themselves" (Il'inskaia 1969, 172). True to the mission at the root of the speech culture movement, the end goal was to foster more civilized behavior, linguistic and otherwise. While pedantic lectures against the ills of youth jargon would only increase its attractiveness ("Everyone knows that forbidden fruit is sweet" [172]), one needed to draw the line when dealing with what the author called "intentional speech rudeness" (*narochitaia rechevaia grubost'*) because it was not only "evidence of spiritual crudeness, insensitivity (*nechutkost'*), and tactlessness, but it [was] also infectious and dangerous for the wider public (*dlia okruzhaiushchikh*)" (172). Grigor'ev drew the link between linguistic and general behavior even more directly in his introduction, suggesting the normative bar should be set particularly high for public role models of proper speech: "Since our relationships to our surroundings are regulated by certain behavioral norms, we naturally must follow these norms. Applied to speech communication, this is expressed in the fact that the literary language is accepted as a mandatory norm for everyone, and its rules serve (or should serve) as a point of orientation, in part, for teachers of schools and universities, radio and television announcers, staff at newspapers and journals, etc." (160).

Despite some lingering resistance from the purist and antiprescriptivist margins, the speech culture industry flourished over the course of the 1960s with the publication of increasing numbers of guides and primers and extended usage discussions regularly highlighted on the pages of the leading cultural authority and widely circulating *Literary Gazette* (which from 1967 to 1971 featured its own "Russian Language Service" rubric).[10] By 1964 Ditmar Rozental's *Kul'tura rechi* was in its third edition, boasting a print run of 150,000 copies. As the successor of *Issues in Speech Culture,* the journal *Russian Speech (Russkaia rech')* brought the technology of *kul'tura rechi* further into the public realm with bimonthly issues dedicated entirely to the linguistic edification of the general population. Inaugurated

---

10. By 1966, even the ex-Marrist Fedot Filin was declaring that the role of the linguist was "to prepare and inculcate scientifically based, rational recommendations that would allow society to consciously remove language superfluity (*izbytochnost'*) incompatible with speech culture" (Filin 1966, 18). For a detailed analysis of the language debates featured in the *Literary Gazette* from 1964 to 1978, including a discussion of the minority "antinormalization" position, see Christians (1983).

in 1967 by many of the same names involved in the earlier project, the journal sought to provide readers with a combination of historical background and concrete advice on Russian language usage and, like its predecessor, to carve out a centrist position on the permissibility spectrum ("The battle for speech culture always takes place on two fronts: against those who pollute language with unnecessary 'novelties,' and against those who stubbornly reject everything new and unusual" ["K chitateliu" 1968, 3]). Here too, from the opening issue, one finds a concerted effort to construct an audience of language users desperate for expert advice. In a sketch of her work at the "Information Desk of the Russian Language Institute of the USSR Academy of Sciences," one contributor described the plethora of questions that came in, full of urgency, sincerity, passion, even desperation. Their needs, she explained, were entirely natural: "The telephone rings without interruption. There are many questions and that is natural. Language is a living organism; at every new stage of language development some phenomena die off, others arise and push out the old.... People need linguistic first aid (*skoraia lingvisticheskaia pomoshch'*)" (Bukchina 1967, 101).

Responding to such calls for "linguistic first aid" remained a central mission of the journal, be it through its explication of perennial puzzles such as the origins of the words *tovarishch* ("comrade") and *dom kul'tury* ("house of culture"), the difference between *vospitatel'* ("teacher," "tutor") and *prepodavatel'* ("teacher," "instructor"), the declension of *Pushkino, Tushino,* and *tufli* (shoes), or lexical novelties such as *aerobus, gidrobus* ("hydrobus"), *lazer,* and *khobbi*.[11] The very existence of such rubrics presupposed the existence of linguist "patients" either in need of expert treatment or proud of their superior mastery, appalled by the mutilation of language they witnessed around them, and in search of affirmation from the authorities. By the journal's fourth issue editors claimed that "hundreds of letters [had] piled up on the editor's desk" and cited a range of examples that testified to the fact that improving one's speech culture was a desire shared by young and old alike: "Pensioner Semen Ivanovich Aleseitsev from *Novaia Kakhovka* suggests introducing into Russian the new word, *mednoe,* in the meaning of 'sweet.' Seventh grader A. Efremov of Leningrad asks, 'How

---

11. "Pochta *Russkoi rechi,*" *Russkaia rech'* 5 (1967): 112–13; "Pochta *Russkoi rechi,*" *Russkaia rech'* 4 (1968): 112–14; "Pochta *Russkoi rechi,*" *Russkaia rech'* 1 (1969): 123–24; "Pochta *Russkoi rechi,*" *Russkaia rech'* 5 (1967): 112–13; "Novye slova," *Russkaia rech'* 5 (1968): 107–9.

do I develop my speech?'" ("Pochta *Russkoi rechi*" 1967, 4:78). The "Mail" rubric documented active participation of folk linguists—citizen readers writing to report grammatical and spelling errors witnessed in the public sector. One concerned resident of Engels, a town in the Saratov oblast', sent in a candy wrapper with four words on it, two of which contained grammatical or spelling errors (*konfety* [pl.] *maliutka,* even though there was only one piece of candy in the wrapper, and *Engel'skii gorpishchetorg,* the first word lacking the necessary double *s*) ("Pochta *Russkoi rechi*" 1967, 4:78). As with earlier vestiges of the speech culture movement, at stake in these concerns about language degradation were broader concerns about the general level of culturedness (*kul'turnost'*) of the population at large: "Is it possible to become a cultured person without mastering the native tongue to perfection? Is not poverty of language the first sign of poverty of thought?" ("Pochta *Russkoi rechi*" 1967, 4:78).

The Soviet citizen of the 1960s and 1970s had more outlets for obtaining linguistic first aid than the professional journals as technologies of speech culture expanded into more electronic spheres of communication. In Moscow beginning in 1958 they could dial up the Russian Language Service of the Academy of Sciences Russian Language Institute, a telephone hotline where trained linguists would field questions ranging from spelling to style (Grishina 2006, 48). Employees of the Leningrad branch of the Linguistics Institute provided similar services in the form of Linguistic First Aid (*Skoraia lingvisticheskaia*) beginning in 1968 ("Skoraia Lingvisticheskaia" 1974). Judging by historical accounts, the services served a dual function—as a means of providing assistance to needy citizens and a mechanism for folk linguists to themselves serve as language monitors, "reporting on typographical errors in newspapers and journals and speech errors perpetrated by radio and television employees" (Grishina 2006, 48).

The speech culture movement first used radio to expand its access to a popular audience with *In the World of Words (V mire slov),* broadcast biweekly on Sundays from 1962 to 1996 (Grishina 2006, 48). While it relied on experts—former students of Vinogradov and Ozhegov (Viktor Deriagin and Lev Skvortsov)—to provide the linguistic expertise, the show adopted a more popularized production tack by relying on professional actors and radio announcers for its actual delivery. Beginning at 12:35 p.m. every other Sunday afternoon, the likes of Vladimir Balashov and Vera

Eniutina would entertain listeners with scripted answers to their usage questions ("V mire slov" 2011).

Beginning in 1970, the popular children's educational show, *Radio Nanny,* filled the airwaves with entertaining lessons in a variety of school subjects, including Russian language. As one of the show's cohosts, Aleksandr Levenbuk ("Alik"), recalled, he, Nikolai Litvinov, and Aleksandr Livshits sought to inject language study with a levity and humor that would promote proper usage in a nonpedantic manner: "We put the textbooks and guides to the side and tried to translate the boring rule into a laconic and lighthearted form. We pretended that we were helping the textbook and the teacher, not replacing them, but in reality that was precisely our goal—to replace the textbook. Because with us, [learning language rules] was more fun and shorter and could be remembered, whereas in the textbook everything was stated in a significantly more complex way. Many foreign countries taught language using the *Radio Nanny* method, but our Ministry of Education regarded us rather jealously" ("Moia prekrasnaia niania" n.d.).

Although it is difficult to assess the size and scope of the listening audience of such popular programs, the limited selection of radio options at the time (when stations were few and all state-run) meant they had access to a significant portion of the national listening audience.[12] As the authors of *In the World of Words* staked their claim to popularity, "over the period of the program's existence we have received hundreds of thousands of letters from amateurs (*liubiteli*) of the Russian language. The questions directed to us by people of different ages, different professions, and different educational backgrounds have helped us to better imagine and define the circle of basic issues of speech culture" (Liustrova and Skvortsov 1972, 6).[13] In their introduction to their second book based on material from *In the World of Words,* Liustrova and colleagues actually listed names and

---

12. Popular language shows made some inroads into television during this time, primarily in the form of *Russkaia rech'* beginning in 1971 (Ulukhanov 1974).

13. In a 1970 interview, one of the hosts of *In the World of Words,* V. N. Balashov, noted the "colossal response" the show received from its listening audience ("'Govorit Moskva....'" 1970); Grishina (2006, 49) claimed that the radio show received "over thirty thousand letters from listeners" in its first three years of broadcasting. A 1974 report on the content and reception of the television version of *Russkaia rech'* pointed to a "multitude of viewers' letters as well as coverage in the central press" as evidence of that show's "usefulness and essentialness" (Ulukhanov 1974, 66).

professions of listeners to provide a more vivid portrait of a constructed audience that spanned the demographic spectrum and viewed the active engagement in perfecting speech culture as a source of joy, reflection, and realization of potential:

> The electrical fitter V. A. Rybin from Iaroslavl', the repairman A. F. Pish-chalov from the town of Andropov, the teacher V. I. Obolonik from the town of Konotop, the pensioner V. G. Pan'shin from Sverdlovsk, Z. I. Vinogra-dova from Magadan oblast', A. V. Silina from Kalinin oblast', R. T. Sozinov from Krasnoiarsk, A. S. Plugareva from Omsk, A. N. Greaderov from Sev-astpol', the Muscovite N. G. Mashkov, and many others talk about their interest in the show and the benefit it brings all lovers of the Russian language. According to the testimony of numerous radio listeners, the show *In the World of Words* forces one to ponder, argue, remember, smile, and search in guides for the answers to questions that arise—in short, it awakens a lively and creative interest in the native tongue (and) adds to it the language's richest expressive capabilities, to its past and its present. (Liustrova, Skvortsov, and Deriagin 1987, 7)

Speech Culture and the Language of the Soviet State

Ironically, but critically for its survival, the speech culture movement made little mention of what arguably posed the greatest threat to the linguistic well-being of the nation—the horribly clichéd and wooden language of the official Soviet language of state. Explicit discussions of political language struck an unwaveringly positive tone, either praising the oratorical skills of Soviet founding fathers or celebrating the linguistic innovation brought about by the revolution (Kozhin 1969; "Navstrechu" 1971; Beloded 1971; Kozhin 1973; Shanskii 1980). More questionable features commonly seen now to be the hallmarks of Soviet newspeak, such as the excessive use of intertextual citation, clichéd turns of phrase, narrative circularity, superlatives, and deverbal nouns (Seriot 1985; Yurchak 2006, 59–74), not only remained unaddressed, but also found their way into politically oriented pieces regularly featured in the professional journals. On occasion journal contributors took on concepts viewed to be anathema to the Soviet way of life, weaving together linguistic and ideological analysis with varying degrees of deftness. In "Where does the word 'hipster' *(stiliaga)* come from?" for instance, the young linguist Vitalii Kostomarov used ideolog-ically charged language to define the term as "a negative indicator of a young person with morals alien to our society," and write off the deplor-able trend as little more than fashionable parroting by a misguided subsec-tion of Soviet youth:

> В послевоенные годы среди некоторой части нашей молодежи пышно расцвело увлечение "западной" танцевальной музыкой; кривлянье под крикливые звуки американского джаз-банда стало модой. «Новизна» казалась «стильной,» и для обозначения ее проявлений в жаргоне низкопробных музыкантов и их поклонников, который возродился в эти годы, появились натасканные из разных источников «модные и стильные» словечки. (Kostomarov 1959, 169–70)

> [In the postwar years a fancy for "Western" dance music decadently burst into bloom among a certain portion of our youth; aping the shrill sounds of the American jazz band became fashionable. The "novelty" seemed "styl-ish," and to signify its manifestation, "fashionable and stylish" little words appeared, hauled from a variety of sources into the jargon of the lowbrow musicians and their fans, who came to life in those years.]

Invoking classic turns from the Soviet ideological discourse to clearly stake out boundaries between normative and abnormal, Kostomarov strayed from narrow linguistic analysis to more global statements of right and wrong behavior: "The Soviet people are carrying out a decisive bat-tle against the influence of taste and morals of the bourgeois 'golden youth,' and playing its role in this battle is the word *stiliaga,* which has become a literary word and is sharply and negatively colored" (175).

Two years later Kostomarov takes on the still more politically charged term "iron curtain" (*zheleznyi zanaves*) and, here too, departs almost entirely from the language of linguistic analysis, opting instead for the sty-listic coloring of state ideology to account for the term's existence:

> Идеология капитализма, стремясь оправдать свою политику раздувания холодной войны, политику вражды и ненависти между народами, выдвинули версию о том, что СССР якобы

отгородил себя от "свободного мира" непреодолимой стеной, с целью тайно подготовиться к завоеванию этого "свободного мира." Среди прочих приемов "обоснования" этой фантастической басни была пущена в ход и лингвистическая подделка: *железный занавес* стало назойливо рекламироваться как название этой несуществующей стены." (Kostomarov 1961, 199)

[Seeking to justify their policy of fanning the Cold War, a policy of animosity and hatred among peoples, the ideologues of capitalism came out with a story of how the USSR supposedly closed itself off from the "free world" with an impenetrable wall, with the goal of secretly preparing to conquer that "free world." Among the various devices deployed to provide foundation to this fantastic fable was a linguistic forgery: *iron curtain* began to be importunately advertised as the name of this nonexistent wall.]

With the generous use of distancing quotes, qualifiers such as "seeking to justify," "so-called," and "nonexistent," and emotionally marked words such as "fanning," "animosity and hatred," "story," "fantastic fable," "forgery," and "importunately," the note reads more like a deconstruction than a definition. And, of course, that was the very function of the piece. (Although Kostomarov did end up acknowledging that despite Soviet lexicographers' resistance to the term, "the iron curtain" nevertheless acquired a stable place in the literary language [201].)

What is notable in such pieces is not the blatantly ideological focus and tone. Such articles were quite common in, if not required of, professional journals of the Soviet era—a product of what Yurchak (2006, 47–54) describes as the "hypernormalization" of political Russian and Soviet discourse in general in late socialism. Noteworthy, instead, is the sharp contrast (at least to today's reader) such passages strike with the surrounding pieces devoted to norms, speech culture, and literary language. The little critical mention of official language that did make it onto the pages of the journals took aim at a more ideologically acceptable bugbear—the convoluted language of the bureaucracy. But this linguistic malady, like vulgarisms and youth slang, tended to be ascribed to individual users, or subsets of users, rather than political discourse on the whole (e.g., "Decisive protest is being expressed against the mangling [*koverkan'e*] of language, vulgarisms, and the misuse of verbal stamps and chancellery writing"

["Pochta *Russkoi rechi*" 1967, 4:78.]).[14] More institutionalized were the critiques of the slapdash, cliché-ridden language of newspapers, but these, too, carefully avoided mention of political discourse. Beginning in 1969, for instance, *Russkaia rech'* ran an occasional rubric dedicated to the language of newspapers, focusing primarily on examples of poor editing, mistakes in grammar, spelling, usage, or dry journalistic style (e.g., "Iazyk gazety" 1969, 3:48–66; "Iazyk gazety" 1969, 4:66–82). Cries against cliché-prone bureaucrats and nameless journalists aside, criticism of the language of state remained strictly taboo.

And yet the two seemingly contradictory sources of linguistic authority—the literary language of the nineteenth-century classics and the political discourse of the classics of Marxism and Leninism—had more in common than first meets the eye. Both perspectives looked to what Bakhtin (1981) called the "epic past" for ideal manifestations of their language of authority—the speech culture movement to the literary language as represented by the nineteenth-century classics, on the one hand, and the political education industry to the speeches of the Soviet founding fathers, on the other.[15] Both relied on a notion of centralized authority—either cultural or political—that reinforced established hierarchies in both realms. Indeed, they were more complementary than contradictory, reflecting different points of orientation more than anything else. The discourse of *kul'tura rechi* described language more in terms of essence and form, while Soviet political discourse underscored its instrumental function.[16] Their differing points of orientation reflected their differing goals—in the one case, the

---

14. Cf. "Главное, очевидно, не отдавать речь во власть шаблона, не засорять ее суконными оборотами: 'всемерно улучшать,' 'в свете поставленных задач,' 'пройти под знаком,' 'иметь место,' 'уделять должное внимание,' 'истинное положение вещей,' 'истекший период,' 'на данном этапе,' 'в переживаемый момент,' 'охватить мероприятиями,' 'вовлечь в борьбу'" (Stepanov and Tolmachev 1966, 212) ["The main thing, obviously, is not to surrender one's speech to the power of the cliché, not to pollute it with woolen turns of phrase: 'to improve in every measure,' 'to have a place,' 'to devote necessary attention,' 'the true state of affairs,' 'the elapsed period of time,' 'at the present stage,' 'at the currently experienced moment,' 'to capture with events,' 'to engage in battle'"].

15. I am grateful to Helena Goscilo for pointing out the link to Bakhtin.

16. Although as Yurchak (2006, 76) rightly argues, the "hegemony" of this form of state-mandated speaking and writing on the abstract, "performative," level allowed for the production of alternative forms and meanings by citizens in everyday life.

goal of fostering linguistic "culturedness" (*kul'turnost'*), in the other case, the goal of fostering a Soviet form of political correctness (and *kul'turnost'*).

By establishing the problem, the public awareness of the problem, the demand that it be addressed, and the need for qualified professionals to assume authority over that task, specialists writing for *Issues of Speech Culture* and other journals over the course of the post-Stalin decades successfully established a formidable institution that complemented overarching political institutions by advocating a model of authority based on top-down institutional power and the canonization of patristic texts. It should be of little surprise, then, that when Soviet newspeak suffered dramatic devaluation with the onset of glasnost in the late 1980s, the linguistic capital of the speech culture movement began to decline as well. Citizens tasting new fruits of democracy and free speech after years of being subjected to official decrees and dictates had a low tolerance for any attempt to prescribe "proper" and "improper" ways of describing the people and world around them.[17] Suddenly, both political and cultural correctness took a back seat to the urgency of democratic, spontaneous self-expression, however noncanonical.

---

17. For a parallel phenomenon in post-Soviet resistance to postmodernism and other grand critical theories, see Emerson (1992).

2

Glasnost Unleashed

Language Ideologies in the Gorbachev Revolution

"Although we used the same words, we spoke about different things."
—Mikhail Gorbachev, *Memoirs* (1996)

One of the chief architects of glasnost, Aleksandr Iakovlev, opens his memoir chapter on the Gorbachev years with a curious metalinguistic rumination, triggered by a single word, *pustoslovie,* which in English can be loosely translated as "empty rhetoric." Recalling how in the spring of 1985 he had penciled the word into the margin of a draft of a eulogy Gorbachev was to deliver to the recently deceased Communist Party General Secretary, Iakovlev contemplates the symbolic significance that the word and the speech practices it represented held at that critical juncture in late-Soviet history:

> My disgust for empty rhetoric had been ground out through the experience of many decades. In conditions where the country had been crushed down by the punitive system of bolshevism, empty rhetoric had become not just a working dialect for the party-state apparatus (*partgosapparat*), but a collective manifestation of a functional character as well. I grew to hate this practice of senseless babble (*bessmyslennaia govoril'nia*). And it makes me nauseated to this day.

The flow of words, the endless exercise in formulas, spectacles that were called discussions...all served for many years to conceal the substantive sides of life and the real course of events, to putty over bad ideas with the abundance of words. Unified to the extreme, the special party-state language (*partgosiazyk*) had become a kind of social narcotic. Society was tired of empty chatter (*pustaia govoril'nia*), which had become overgrown into a kind of psychological illness of the system.

I think Gorbachev also understood this. As we discussed the upcoming speech, he spoke for a long time about how babble was suffocating party-state work and sapping the CPSU of its authority, how words were veiling thoughtlessness and inaction, and all that sort of thing. His tone impressed me and gave birth to hope, and, most important, trust in the man.

The reader may not believe it, but it was this very episode, purely lexical it would seem, that provided the ideological and psychological impulse for the new policy that later...found expression in the generalized formula of "perestroika." The criticism of empty rhetoric rang out like a shot at the epoch of words and simultaneously served as an invitation to real deeds. (Iakovlev 2001, 9–10)

Rich as it is in its description of Soviet newspeak—the deadening babble of formulaic words and phrases that turn discussions into spectacles, putty over bad ideas, conceal thoughtlessness, and act like a narcotic to the psychological detriment of a nation full of citizens who have mastered it—the passage is striking for another reason. Of all the dramatic anecdotes someone so close to such an important historical figure could begin with, Iakovlev remembers the language. We can question the degree to which he exaggerates its role, but this extended discourse on language, or talk about talk, and its central role in shaping the political destiny of a country certainly gives reason to pause and consider: What is the role, in periods of social and political change, of language and *language ideologies*—of the ways people in positions of power perceive and discuss contemporary language change, how they frame that discussion, and how those discussions quite often serve as surrogate debates about broader issues of identity and authority? How do language ideologies help shape or reshape political authority? And how, in particular, did they figure in the struggle for symbolic authority during the era of Gorbachev's reforms from 1985 to 1990? More than any other keyword of the Gorbachev era, *glasnost* provides an excellent entry point into an exploration of these fundamental issues. In this chapter I use it as a lexical case study of sorts, of the manner in which language is used as a battleground for symbolic (and real) authority, and of the more specific voices or models of authority that figured most prominently in the ideological battles of the day.

Glasnost as Keyword

The prominence of the word itself in the annals of late-twentieth-century history is attested to by the fact that it has found a place for itself as a loanword in authoritative foreign lexicons. According to the *Oxford English Dictionary,* it is the most recent nonscientific Russian word to date, together with *perestroika,* to have earned citizenship in the English language.[1] This, ironically, makes translation more difficult. English-language dictionaries attest to this by avoiding all one-word synonyms, as in the *American Heritage Dictionary,* where it is defined as "an official policy of the former Soviet government emphasizing candor with regard to discussion of social problems and shortcomings."[2] The *OED* comes closest to capturing the evolutionary nuances of the term as policy: "In relation to the affairs of the Soviet Union: a declared party policy since 1985 of greater openness and frankness in public statements, including the publication of news reflecting adversely on the government and political system; greater freedom of speech and information arising from this policy."

Literally, glasnost, which comes from the adjective *glasnyi* (public), means something approximating "publicity" in English and dates back in the Russian political lexicon at least to the early nineteenth century. Derived from the root *GLAS/GOLOS* ("voice," "vote"), the term's etymology underscores the tight link between speech and politics. But as with most political concepts, the literal meaning only scratches the surface. Even the best word etymology will fail to do justice to the complexity of glasnost, in part because of the rich history of the concept and in part because of the additional layers of meanings and nuances it acquired as it passed through

---

1. Nonscientific loanwords from Russian that preceded it almost all reflect American preoccupation with Cold War controversies: *refusenik* (1975), *tamizdat* (1974), *Kalashnikov* (1970), *stukach* (1969), *zek* (1968).

2. By comparison, the *Merriam Webster Dictionary* defines it as "a Soviet policy permitting open discussion of political and social issues and freer dissemination of news and information."

the ideological and pragmatic filters of the Gorbachev era, especially once the word became policy. As it turns out, it meant a variety of things to a variety of key political players, and it is precisely the protean nature of the term, the ambiguous semantic and pragmatic values it carried during the critical years of the Gorbachev reforms, that made it so powerful. As with all successful policies, its success stemmed largely from its ability to absorb and "speak for" a broad range of political agendas. And, like all protean concepts, glasnost became a key battlefield in the broader struggle for meaning, power, and authority as the *pustoslovie* of the Soviet epoch came increasingly under fire.

A Brief History of the Concept

To appreciate the concept's subtle versatility we need to set aside contemporary associations of glasnost with "freedom of speech" and go back to the early part of the nineteenth century to the publicist and writer Faddei Bulgarin. As a strong supporter of Tsar Nicholas I and his policies, Bulgarin first used the term in a 1826 essay, "On Censorship in Russia and on Book Publishing in General." Expounding on ways in which the tsar could win over the support and adoration of his people, Bulgarin writes:

> Не надобно больших усилий, чтобы быть не только любим ею, но даже обожаемым. К этому два средства: *справедливость* и некоторая *гласность* (publicité). Нашу публику можно совершенно покорить, увлечь, привязать к трону одною тею свободы в мнениях на счет некоторых мер и проектов правительства, как сие было до 1816 г. (Altunian 1998, 173)

> [It does not take great effort to not only be loved by the people, but also adored by them. There are two means for doing this: *fairness* and a certain *glasnost* (publicité). It is possible to completely subject, capture, and bind our public to the throne by [giving it] the freedom of opinions about certain government measures and projects, as was the case before 1816.]

Central to Bulgarin's understanding of the concept was the idea of glasnost as a state-sanctioned means of publicizing enough information for the reading public to understand and support the policies of the tsars.

Public opinions and feedback were welcome, but only to the very limited extent that that feedback created a sense of "buy-in" on the public's part. Limited glasnost functioned to shape public opinion, rather than leave it to its own devices. The alternatives, in Bulgarin's view, were either "unlimited glasnost" or total silence, each of which carried its own set of dangers for the tsar: "Complete silence (*bezmolvie*) breeds lack of trust and forces the contemplation of weakness; unlimited glasnost leads to willfulness (*svoevolie*); whereas glasnost inspired by the government itself reconciles both sides and is useful for both" (Altunian 1998, 173).

The term took on added importance in the Great Reform debates in the 1850s under Alexander II, where the battle against bureaucratic corruption and excess (*proizvol*) required "holding up to public scrutiny the actions of those who served the people and the state" (Lincoln 1982, 184). This time, however, more radical advocates such as Petr Dolgorukov and Alexander Hertzen challenged the restricted, state-sponsored model of glasnost by speaking out in ways that could not always be seen as justifying and supporting the reform policies of the state. For them, glasnost should serve as "the mortar to bind Tsar, educated opinion, and the masses into an invincible force that could overcome all reactionary sentiment and all self-interested opposition to reform in Russia" (Lincoln 1982, 185). This more liberal or democratic understanding served as a clarion call for democracy and free speech, but ultimately led to a tempering reaction by Alexander and members of his Main Censorship Administration, which sought to redefine glasnost in a narrower manner that viewed "public opinion" as little more than "public support for the government" (Lincoln 1982, 188). A quite similar sort of semantic wrangling over the keyword would re-emerge in the reform debates of the perestroika era, with apparatchiks embracing the more limited understanding and more liberal "democrats" pushing for full-blown freedom of speech.

Glasnost figured nominally in Soviet discourse on language and information, beginning with early pronouncements by Lenin that "without glasnost it would be ridiculous to talk about democracy (*demokratizm*)" (Lenin 1902).[3] The principle found its way into the 1977 version of the

---

3. It was statements such as these, according to A. Iakovlev reflecting on the days of glasnost, that helped him and others contextualize the concept in a form palatable to conservative apparatchiks. When asked, in a 2000 interview, how he managed to persuade the "orthodox" members of

Soviet Constitution, where it was listed as one of several conditions required for "the continued expansion of socialist democracy," "the increasingly broad participation of citizens in the management of the affairs of the state and society," and the "broad recruitment (*privlechenie*) of citizens to participation in the work [of the councils of Soviets—MSG] ("Konstitutsiia Soiuza Sovetskikh Sotsialisticheskikh Respublik," chap. 1, 12, article 94).

Invocations of the term in the late-Soviet press reflected a similar ambiguity, though their context suggested that the concept's main function was similar to that envisioned by Bulgarin under Nicholas I—to engage the public enough so as to ensure a minimum level of support for state organs. Encouraging citizens' active participation in government affairs— primarily through the more open publicity of policies and agendas and the call for public input—served as a means of strengthening the authority of the state and the nationalization of its views:

Ленинский принцип гласности—действенный способ приобщения широких масс к участию в многогранной работе органов власти, к умножению их актива. ("Glasnost' v rabote sovetov" 1980)

[The Leninist principle of glasnost is an effective means of attracting the broad masses to the participation in the multifaceted work of the organs of power, to an increase in their active component.]

Гласность—живительная связь Советов с населением. Ей служат средства массовой информации—печать, радио, телевидение....Практика показывает: стоит широко оповестить избирателей о повестке дня очередной сессии Совета, как в исполком поступает много предложений по вопросам, которые она содержит. ("Glasnost' v rabote sovetov" 1980)

---

the party to support glasnost, he notes, "It was complete demagogy, but it had to be done. I quoted all the classics right down to Lenin. He has an amazing line in this regard about how the people must know everything and pass judgment on everything consciously. It was another matter that nothing of this sort existed either during his time or later" (Zhirnov 2000).

[Glasnost is the living link of the Soviets to the population. It is served by the mass media—the press, radio, television.... Practice shows that all it takes is notifying voters widely about the agenda of the upcoming session of the Soviet for a multitude of suggestions to come in on the agenda items.]

«Для дальнейшего развития демократических основ Советского государства,» говорил К. У. Черненко на встрече с избирателями 2 марта 1984 года, «неоценимое значение имеет расширение информированности людей о реальном положении дел, гласности в работе партийных и советских учреждений.» ("Sila glasnosti" 1984)

[As K. U. Chernenko said at a meeting with voters on 2 March 1984, "Expanding the degree to which people are informed about the real state of affairs and glasnost in the work of party and Soviet institutions has invaluable significance for the further development of the democratic foundations of the Soviet state."]

Gorbachev on Glasnost

The same conceptual ambiguities and tension—between state-sanctioned access to information and outright "freedom of speech"—can be seen within the pronouncements on the theme by Gorbachev himself over the tenure of his leadership. Closer tracking of the term through his collected works reveals something of a three-stage evolution. In his original use of the term (dating back to 1978 and continuing roughly until the early part of 1986) Gorbachev viewed glasnost in terms quite similar to the reform-minded statesmen before him—as a mechanism that, through the more open publicity of various state-related facts and information (however negative), would shake up the entrenched party-state bureaucracy, beat back the growing tide of economic stagnation, and give rise to a new, invigorated form of what he repeatedly called "democratic socialism"—a concept that still envisioned a single-party state run by the Communist Party. Glasnost thus served as a new party-state ideology—no more and no less—that promoted criticism and self-criticism as a means of reviving a stagnant party apparatus and giving a new sense of empowerment to the people, a heightened sense of vested interest in a restructured socialism.

Looking back at the inception of his reform efforts, Gorbachev noted that "the reform began as an attempt to extricate our country from economic stagnation, not as a desire for pluralism" (Gorbachev and Mlynar 2002, 115).[4] In his first speech as General Secretary, he invoked Lenin ("the state is strong as a result of the consciousness of the masses") to justify the rationale for glasnost on the organizational level, deeming it a means of enhancing party authority: "The better informed people are, the more consciously they act, the more actively they support the party and its plans and programmatic ideas" (Gorbachev 1987, 2:130–31). A 1986 reference to glasnost as a "feedback mechanism of the leaders with those being led (*obratnyi sviaz' rukovoditelei s rukovodimymi*), of the party with the people" left no doubt that the party remained in full control (Gorbachev 1987, 3:415). The Central Committee's chief theoretical journal, *Kommunist,* offers an excellent example of the manner, in June 1986, in which glasnost was to function as an organizational cleansing and strengthening mechanism— not through any change in the ruling authority of the party, but rather through greater access to isolated examples of corruption. The story featured an exposé of drinking, bribery, and graft on the part of officials in the Volgograd party apparatus and the director of a local chemical plant. Its concluding paragraph, in a dazzling display of Soviet language of state, spoke in moralistic tones about the need for informed awareness of the masses as a means of preserving, if not strengthening, the authority of the party-state:

> The general informational awareness of the masses enables their political consciousness, involvement, and deep personal investment in social matters, strengthens in them the feeling that they are true masters, and mobilizes them in the solution of the vital tasks of communist construction.

---

4. This more internal party-oriented definition appears as early as 1984, in a speech by Gorbachev to party ideologues: "In the work of party and state organs, glasnost is an effective means of struggling against bureaucratic distortions (*izvrashcheniia*) [by] requiring a more thoughtful approach to making decisions, to the organization of oversight over their execution, and to the correction of shortcomings and flaws. The very credibility of our propaganda, the effectiveness of our training (*vospitanie*), and the guarantee of the unity between word and deed all largely depend on this" (Gorbachev 1987, 2:95).

Only under the conditions of the expansion of glasnost will each party organization, each party organ, have the capacity to provide that high level of political leadership that meets Leninist demands and distinguishes the multifaceted activity of the CPSU Central Committee and Politburo in this critical period, so saturated with the revolutionary pathos of creation, in the life of the party and all of Soviet society. (Kalashnikov 1986, 47)

If in the glasnost of the first period the emphasis fell on the socialist side of "democratic socialism," the role of publicity, and broader information awareness as a means of strengthening it, in the second period (roughly from the Twenty-seventh Party Congress in February 1986 to the June 1987 Plenary Session of the CPSU Central Committee) that emphasis shifted to the "democratic" part and more active public participation in reform. Glasnost, Gorbachev insisted in a July 1986 speech, was not a one-time campaign slogan that would come and go, but rather "a norm of contemporary Soviet life."[5] Instead of the party as the focal point, the media became the critical institutional mechanism for reform. Characteristic of this phase was his praise for the press in glasnost: "They do much for the expansion of glasnost, for the practical realization of the democratism of our society, and for the posing of series socially significant issues" (Gorbachev 1987, 3:454).[6]

Concurrent with this shift in institutional focus was an increased premium placed in public discussion and debate. Mere access to information was no longer sufficient. In a September 1986 speech to Krasnodar party activists, Gorbachev used psychological terms (largely echoing those invoked by Iakovlev in the opening statement in this chapter) to characterize the positive role that heated debate played in bringing about political reform: "Through discussion, debate (*diskussiia*)—at times, perhaps, heated, even overly heated—through the juxtaposition of outlooks (*vzgliady*) and points of view, through reflection (*razdum'e*), perestroika penetrates people's thinking (*myshlenie*) as well as the psychology of understanding

---

5. In his memoirs, Gorbachev goes so far as to pinpoint New Year 1987 as the real inception of glasnost as a means of demonstrating that perestroika was not "just another campaign" (1996, 185).

6. In a blunter retrospective characterization of the effect, he notes that "freedom of speech made it possible to go over the heads of the apparatchiks and turn directly to the people…" (Gorbachev 1996, 203).

the uniqueness of the contemporary moment" (Gorbachev 1987, 4:88).[7] While this process of psychological penetration through the power of heated debate and reflection presumed a freer exchange of opinions and information than the more narrow meaning of the term used earlier, it still implicitly functioned as a mechanism for realizing Gorbachev's reform policy, a means of allowing perestroika's successful "penetration" of the public consciousness. "Freedom of speech," as a civic right in and of itself, while occasionally entering into the equation, was always subordinate to the policy of reform.

In the third stage of glasnost's semantic evolution in Gorbachev's writing (roughly from the June 1987 Central Committee Plenary Session to the Nineteenth Party Conference of June 1988), the implicit subordination of free speech (strategy) as an instrument for bringing about perestroika reforms (policy) became more explicit, marking a corrective rebalancing of the first two in the face of what was perceived to be glasnost run amok, largely due to excesses on the part of the mass media. In most cases it was the broader notion of "socialism" rather than some narrower notion of party control that served the rebalancing function. Glasnost, Gorbachev insisted at one of his regular meetings with representatives of the media, was "by no means tantamount to a license to say and do anything and everything, but rather a means of strengthening socialism.... Glasnost is the criticism of deficiencies. But it is not the undermining (*podkop*) of socialism, of our socialist values" (Gorbachev 1987, 5:218–19). Gorbachev performed a deft rhetorical twist at a similar sort of meeting several months later when he managed to set limits on the limitlessness of glasnost: "We are for glasnost without any reservations (*ogovorki*) or limitations. But [we are] for glasnost in the interest of socialism. And to the question as to whether there are limits to glasnost, criticism, and democracy, there is but one answer: if glasnost, criticism, and democracy are in the interest of socialism, in the interest of the people, they are limitless" (Gorbachev 1987, 6:28).[8]

---

7. This statement suggests that, like Iakovlev, Gorbachev realized the detrimental role that the party-state language had in promoting and perpetuating thoughtlessness (*"slovami prikryvaetsia bezdum'e…"*), and leading ultimately to a "psychological illness of the system."

8. For a similar rhetorical bait and switch game, see his comments issued to the same audience later that year: "We're not talking about some sort of limit to glasnost or to democracy.

The balancing act appeared in Gorbachev's 1988 book, *Perestroika and New Thinking,* when he openly acknowledged the tension between the "Right" and "Left" (here, shorthand for conservatives and reformers) and paid equal tribute to their institutional strongholds—the party and the media—as "two real and mighty forces" that often wound up combating rather than complementing each other (Gorbachev 1988, 127, 73). At the same time he issued warnings to both camps, cautioning the Left not to "babble away (*zaboltat'*) democracy [and] glasnost," and the right not to "surround the development of democracy, criticism, and glasnost with all sorts of conditions and exceptions (*ogovorkami*)" (Gorbachev 1988, 74–75).[9]

The Battle for Glasnost at the Lectern

Two main points emerge from this abbreviated survey of "Gorbachev on glasnost"—first, that Gorbachev offered a range of interpretations capable of accommodating different ideological leanings, linguistic and otherwise; and second, that the evolution of his own thinking was such that his most "centrist" or "fence-sitting" position coincided chronologically with the two political gatherings that arguably proved the most decisive with respect to the future direction of the party and the state. The first of these events was the Nineteenth All-Union Party Conference of June 1988, at which the fate and future of the party was largely forged. The second was the First Congress of People's Deputies, the inaugural meeting of the pseudo-democratically elected legislative body in May and June 1989. Attesting to Iakovlev's claim about language's role as the motivating impulse to political reform, both events featured extensive commentary on the appropriate form and function of public language, glasnost, and the media in the Soviet Union under perestroika. The party conference served primarily as a gripe session for those espousing what I will call a "deed-oriented" language ideology that de-emphasized language as a tool for reform. The Congress of People's Deputies provided a platform for a word-oriented

---

What limits? Glasnost in the interest of the people, in the interest of socialism, should be limitless. I repeat—in the interest of the people, in the interest of socialism" (Gorbachev 1987, 6:575).

9. It is this modified definition that became codified in the 1989 edition of the party publishing house's political lexicon (*Kratkii politicheskii slovar'* 1989, 112–13).

language ideology that viewed language as a powerful weapon for bringing about at least the fundamental reforms proposed by the General Secretary, if not the wholesale undermining of the central authority of the Soviet state itself. Particularly given the growing ambiguity of Gorbachev's own understanding of glasnost at this point, the gatherings proved instrumental in defining the legitimate contour and scope of both the policy of glasnost and its more long-term implications for reform.

The two basic language ideologies on display at the meeting debates reflected two quite different visions of language, authority, and political reform. The deed-oriented one, advocated by the more conservative members of the party-state apparatus, or apparatchiks (a word that found a place in the codified English lexicon in 1963), viewed glasnost in a manner akin to Gorbachev's earliest use of the term—as an institutional reform mechanism for heightening efficiency and productivity. This view, more in line with the term's invocation by nineteenth-century imperial reformers, highlighted the notion of openness of and access to information as a means of weeding out the bad apples from the party-state apparatus and thereby making that structure stronger and more viable in its role as the people's vanguard. With its focus on structural efficiency, productivity, and cleansing, it de-emphasized the importance of speeches and talk, underscoring, instead, the need for action as a means of bringing about (primarily internal) change. In contrast, the word-oriented language ideology embraced by the "democrats"—the more liberal members of the media, intelligentsia, and party itself—viewed glasnost primarily as the basic right to speak one's mind, publicly and freely, and thus accentuated the "word" as a means of bringing about change—potentially of a revolutionary sort. If for the apparatchiks the party was the sustaining institution of choice, for the democrats it was the media.

The Deed-Oriented Glasnost of the Apparatchiks

In the age-old tension between words and deeds (by no means unique to Russia), words almost always get the short end of the stick. The brief, introductory survey of Russian proverbs on language suggest as much, and it was certainly the case in the vast majority of speeches addressing glasnost at the Nineteenth Party Conference, where "deed" and "word" made frequent appearances, almost always with a strong bias for action and against the spoken and printed word as tools for reform.[10] Some delegates spoke of free speech as a luxury of the intelligentsia, such as the Kemerovo party official who declared that the worker collectives of Kuzbass did not measure perestroika based on "the degree of freedom for individual self-expression disconnected from the degree of responsibility for the deed, but rather directly according to the deed, only the deed, and the deed alone" (*XIX Vsesoiuznaia konferentsiia* 1988, 1:94).[11] In his own speech, Minister of Health Evgenii Chazov took a different line of argumentation, warning of the possible "devaluation" of glasnost by equating it "simply" to "freedom of speech" (something, he noted, that was already guaranteed by the constitution). His alternative resembled the party-operated mechanism seen in Gorbachev's early pronouncements, more akin to an ideological technician with a tool box than an impassioned orator at a public rally: "Are we not repeating the mistakes of the past when we forget the deeds behind the words? Glasnost today, comrades, is, after all, a lever for the exposure of the causes of the braking mechanisms, [and] for the development on this basis of techniques for renewal in our country" (1:121).

The lion's share of references to glasnost came in the form of attacks on those responsible for the distortions and excesses of the policy, on those who worshiped the word at the expense of the deed. The rich vocabulary of epithets used to label the democrats and their speech acts clearly defined a language ideology suspicious of all political discourse located outside the bounds of the codified language of the party-state. The highest-frequency terms referring to the speakers themselves included such colorful gems as "blabbermouths" (*boltaiushchie*), "demagogues," "loudmouths" (*krikuny*), "extremists," and "liars" (1:226–27, 139, 141). Terms describing their speech acts were still richer and included, in their order of appearance:

---

10. The Nineteenth All-Union Party Conference (held from 28 June to 2 July 1988) proved of rhetorical import for several related reasons. It marked the first significant public display of fissures within the party, which, though by later standards seem tame, were dramatic relative to unified party displays that had preceded them. It also put the party on record as favoring reform, producing, for example, the first official formulation of a party policy of glasnost. Finally, and more important for my purposes, its still-lopsided pro-apparatus makeup provided an opportunity for party managers to air their grievances over what they saw to be a glasnost run amok.

11. All further references to this source will be cited parenthetically in text by volume and page number.

"phrase-mongering" (*frazerstvo*), "mere slogans," "anarchism," "demagogic deviations and whippings (*perekhlesty*)," "demagoguery and empty rhetoric (*pustoslovie*)," "screaming," "invective," "anarchist babble (*boltovnia*)," "cheap demagogic dalliances" (*deshevo stoiashchie demogogicheskie zaigryvaniia*), "despotism," "slander," "shrillness" (*kriklivost'*), and, particularly noteworthy in light of chapter one, "lack of culture" (*beskul'tur'e*) (1:108, 110, 121, 139, 226–27, 2:47, 1:141).

The list highlights several other basic oppositions that complement the "deed—word" contrast and link language symbolically to broader issues of power: substantive—insubstantial, trustworthy—untrustworthy, constructive—destructive, orderly/disciplined—anarchic. All of them factor into what might be called the "discourse of antidemagoguery"— arguably among the most important indices of legitimacy. Although in ancient Greece a "demagogue" was (not unlike "vanguard") simply "a leader of the common people" (as indicated in its root *demos* [people] + *agogos* [leading]), the word in modern English and Russian has a distinctly negative meaning, namely, "a leader who obtains power by means of impassioned appeals to the emotions and prejudices of the populace."[12] In the language of the perestroika era, when the notion of democracy become embraced by nearly all sides, the answer to the question, Who is or should be leading whom? depended largely on the ability to establish authority as the representative of the people. If you could do this successfully, then you could lay claim to democratic foundations to buttress your opinion; if you could not, you were a noise-making demagogue who, in some self-serving pursuit of "free speech," devalued the essential worth of language. It is of little surprise, then, that, first of all, the theme of demagoguery (applied to the democrats) should resound so forcefully in the speeches of the apparatchiks, and that, in their own defense, they should consistently invoke the name and good will of the "people."[13] Gorbachev himself tried to assuage the fears of the apparatchiks over the media's role in glasnost by assuring them in his opening speech that, even after a variety of thought and personal expression had been permitted, "the people

---

12. *American Heritage Dictionary,* 4th ed. (2000). By comparison, both languages understand a "democrat" to be one who espouses the principle of leadership *by* the people.

13. The apparatchiks frequently enlist a wide range of terms derived from *narod*, including *obshchenarodnyi* and *vsenarodnyi* (both of which correspond roughly to "nationwide," "national").

still chose socialism" (1:89). A Moscow party secretary nicely illustrated the demagoguery/democracy tension when, in a matter of sentences, he spoke on the one hand of "fruitless demagoguery" that involved "the juggling of slogans of democratization," "anarchism," and "political confrontation," and contrasted it on the other hand to a party that engaged in "constructive work," was committed to a "socialist pluralism of opinions," and "the formation of a nationwide (*obshchenarodnyi*) movement for the renewal of society." Once all the positive and negative signs were assigned from the rich store of discursive oppositions, it became quite simple to solve the symbolic legitimacy equation and determine who was filling the "vanguard role in perestroika" (his answer: the party) and who was merely a demagogue (1:110).

It is ironic, though perhaps not unsurprising, that despite the most colorful and emotionally charged words and phrases they recruited to damn the opposition, the apparatchiks themselves favored a speech style that remained largely ensconced in thickets of what Iakovlev called the party-state language, or *partgosiazyk,* as if in the shadows of their functionary actions persuasiveness and eloquence were of little to no consequence. One notable exception came from the Moscow party chief, Valentin Mesiats, who not only employed the full power of the pro-party linguistic arsenal, but also recognized the power of the media and the need for party members to defend themselves publicly in order to secure (or regain, as the case may be) their rightful leadership role:

> Outbursts of demagoguery have drawn attention to themselves as of late. All sorts of spiteful critics (*zlopykhateli*), loudmouths, and anarchizing elements have raised their heads, and, under the flag of democracy, have tried to sow a lack of faith in the path of the party and essentially defile (*porochat*) perestroika. Voices ring out about the party's loss of trust, about the introduction of a multiparty system. The issue is complicated by the fact that many party, Soviet, and managerial leaders, afraid of becoming reputed as enemies of democracy, fail to give all this "scum" the squelching it deserves, and instead retreat from sharp debates, not infrequently displaying bewilderment, indecisiveness, and at times even total ideological helplessness. The task of the day is to teach party-managerial activists to distinguish clearly democracy from demagoguery and wage uncompromising battle against the latter. (Applause.) (2:7)

The Word-Oriented Glasnost of the Democrats

Despite a level of open debate and dissent that was remarkable for its time, the apparatchiks still dominated the floor and set the tenor for the Nineteenth Party Conference, and their discourse of antidemagoguery and deed-oriented glasnost held sway. At the First Congress of People's Deputies of May–June 1989, however, they paid a price for their general failure to appreciate the power of eloquence and persuasion, and of the media, which broadcast it to a broader national audience. Although this inaugural meeting of the first pseudo-democratically elected national body produced concrete systemic changes (including the election of leaders and members of the smaller bicameral legislative unit known as the "Supreme Soviet"), its symbolic and rhetorical import was as important as its legislative. On stage together for the first time were the two dominant voices of authority, engaged in a thirteen-day dialogue over the fate of the country and the state of its political system.[14] It not only provided the first public confrontation of the two voices, but it also did so on live television, in its entirety, for the entire nation to see and hear.

And tune in they did to this unprecedented, largely unscripted event. According to several sources, labor productivity in the Soviet Union dropped 20 percent during the transmission of the congress (Mickiewicz 1991). In a country accustomed to having party-state conferences function as rubber-stamping formalities dominated by speeches that, in style and substance, differed little from one another, suddenly the word regained import and urgency. For the newly elected delegates unaccustomed to such a forum, the rhetorical stakes were as unpredictable as they were high.

Makeup of the body still favored the apparatus, with one-third of the 2,250 seats going to representatives of various corporate groups, such as the Communist Party itself, the Communist Youth League, and trade unions, and many of the remaining "open" seats being controlled by local party

---

14. Reflecting later on the political significance of the congress, Gorbachev noted that it "brought many new people into our political structures to take their place alongside representatives of the old *nomenklatura*" (Gorbachev and Mlynar 2002, 12).

bosses.[15] But in a forum where the national audience was at least as important as the immediate audience, and television the primary medium between the two, raw numbers were not as important as who actually spoke, when they spoke, what they said, and how they said it. In this regard, the vocal minority of democrats more than held its own against the largely complacent majority.

A large portion of their symbolic clout derived from their early access to the podium. The timing and frequency of their appearances allowed the democrats to disproportionally influence the tone, if not the agenda, of the meeting. At the congress's first session, for example, the lack of clear protocol for determining and regulating speakers became painfully clear to the apparatchiks as work on the first, procedural, items of the agenda was repeatedly interrupted by a handful of well-prepared delegates (mostly from Moscow) with a variety of concerns, all somehow related to issues of democratic expression and free speech. In the first address to the congress by a delegate from the floor, the distinguished physicist and former dissident Andrei Sakharov called for a decree on the legislative authority of the congress (above and beyond that of the Communist Party), justifying his use of "decree" under the reasoning that "perestroika [was] revolution." In an attempt to clarify names behind votes, another Moscow delegate, Sergei Stankevich, proposed an amendment to the standing order that required roll-call voting instead of a simple show of hands (as had been the case up until that point). Then Aleksandr Adamovich called on the congress to rescind immediately the "Decree on the Procedure for Organizing and Holding Meetings, Rallies, Street Processions, and Demonstrations in the USSR," a law enacted in July 1988 that placed heavy restrictions on citizens' right to organize and attend public gatherings. Similar intrusions set a confrontational, pro-democratic tone early in the second session, when the Moscow sociologist Tat'iana Zaslavskaia took the floor with an "out-of-turn announcement" relating to the same "decree," complaining of police intimidation at a public rally held in downtown Moscow on the first evening of the congress. Her remarks provoked a rebuttal from the Minister

---

15. Seven hundred fifty of the deputies were elected from territorial districts and the same number came from territorial-ethnic districts. According to the estimate of the sociologist Tat'iana Zaslavskaia, herself a deputy at the congress, approximately two hundred delegates from a more radical orientation came to the meeting (Rollins 1993, 1:xii–xiv; Theen 1991, 1:xix).

of Internal Affairs and counter rebuttals from Sakharov, Stankevich, and others (*Pervyi s"ezd* 1989, 1:10, 26, 32–33, 113).[16]

The real fireworks began in the opening speeches of the third session, just following the announced results of voting for the Supreme Soviet, which reflected the more conservative preferences of the silent majority. The historian Iurii Afanas'ev spoke first, charging that the body had "set into motion the usual machine: several didactically-stigmatizing speeches (*nravouchitel'no-kleimiashchie vystupleniia*)...followed by the torporific voting of the majority," a majority he later infamously labeled "aggressively obedient" (*agressivno-poslushnoe*). Directly after Afanas'ev, the Moscow economist Gavriil Popov rose to the tribune to invite all those "deputies of a democratic orientation" to form an "interregional group" to fight for the democratic cause. Like Afanas'ev, he portrayed them as automatons by referring to the previous day's "machine of voting by the mechanistic majority." Several speakers later, the same Adamovich used morphological variants of "obedience" four times in a matter of several sentences to refer to the behavior of the apparatchiks, further denigrating them with modifiers such as "aggressive," "furious," and "belligerent" (1:223–24, 234).

Through a combination of their timing, their own notoriety, and the rhetorical flair of their declarations, the Moscow democrats set the tone for the congress, despite their small numbers, and to a large extent established the metaphorical rules of engagement.[17] Their ability to manipulate the media to advance their political agenda, often in ways that were clearly premeditated, might be seen as one of the early examples of what under Yeltsin and Putin after him would become an established, if notorious, practice of "political technology." One of the primary rhetorical means by which they did so was to replace the conservative call for *deed* over *word* with one that placed the onus on delegates and, perhaps more important, the viewing and listening nation to buck obedience and exercise their democratic right to speak out against the silently subservient apparatus.

---

16. All further references to this source will be cited parenthetically in text by volume and page number. Sakharov also protested plans for an immediate vote on the position of the Supreme Soviet Chair (even though by his own admission Gorbachev was the only realistic candidate), arguing that an open debate of the candidates and their platforms should precede any election.

17. On the issue of notoriety, the nature of a delegate's invocation of "Yeltsin" alone sufficed as a reliable ideological litmus test.

That majority, in turn, largely reinforced this image in the early days of the congress by not responding directly to the attacks of the liberals, remaining, by and large, silently obedient. (In Russian the word "obedient" [*poslushnyi*], in fact, is derived from the basic root of "listen" [*slushat'*].) Its most common form of protest came in the form of critical disruptive applause or murmurs of discontent (noted in the stenographic record as "noise in the hall"), which only reinforced its image as an aggressive and belligerent beast.[18]

Timing and preparation aside, one must also not discount the shock factor that the democrats' rhetorical style itself had on the stupefied apparatchik majority and the congress's broader national viewing audience. Several styles stood out as potent verbal antidotes to the traditional party-state language that dominated the carefully organized political congresses and conferences of the past. Among the more prominent were the voice of the non-Russian national revolutionaries (particularly from the Baltic republics and Georgia), the voice of the periphery (rebels from Siberia complaining about the domination of the center), and what might be called the "prosecutorial voice."

This last one is most noteworthy because of the success with which it employed the confrontational rhetorical style of the prosecutor to turn the congress into a nationally broadcast trial of a corrupt party-state. The two delegates attempting to conduct the impromptu trial were themselves public prosecutors, Telman Gdlian and Nikolai Ivanov, who had been involved in a controversial and highly publicized investigation of corruption and cover-up among high-ranking Uzbek and Moscow party officials.[19] First in their speeches on the nomination of Anatolii Luk'ianov to the position of Deputy Chairman, and then in more aggressive presentations on the confirmation of Aleksandr Sukharev to the post of USSR Prosecutor General, the two jurors peppered the candidates with highly detailed and often accusatory questions concerning their involvement in the cover-up of the investigation. (Sukharev had already been serving as Prosecutor General and thus had been instrumental in shutting down the special

18. See the writer Yurii Vlasov's charge that the "booing and rush to muffle orators" reflects a style of intolerance that had its origins in the Brezhnev era (2:80).

19. The special investigation itself had been shut down and subject to investigation, and Gdlian, Ivanov, and hundreds of their co-investigators fired just weeks before the congress—largely as a result of Ivanov's nationally televised claim that prominent conservative Politburo member Egor Ligachev was part of a corrupt Soviet "mafia" (Theen 1991, 302–3).

investigation headed by Gdlian.) Gdlian's interrogation of Sukharev was particularly confrontational, mixing the rhetorical precision of a trial lawyer with the liberties afforded a politician in a highly charged partisan confrontation. The following extended excerpt from the stenographic record attests to the cognizance on all sides of the greater symbolic import of the confrontation and efforts to contain it on the part of the nominee and the chair (who at this particular session happened to be Gorbachev):

Gorbachev:	Please begin, Comrade Gdlian.
Gdlian:	Comrades, this is what is at issue. I would like to put a question to Aleksandr Iakovlevich Sukharev, the candidate for the post of USSR Prosecutor General. Aleksandr Iakovlevich, you still have not answered the question of whether or not party organs, including the CPSU Central Committee, and the USSR Supreme Soviet Presidium intervened [in the special investigation—MSG].
Sukharev:	I reply that during my work as USSR Prosecutor General and when I was first Deputy Prosecutor General for three months there were no such incidents....I declare this with total responsibility, and this can be established from documents.
Gdlian:	In that case I must expose (*razoblachit'*) the USSR Prosecutor General in the presence of everyone.
Gorbachev:	Wait, you are to ask questions.
Gdlian:	One moment, why questions?
Gorbachev:	You will make a statement later.
Gdlian:	Today?
Gorbachev:	Yes, today. Now ask your questions.
Gdlian:	Okay. Because these are fundamental issues. Understand, comrades, we are rushing, we....But....
Gorbachev:	Ask the questions.
Gdlian:	Tell me, Aleksandr Iakovlevich, why did you yourself participate together with your subordinates in causing the collapse of the case that you and other comrades quite unjustly call, for some reason, "Uzbek," although there is no "Uzbek" case? Remember, Prosecutor General, it is sooner a "Moscow," "Kremlin" case than an "Uzbek" case.

Gorbachev:	Comrade Gdlian, listen....
Gdlian:	Go right ahead.
Sukharev:	Well, comrades, it seems to me that a thing or two is already clear.
Gorbachev:	Comrade Gdlian, formulate your questions, and the Prosecutor General will answer them.
Gdlian:	I have already done so.
Gorbachev:	Ask all your questions.
Gdlian:	Together with his subordinates and workers—certain workers of the USSR KGB—he participated, as USSR Prosecutor General, in the collapse of the case, committing unlawful actions with respect to what he called the "Uzbek" case, although I have said what kind of case it is. This is a specific question.
Gorbachev:	Have you any other questions?
Voices from the floor:	Yes, ask questions!...
Gdlian:	We will not get to the bottom of it like this, comrades. You understand how it is. One person asks, the other person answers.
(Noise in the hall).	
Gorbachev:	Comrade Gdlian, this is not a television debate. You ask as many questions as you have, and we will listen to the answers.
Gdlian:	Okay. Tell me with what the dismissal of Gdlian and Ivanov from the leadership of the USSR Prosecutor's Office investigative group was connected. Were there, to put it more accurately, legitimate grounds for this or were you carrying out someone's instructions, someone's social imperative (*sotsial'nyi zakaz*)?[20] I mean in this case the party organs in the form of the CPSU Central Committee. Precisely those circles, I emphasize, so that there is no demagoguery here, those circles that are not interested in further investigating this now essentially tragicomic affair....If you beat your chest with regard to your fidelity to principles, stating that you declared war on Mafioso groups and that you

---

20. *"Sotsial'nyi zakaz"* or *"sotszakaz"* was a notorious neologism of the Soviet era referring to pressure placed by the state on citizens to conform to the mandates of party-state ideology.

will see all this through to the end—in particular, the case that we were investigating—then tell me why approximately seventy investigators, the very best investigators of this investigative group, people who spent years going through this school and who knew everything, were sent packing by your orders. Professional specialists will understand what it means to change horses halfway into a crossing, so to speak. Why did you do this, and will new people ever get to the bottom of it, particularly when, as you put it, people have been in custody for so many years? We, too, are against people sitting in custody for many years. This is my question, please.

Gorbachev: Do you have any other questions, Comrade Gdlian?

Gdlian: Yes.

Gorbachev: Go ahead.

Gdlian: He still has not answered the questions. (Noise in the hall.) Wait, it is necessary to answer when questions are asked. When he gave an answer at the Nineteenth Party Conference as general prosecutor, he misled the entire party forum. He said that criminal proceedings were not instituted, and so no investigation was conducted. This is a fundamental issue, comrades. Why? Because it just will not do when the general prosecutor lies. And we will prove this, because there are lawyers here who will give an opinion. One minute. They will give an opinion on whether or not criminal proceedings must be instituted. And now, in order to confirm this, I will tell you....

Gorbachev: Ask questions, comrade Gdlian. Have you asked them all?

Gdlian: No, not all.

Gorbachev: Well, ask all your questions.

Gdlian: When is it that I will make a statement? Today?

Gorbachev: Today, today.... (Rollins 1993, 2:231–32)[21]

---

21. The English translation comes from this source, with a number of small but significant alterations. For the Russian-language stenographic record of the exchange, see *Pervyi s"ezd,* 2:196–202.

This tense and dramatic exchange highlights a variety of discourse strategies that collectively underscore Gdlian's desire to put the party-state on symbolic trial. He threatens to expose Sukharev on live, national television; he recasts the scandal in a manner that shifts the guilt from Uzbekistan to Moscow and the Kremlin; and, despite Gorbachev's best efforts, he issues a laundry list of imbedded accusations—the more linguistically damning of which are lying and using lofty moralistic words to conceal immoral and illegal deeds.[22] Equally blatant are Gorbachev's and Sukharev's efforts at containment. Gorbachev limits Gdlian to five minutes, restricts the prosecutor's speech acts to questions (with only partial success), rejects what he calls the "television-debate" format, and ultimately ignores his promise to give Gdlian a separate opportunity to make his case on the congress floor. Sukharev, for his part, limits his responses to dodgy generalities and repeatedly invokes the authority of "documentation" in his defense (good manager that he is).

A final voice of authority that proved a potent rhetorical weapon was that of the electorate. Far more than their apparatchik counterparts, a large portion of whom received their mandates either thorough organizational channels or single-candidate balloting, the democrats invoked the "voter" (*izbiratel'*) in defense of their right to speak and be heard. The "voter" for the democrats, in fact, served a similar legitimizing function as the *narod* (the people) did for the apparatchiks in the traditional formulations about the party's role as vanguard. As Stankevich protested when interrupted by "noise in the hall" and applause, "This is outrageous. I was sent here by 380,000 voters. You have no right to muzzle me" (*zatykat' mne v rot*). In response to similar disruptions, another delegate declared, "Don't interrupt me, comrades! One hundred twenty thousand voters stand behind me" (1:115, 297).

It was also mostly democratic delegates who took to the podium with communiqués ostensibly sent from voters during the conference. In the most extended of these, a regional delegate filled his time at the podium almost entirely with passages from "calls and telegrams from the city

---

22. Ironically but not surprisingly, Gdlian's abbreviated trial carries dramatic echoes of the public shaming techniques perfected by party operatives in early Soviet Russia show trials, although here, of course, he is turning the technique against a perceived corrupt state (through one of its officials) (Wood 2005; Cassiday 2000).

of Arkhangel'sk." The first, addressed to the entire congress, offered encouragement to the resistant minority in their rhetorical battle and warnings over the pretenses embedded in the language ideology of the apparatchiks:

> "Comrade Peoples' Deputies! I am one of those whom you represent at the congress. We sent you to the congress to determine the fate of the country. So first of all, don't be afraid of discussions, don't let yourselves be shoved from behind in a rush for decisions. Deliberate. Doubt. Approach the truth through disputation (*spor*)....Be patient and tolerant, but do not allow yourselves to be knocked down by the sort of appeal that was pronounced by one deputy...: 'Enough bantering—down to work!' (*Khvatit boltat'—za rabotu!*). This is a hidden appeal to 'Obey your elders' (*Slushaites' starshikh*), an attempt to steer your work back onto old tracks." [1:414–15][23]

Equipped with concrete electoral tallies and telegrams, the democrats were less vulnerable to the discourse of demagoguery. Few, nevertheless, harbored illusions of swaying the majority opinion of the congress, stacked as it was against them. In most cases, however, just getting the word out was as important as getting concrete action from a congress that was so obviously ill-disposed toward them. Procedurally, theirs were largely quixotic efforts at undermining party-state authority and control. But on the symbolic level those efforts were not nearly as futile as they appeared—especially considering that their real target audience was primarily the mass media and the tuned-in nation. They were far more successful as political technologists than parliamentarians, but in this unprecedented national forum, mastery of the medium proved a more potent weapon than getting laws on the books. Given the live broadcast, Gdlian and Ivanov still managed to create a situation in which the party-state was put on trial (however briefly) for its corruption, and Sakharov, in the manner of a modern holy fool, on a number of key occasions (directly at the beginning and the end) still managed to place at Gorbachev's feet awkward but fundamental issues of power and democracy.

---

23. For other examples, see 1:334, 336, 395, 403–4.

Rhetorical Impotence of the Apparatus

By arguing that the conservative majority ceded substantial rhetorical ground in the early days of the congress, I do not mean to suggest that it did not make itself heard. In terms of mere time at the podium, in fact, this contingent had the upper hand from the start. When it did take the floor, however, it tended to fall back on the unremarkable oratorical style typical of the party plenums and conferences of the past. Perhaps not fully anticipating the symbolic impact of the congress, scores of local party bosses took the podium to rattle off regional needs and accomplishments.

It actually took a call to arms from some of the working-class delegates to stand up to the attacks of the liberals. A truck driver from Tashkent complained that "demagoguery" was getting in the way of solving the country's real problems. A machine operator foreman from Ivanovo questioned the pluck of the party apparatus ("I am amazed at how the party workers of the congress remain silent. Why do they not squelch these obviously extremist attacks on the party?") (1:117, 2:59). When they did catch on to the need to fight back, the apparatchiks employed many of the rhetorical strategies witnessed during the Nineteenth Party Conference, with notably heightened attacks on "rally-style democracy" (*mitingovaia demokratiia*), the "pinning of labels" (*nakleivanie/naveshivanie iarlykov*), and "slander." One of the more concise formulations of a position voiced over again by the apparatchiks came from a regional party chairman from Belarus, who issued the following qualified support for the movements of the day: "I accept democratization and glasnost only under the condition of acute self-discipline, organization (*organizovannost'*), and responsibility for the assigned task (*poruchennoe delo*). . . . Under all of their other manifestations they take on the form of demagoguery, with elements of anarchy and laxity (Applause)" (2:189).

Gorbachev, for his part, in the face of aggressive tactics by the democrats and growing discontent from the apparatchiks, struggled to maintain a balance between democracy and order. Though startlingly accommodating to the liberal minority in the opening days, he did not hesitate to draw the line in the later stages of the congress—as seen in the encounter with Gdlian, and also evident in his clamping down on Sakharov, who quixotically attempted to push through a "decree on power" in the final minutes of the last day of the event. Gorbachev's main method for doing so in this last case was by restricting Sakharov to five minutes (when the

Nobel Laureate had requested fifteen) and demonstrably cutting him off when he exceeded that limit ("I ask that you come to a close, finish. That's all! Gather up your report please! [Applause]. I ask that you be seated. Turn on the third microphone....") (3:328). But again, while Gorbachev clearly had the upper hand in the procedural and technological sense—with the power to deprive Sakharov of a voice altogether—this and other rhetorically disruptive incidents sent the sort of symbolic message to the unprecedented viewing audience that Gorbachev, not to mention the ap-paratchiks, could hardly have endorsed.[24]

His own closing remarks, delivered at the outset of the final session, reflected a centrist position that, in the wake of the polarizing thirteen-day gathering, seemed more than a bit idealistic. He welcomed the contentious debate that dominated the congress as a positive sign of progress, "pluralism," "democratization and glasnost," but hastened to add that it had to happen "within the framework of the Soviet political system." He affirmed his belief, on the one hand, in "the new boundaries of the revolutionary renewal of socialism" and the "unlimited potential of socialism," but insisted that that form of socialism be based on democracy, glasnost, humanism, and individual, law-governed human rights. In defense of the party, he warned that the baby not be thrown out with the bathwater, and urged that the "command-administrative" system that rightly served as the object of attack and reform not be equated with the "apparatus," which he defended as a necessary component of any normally functioning government. In the end, he remarked, "both extremes—conservatism as well as leftism—meet. And putting either one of those extremes at the center of political activity can lead to only one result—an irreparable blow to perestroika" (3:255, 261–62, 263, 264).

Givi Gumbaridze, the First Secretary of the Georgian Communist Party and professed democrat, opened his speech to the congress with an extended metalinguistic allusion that nicely encapsulated the heightened

---

24. Gorbachev acknowledges as much when he takes time to single out and reject Sakharov's criticisms of the congress in a brief summary statement at the very end of the final day's proceedings—a defensive tack he would probably have preferred to avoid in the closing minute of the closing day. Ironically, although he was successful at cutting the microphones within the conference hall during Sakharov's speech, the television audio transmission continued uninterrupted (Sakharov 1992, 149–50).

importance that the spoken word had acquired by this point in late-Soviet history: "Our dialogue with one another is first and foremost an open conversation with the people and the country. Never before, in all likelihood, has the value of the spoken word been so high" (3:91). Although he meant it in reference to the congress, it could just as easily have applied to the role of public discourse in general during the Gorbachev era, largely because of the powerful and protean notion of glasnost. "From the end of 1987 on," Gorbachev would later note, "there was practically never a single session of the Politburo without debate over glasnost" (Gorbachev and Mlynar 2002, 71).

Initiated originally as a means of loosening the control over information and reforming the party apparatus in order to preserve its authority, glasnost quickly transformed into a language ideology that viewed free speech in the name of any set of ideas as a fundamental civil right, and in this transformation extended well beyond the discursive bounds originally envisioned by the policy's initiators. Gorbachev himself acknowledges this directly in his memoirs, writing that "glasnost broke out of the limits that we had initially tried to frame and became a process that was beyond anybody's control" (Gorbachev 1996, 210). Its initial strength grew out of its flexibility, its flexibility from its ambiguity—its ability to encompass language ideologies at all points of the political spectrum. But the more the debate evolved, the fewer voices there were in the center of that spectrum sharing the belief along with Gorbachev in a "synthesis" that would lead to a truly viable form of socialist democracy or democratic socialism (Gorbachev 1996, 251). And largely because of the publicity of that debate and the heightened import of the spoken word, it was the democrats—who appreciated the word as much as, if not more than, the deed—who came away with the upper hand. The apparatchiks, in contrast, lacked a compelling story to tell or case to make, and, by and large, a compelling language in which to do so. By the summer of 1989 they found themselves more often than not in the position of a tongue-tied defendant at the mercy of a fiery prosecutor who made his living using words to incite and inspire in the courtroom of public opinion.

Economies of Profanity

Free Speech and Varieties of Language Degradation

«Для оценки положения в стране нет слов! Остались одни выражения.» [There are no words for what's happening in Russia! Only (obscene) expressions.]

—UNIDENTIFIED RUSSIAN POLITICIAN (QUOTED IN BERNASKONI 2001)

In the aftermath of the failed coup of August 1991, it became clear that it was the democrats who had won the rhetorical battle over glasnost. For a variety of reasons, their broader interpretation of the term as a close cousin to "free speech" eclipsed the narrower notion of glasnost as "greater public access to information" espoused by the party apparatchiks. But by winning the battle over words, they also helped trigger the devaluation of the term itself. Gorbachev escaped captivity but suffered an irreparable blow in legitimacy, leading to the deflation of his own political authority and that of glasnost as well. It had become a compromised concept, weakened by half measures and the perception of retrenchment. In its place, the more uncompromising notion of *svoboda slova* (freedom of speech) came to the fore to assume a dominant role in the language culture of the early Yeltsin years. As one observer put it, "The opposition to glasnost had now become not silence [as was in the earlier perestroika years—MSG], but rather 'freedom of speech.' Glasnost itself grew to be seen as a conscious policy of the authorities, as a lie" (Altunian 1998, 136).

And yet as a newly authoritative language ideology, *svoboda slova* was not lacking in its own symbolic ambiguity. Its mixed, largely non-Russian origins left it open to criticism as a Western import that disregarded more time-honored Russian attitudes toward the word and allowed it to be associated with metaphors of linguistic, social, economic, and moral excess—encapsulated by the two keywords most central to the attacks on the wild years of the 1990s—*proizvol* (arbitrariness) and *bespredel* (criminal slang for "lawlessness"). How is it that, over the course of a decade, the hallmark of liberal society came to be reduced in the minds of many Russians to the equivalent of the right to swear in public?

Language as Civic Empowerment

In the dramatic live broadcast of the First Congress of Peoples' Deputies discussed in 1989, Soviet citizens witnessed a revolutionary call for new civic rights and responsibilities in the realm of free and meaningful dialogue. The unprecedented show of open and contentious debate over the past, present, and future of the country had as profound an impact on the contemporary language culture as it did on the political one. But even before that, with the onset of glasnost in 1987, speaking one's mind in public—without necessarily employing the official voice of the Soviet state—became not only permissible but also encouraged. The event helped set off a revival of interest in the formerly taboo discipline of rhetoric, precisely as an instrument for social change, civic empowerment, and creative expression.

The two main journals specializing in the language culture of the schools and society at large—*Russian Language in School* and *Russian Speech*—first embraced the policy of glasnost in firm keeping with Soviet convention, couching it in the "revolutionary" tradition of Soviet political discourse and codifying it through the time-honored practice of extensive quotation from the General Secretary and other leading political figures (Piniashev 1987; "Istochnik dukhovnogo obogashcheniia" 1986). Despite the old forms of practice, however, the early efforts helped circulate a new vocabulary that slowly enabled more fundamental shifts to take place. The journals regularly featured word histories of new political keywords such as *perestroika, glasnost, demokratiia* (democracy), *parlament* (parliament), *oppozitsiia* (opposition), *referendum,* and *alternativ* (alternative). They also published critical exposés of the contradictory or totalitarian features of terms and concepts relating to the Stalin and Brezhnev periods, such as *apparatchik, funktsioner* (functionary), *chinovnik* (government bureaucrat), *biurokratizm* (bureaucratism), *Stalinizm* (Stalinism), and *stalinshchina* (a derogatory term referring to atrocities or excesses of the Stalin era) (Varichenko 1990; Khan-Pira 1990; Iatsiuk 1991).[1] With few exceptions, the implicit foe throughout the discussions was the stagnated, monologic, and text-based canonical language of the pre-perestroika Soviet era.

Perestroika-era pedagogical journals likewise displayed a shift in their functional orientation toward language. If previously they focused on language as an emblem of Soviet patriotism, underscoring the role of Russian as a unifying force in a multiethnic state and source for transnational pride, their new perspective emphasized a more instrumental role of language as a tool for social and political reform.[2]

This metaphor of language as instrument assumed a variety of forms in discussions from the late 1980s and early 1990s. In one, language became a mechanism for innovation, coupled in methodological discourse with terms such as "creation" (*tvorchestvo*) and "renewal" (*obnovlenie*), and enlisted in "the destruction of...stereotypes and clichés" (Dudnikov 1988, 43). Another called for the resurrection of true verbal exchange: "With particular acuteness perestroika demands from members of society a new thinking (*novoe myshlenie*)—flexible, multidimensional, and new communicative speech skills, including the ability to conduct discussions, debates, and polemics" (Dziubenko 1988, 30). In contrast to the old world of written doctrine and decree, the citizen of the new society had to "convince (*ubedit'*) the listener, motivate (*pobudit'*) him to specific

---

1. For later, more comprehensive discussions of the language associated with the Soviet epoch, see Mokienko and Nikinitan 1998 and Sarnov 2005.

2. One can find ample evidence of language recruited in the name of state patriotism in didactic journals from the pre-perestroika years. Starkovskii (1986, 34), for example, offers an array of language-related terminology that points to the broader organizational concerns of the Soviet state: words and phrases such as "pedagogical collective," "plan," "diligence," "industriousness," "a unified orthographic and speech regime," and "the implementation of controls" are all used in unmarked fashion to explain the need for nurturing proper use of Russian. Toward a similar end, methodological papers on the instruction of patriotism through language and literature offer model exercises identifying lexical groups relating to "Motherland" (*Rodina*) and "Red Army" in the works of Arkadii Gaidar, and contrasting them to those surrounding the White Army and the bourgeoisie (Vozniuk 1986).

actions and conduct" (Emirova 1990, 81). According to another methodologist, "democratization [had] weakened the power of the command and
strengthened the meaning of persuasion. Which means we must teach how
to persuade" (Ryl'nikova 1990, 27). Coauthors writing on the importance
of discussions in schools declared that "the times of undivided monologue
on the part of the teacher [were] departing into the past. The monologic
discourse of the teacher, if it [did] not contain at least elements of dialogiza-
tion, must be regarded as a manifestation of authority, the result of a state
of inequality among the participants of verbal interaction. Collaboration
[was] made possible through a dialogue of equality (*dialog ravnopraviia*),
that is, through such an organization of discourse in which all of its participants [are] active to the same degree" (Rodchenko and Koreneva 1990, 7).[3]

The new focus on public debate and expression also raised concerns about Soviet citizens' oratorical deficiencies. As one commentator
explained,

> The democratization of society and glasnost presuppose the ability of all
> people to express their point of view, but this requires first and foremost the
> ability to express one's thoughts in a manner that will lead to understanding
> and support. In a sense, we have said to people, "Speak!" but how can they
> speak if they are either accustomed to keeping silent or incapable of defend-
> ing their position? A person who holds a just position but who has not mas-
> tered the word can be compared to a well-armed soldier who holds in his
> hands everything needed for victory, but lacks just one thing—the ability to
> shoot well. (Annushkin 1988, 81–83)[4]

Employing similarly instrumental metaphors to stress the importance
of public speaking, a rhetoric textbook for grade school and high school

---

3. This same type of emphasis on the Bakhtinian notion of "dialogue," "multivoiced" discourse, and "polyphony" can be found in discussions about the changing needs in school literature
instruction; for example, in Aizerman 1990.

4. Suspicion toward rhetoric has its most recent roots in the early Soviet period, when Lenin
and others generally viewed it as a form of "fine speaking" (cf. *krasnorechie*) that actually veiled the
truth and functioned as a means of perpetuating power and control in bourgeois forms of government. The suspicion itself dates back to Plato, who drew clear distinctions between oratory that
promoted proper moral and ethical values and public speaking that depended primarily on its aesthetic qualities for convincing an audience. See, for example, Plato 1994. For a detailed study of
changing attitudes toward public speaking in the early Soviet period, see Gorham 1996. For comments on this taboo in more recent times, see Ivanova 1991b.

students explained that "the preconditions for the development of creative initiative in the country have been established; a broad expanse for the expression of various opinions, convictions, and evaluations has been opened. All this requires the development of the communicative potential of the modern person....As the talented pedagogue V. A. Sukhomlinskii wrote, 'By means of the word, one can kill and revive, wound and cure, sow confusion and hopelessness, and inspire'" (Graudina and Shiriaev 1994, 3). In a discussion of the tripartite notions central to classical rhetoric—ethos, logos, and pathos—another methodologist concluded that "these basic features of responsible and persuasive speech must be mastered by students...in the process of their entire training, so that...they [became] the principles of speech behavior (*rechevoe povedenie*) in the real lives and activities of the person-citizen" (Ivanova 1991a, 12). Given the emphasis on language as an implement of power, persuasion, and creative initiative, it was not unusual to find, alongside quotes from such classics of rhetoric as Aristotle and Cicero, gems from more modern men of influence such as Dale Carnegie and even Lee Iacocca (Andreev 1995, 41–45).[5]

New Technological and Economic Realities

While developing the "communicative potential of the modern person" may have been forefront on the agenda of pedagogical journals, broader print and television media faced other pressures that sometimes flew directly in the face of all didactic goals. Once the state loosened its ideological, legal, and financial control of the media in the early 1990s, papers and programming became not only more democratic but also more market oriented. A flurry of niche papers, magazines, shows, and channels emerged to appeal to more targeted subgroups of the community, each doing its best to cut a linguistic profile that would appeal to its readers and viewers. The in-your-face style and content of the weekly magazine *Ogonek* and the television news shows *Vzgliad* and *600 sekund* reflected the new premium placed on free speech and open expression of opinion that, along with the relaxation of censorship (of both content and form), helped radically

---

5. Note also the appearance of such interest groups as The Association of Rhetoricians of Russian and Other Sovereign States, reported in *Russkii iazyk v shkole* 3–4 (1992): 69–70.

change the style and tone of the language of the mass media. Political and economic factors converged to promote a less censored, more freewheeling, informal, and, at times, crude writing style on the pages of the press. While the old style of speaking and writing had not disappeared entirely, by the final years of Gorbachev's rule the more open, fast-paced, democratic— some would say brash and even vulgar—language of glasnost and *svoboda slova* held a majority stake in the market of linguistic capital.

While many view the period from August 1991 to the end of 1995 as something of a golden age of the Russian media, in which it functioned as a Fourth Estate truly independent of the state in terms of both finances and views, the new democratic and market orientations came at a price (Zassoursky 2004, 27). New dependence on advertising changed both the look and sound of print and electronic media. Increasing pressure to appeal to a mass market led both spheres to think more in terms of entertainment than education and enlightenment—the primary goal of Soviet mass communication—a dynamic that has been shown globally to lead to a general tabloidization of the media (Tumber 2001). Newspapers, magazines, and publishing houses alike found it hard to resist the allure of pulp fiction and trashy TV (soaps, serials, game shows, and sensationalist "news" exposes), much of which was imported from the West because of the lack of experience, financing, and infrastructure to produce homegrown versions.[6] And separate trends of *chernukha* (exceedingly negative exposés of life in Russia, present and past) and "black PR" added further linguistic ambiguity to the mix.[7]

Economically and technologically, many of the linguistic changes that accompanied these radical shifts in the information industries were both natural and essential. A market economy and democratic political system required new terms to describe those processes, many of which did not exist in Russian. Hence the great influx of loanwords from the West and from English in particular. The new market for freer, more open discourse also inevitably meant more spontaneous language production that tended

---

6. For an excellent discussion of the spread of formerly taboo topics of sex and violence in pulp fiction of this era, see Borenstein 2008.

7. A term in common circulation in the 1990s, *chernukha,* derived from the root for "black" (*chernyi*) combined with the derogatory nominalizing suffix *–ukha,* was used to describe news and other forms of mass communication that transmitted predominantly negative portraits of Russian history and contemporary society. Cf. Graham 2000; Borenstein 2008, 17–23.

to be more colloquial in style, a trend exacerbated by the influx of a new generation of journalists and TV personalities lacking traditional Soviet training. On one level, this meant a general "coarsening" of the language of the print and electronic media; but from another perspective, it could also be seen as the price to be paid for democracy—where the people and their language (the "vernacular" or "vulgate") held more sway in public discourse.[8] And this inevitably included the rise in prominence of profanity, or *mat*.

Symbolic Authority of Profanity and Violence

Profanity has always had its place as a mark of distinction in a variety of settings in everyday life. In some settings its proper use actually functions as a source of linguistic capital (Thompson 1990, 27). Uspenskii (1996, 14) points out that, historically, *mat* shared much in common with the sacred language of the Church. Both were prohibited from being pronounced out loud or used in a dismissive or matter-of-fact way: "in actuality, a special stress on unconventionality of the linguistic sign is intrinsic to the sacred sphere because of the taboo placed on expressions associated with it, and in this regard, in a paradoxical way, the lexicon of the profane is entwined with that of the sacred." In fact, throughout Russian folklore we see examples where the invocation of *mat* and *skvernoslovie* (foul language) actually served as a more potent means of warding off diabolical forces than prayer (Uspenskii 1996, 19).

In the context of the chaotic early 1990s, those diabolic forces manifested themselves in multiple arenas, including political, economic, social, and cultural, creating an environment ripe for the cathartic power of *mat*. Put differently, the vulgarization—not to mention the criminalization—of

---

8. Anderson (1995) argues that greater proximity to the vernacular of public discourse is one key indicator of a successful transition from an authoritarian to a democratic society, as it signals a greater connection between institutions of power and the populace. John Joseph (2006) makes a related point but in the opposite direction when he argues that "standard" language is an imagined ideal that serves the purpose of justifying the use of language as an essential marker of national identity: all class, regional, and individual variations to the standard are reduced to "dialects." If this is so, than a logical result of the rejection of such state order (particularly a more authoritarian one) would be a general devaluation of the "standard" language of that state and a celebration of variations, dialects, and deviations—a phenomenon we certainly witness in Russia of the 1990s.

language in the late 1980s and 1990s simply reflected social and economic conditions that had themselves become vulgar, brutal, and criminal. *Mat* and *blatnaia muzyka* (criminal argot) not only acted as a living, breathing testament to the difficult times, but they also provided speakers with a useful outlet for anger and frustration. Such a function is fairly clearly reflected in the aphorism quoted in the epigraph to this chapter and widely circulated at the time. Or, as Viktor Erofeev (2003) put it in his essay "Dirty Words," "the syllables blya-blya-blya and yob-yob-yob echo through the air above Russia like the bleeps of a sputnik. Decode these sounds and you have a general distress signal, the SOS of national catastrophe."[9] *Mat* also apparently could serve as a form of physical therapy—at least so claimed a 2005 clinical study that demonstrated that injured soldiers who were nurtured in a hospital environment of free-flowing *mat* actually healed more quickly because it provided a "sexual boost of emotion that mobilize[d] their androgen levels," functioning as what the author called a "verbal prosthesis":

> Our research has shown that wounds scarred over and bones coalesced more quickly in wards where *mat* was audible from morning to night, regardless of whether there were workers or intellectuals there. In the wards "purified" of *mat,* in contrast, the revitalization process was not quick. Historically, during "transitional" periods there emerges a mass debilitation in society, where it becomes necessary for the most vulnerable layers of society (youth and people with insufficient education) to use the eroticization of their verbal activity as a cultural (anticultural!) defense. Their speech is laden with verbal prostheses—sexually scabrous expressions (as a subconscious protest against social pressure). (Kitaev-Smyk 2005, 18, 21)

Vladimir Zhel'vis, explaining that a big reason for invective's popularity lies in its ability to express emotion that is otherwise difficult to "transmit with the help of codified resources," likened its force in these instances to that of the Aristotelian sense of catharsis, "a purification through

---

9. The monosyllabic *blya* and *yob* clearly evoke for any Russian ears two of the more high-frequency obscenities in Russian, *bliad'* (whore) and *ebat'* (to fuck). Writing on the verge of the Soviet Union's collapse, another commentator soberly described *mat* as a weapon that enabled speakers to "most appropriately evaluate the state of a country that is decisively changing its social order" (Potapov 1991).

experiencing a hero's high tragedy in all its twists and turns" (although in this case, the "hero" may be the *mat* user him- or herself) (Zhel'vis 1997, 138, 29–30). Zhel'vis also wrote of the resulting relief the profanity user experiences as a "defiant harmony" (*poprannaia garmoniia*) of the sort that breaking rules sometimes brought—being at once aware of the norms and gratified, however fleetingly, by participation in their violation (Zhel'vis 1997, 32). In this sense the use of profanity acted in a carnivalesque way to actually sustain the sacredness of the very standards it was, on the surface, undermining (Zhel'vis 1997, 18).[10]

Institutional Authorization

The cultural currency of *mat* also increased thanks to endorsements of various kinds from prominent institutional authorities in the realm of language—linguists, writers, and politicians, in particular. In popular linguistics we find, from the perestroika era through the mid-1990s, a booming industry of books on *mat* and criminal argot that effectively enhanced their linguistic capital and brought them back from beyond the pale of taboo. They did so ideologically by anchoring it in the long-standing romantic project of identifying and celebrating ethnic Russian roots, and economically by developing a self-sustaining market for reference books—however dubious their methodological grounding.

Scholars have aptly shown that the history of these specialty dictionaries dates back at least to the nineteenth century and is rooted in the mythology of the outlaw and in romanticism in general (Plutser-Sarno 2000). Even in the midst of high Stalinism, the young Dmitrii Likhachev, who later became an icon of Russian philology, took on the subject with a palpable strain of romanticism and mythologization, writing of the "magical" and "incantatory" nature of thieves' argot and arguing that it only appeared "substandard" to the outsider; insider thieves deemed it to be "heroic and elevated" (Likhachev [1935] 1992, 360–65, 369).

With the emergence of democratic institutions and the collapse of the Soviet Union, the symbolic capital of this sort of discourse of heroicism attached to "substandard" speech styles surged, so starkly contrasted as it was

---

10. For a more detailed Bakhtinian analysis of *argot,* see Elistratov 2000.

to the wooden and now discredited language of the Soviet state. Strains of more or less effusive praise colored the majority of introductions to the volumes of newly published lexicons devoted to the topic. The editors of one of the first post-perestroika dictionaries of criminal argot invoked the same metaphor of profanity as physical therapy previously mentioned:

> The language long ago felt and understood that it had become stock and rubbery *(derevianno-rezinovyi)* and had forgotten that it was Russian, and, tired of being the Soviet-style submissive do-gooder, turned to its roots. Like a sponge, all of those years—without asking permission—it has soaked up the expressive, vivid lexicon of the zone, the thoroughly forgotten, correct, (real!) Russian of the finally permitted Nabokov, Dovlatov, Siniavskii, Aleshkovskii, Platonov.... And in this manner, it seems, it is healing itself of the metastasis of pharisaism, cliché, official tongue-tiedness, ideologism, and mediocrity. (Baldaev, Belko, and Isupov 1992, 6–7)

To underscore the legitimate status of this long-suppressed part of the language, compilers even invoked Turgenev to explain how the lexicon of the camp led to the "replenishment" *(popolniaetsia)* of the "*velikii i mo-guchii*" (Baldaev, Belko, and Isupov 1992, 9). Echoing these sentiments from his political rostrum, Vladimir Zhirinovskii invoked the discourse of linguistic wealth and "rehabilitation" when he railed against those of his fellow politicians who called for laws forbidding the use of *mat:* "Russian is the most expressive language in the world! But we have a hatred of our own tongue. We reject the wealth of the language, and this has led to a rejection of Russian wealth in general. We need to rehabilitate *mat*" (Erofeev 2003, 48).

Even in more serious studies of Russian *mat* and criminal argot we see evidence of aggrandizement, if not romanticization, of the subject matter. In *Russian Sacred Idioms,* the coeditors and Academy of Sciences linguists Baranov and Dobrovol'skii deploy an elaborate and creative play on the romantic myth of *mat* as the authentic voice of the people by adopting the device of the "found manuscript" (in the spirit of Gogol' and Pushkin, among others), inventing and introducing the fictional collector of *mat,* Vasilii Bui (rhymes with *khui,* or "prick," and also suggests *buinyi* [impetuous]), whom they lionize as an "elite linguist and Citizen with a capital 'C'—a Russian patriot," who roams the Russian provinces in search of new pearls of folk vulgarity: "We tried…to contact the author but it turned out that he no longer lives at the address shown. Over the course of four years we received from him from Briansk, Rostov, Saratov, Paris, Ekaterinburg, Gomel', and Baden-Baden short notes with addenda and editorial instructions. All of this material has gone into the 'Vasilii Bui' archive, which we preserve with great care" (Bui 1995, vi).

The romantic gloss they use to highlight Bui's folk authenticity is equaled by the editors' declared amazement over his impressive linguistic pedigree ("The symphonic personality of Vasilii Bui is veiled in mystery. We know nothing about his professional activity, about where he received such an elite linguistic education and what his creative plans [for the future] may be" [Bui 1995, vii])—a device that serves to increase the value not only of the collection, but also of the legitimacy of the language itself as an object of study. The back cover of the second, 2005, edition plays up these parallel sources of authority by featuring one quote comparing Bui to Koz'ma Prutkov, the fictional nineteenth-century author of folk aphorisms, and a second, from the Academy linguist Aleksei Shmelev, praising the dictionary for fulfilling "the highest demands of linguistic scholarship."

Of course, above and beyond any romantic or essentialist motivations for producing dictionaries of *mat,* a simpler and more concrete rationale rested on the basic fact that reference books devoted to these forms of once-taboo discourse had enormous market appeal. As one reviewer caustically pointed out, many of the books posing as "dictionaries" "have more in common with pornography than lexicography," with even those who are trained as philologists sacrificing their scholarly principles to make a quick buck: "Thus the helmsmen of great Russian literature make money on Russian *mat*" (Plutser-Sarno 2001, 66).

The cultural currency of *mat* benefited from political endorsements as well, as the statement from Zhirinovskii suggests. The most notorious example of high-placed invective probably comes in the form of Vladimir Putin's 1999 press conference promise as prime minister to "waste Chechens in the outhouse" (*Esli my ikh naidem v tualete, to my ikh i v sortire zamochim v kontse kontsov*), a statement that without doubt cast him as a strong and decisive ruler for most Russians and went far to smooth his path to the presidency (a phenomenon explored in greater detail in chapter 5). Yeltsin was apparently more of a purist about the use of profanity, although rumors from commentators attributed his distaste for *mat* to the principle that "only the leader should retain the right to curse" (*pravo rugat'sia imeet tol'ko sam khoziain*) (Korolev 2001). Gorbachev had his own *mat* moment at a critical juncture of his presidency, referring to his captors in the aftermath of the coup as *mudaki* (dickheads) and recounting on television how during captivity he had "sent them where Russians send people" (Guseinov 2004, 146). All three episodes involving presidential profanity not only point to a pattern of political authorization of *mat* but also underscore its place and role as a discourse of power, reserved for rare instances either to convey anger or threat or to reiterate the special position of the *mat* user himself (and it is predominantly a *male* discursive zone as well).

Writers also turned to *mat* as a mark of distinction. Well known by now is the role that profanity plays in the works of two of Russia's best and more controversial writers, Erofeev and Vladimir Sorokin, not only contributing to the texture of their postmodern allure (or revulsion) but also in bringing them publicity through public demonstrations and court cases.[11] In fact, a number of writers and intellectuals are on record as believing that the more *mat* is used by the general public, the more precipitously its cultural capital will actually decline. Hence the curious phenomenon of declarations calling for the "protection" of the sacred status of profanity itself against the overuse and misuse by commoners that would lead to the ultimate defusing of the discourse as either a source of catharsis or of aesthetic innovation. As Viktor Erofeev put it, "Opponents fear the degradation of society. Supporters worry that the legalization of profanity will release the tension and weaken the possibilities of Russian" (2004, 16).[12] In a similar manner, Zhel'vis (1997, 135–36) warned of the danger of the "devaluation" of invective with overuse and the cessation of its "purifying" function and society's deprivation of "one of its means of realizing negative emotions and forcing it to seek catharsis in other types of activities that are not always safe from a social standpoint." And Zorin (1996, 136) concludes his essay on profanity by predicting the reduction in the breadth and wealth of *mat* as a result of its "legalization," "changing from a special language into one of the stylistic registers of the literary language."

---

11. For an overview of initiatives taken by the Kremlin-backed youth group Walking Together (*Idushchie vmeste*) against the "pornographic" works of Vladimir Sorokin, Viktor Erofeev, and Viktor Pelevin, see Birch 2002.

12. Elistratov (2000, 651) refers to it as the "complete plebianization of the sanctuary of the thieves' hermetic system."

Perhaps even more important than the endorsement profanity received from political and intellectual elites was the allure and coverage of such topics in the mass media, ranging from pulp fiction and cop shows to the plethora of shows and genres imported from abroad, including advertising. Explaining the effect of the media's inundation of the public sphere with this language, Plutser-Sarno, in a somewhat hyperbolic manner, wrote of the "criminalization of linguistic self-consciousness":

It [criminal argot] only serves to ignite the curiosity of well-intended citizen. Bards sing songs in criminal argot, literati write entire novels [in it]. Thousands of films about the criminal world are shot, where noble bandits waste (*mochat*) the ignoble right and left, and vice versa. The media commonly circulate the myth about the mafia-like nature of society and the state. And the 'thieves" dictionary plays a significant part in this circulation process.... In fact, thieves' jargon itself has slowly begun to leave the dictionary of argot and assume the status of widely used colloquial speech.... Thieves' language is becoming the language of the reader, in a kind of criminalization of the linguistic self-consciousness. Well-intended philistines and everyday law-abiding citizens, we are beginning to see ourselves in the role of noble bandits, offended paupers, and fearless slum dwellers. (Plutser-Sarno 2000, 217)[13]

Drawing similar conclusions, Anatolii Chudinov describes the two-way process of legitimation in terms of "metaphorical expansion":

It has been clear for a long time that phenomena located at the center of public consciousness have become a source for metaphorical expansion. Moreover, the active use in speech of criminal metaphor (together with the nearly constant stream in the media of pictures of real crimes) has clearly influenced the public assessment of the situation in the country, engendering the idea that society is actually penetrated by criminal ties and relationships, that in Russia crime is the norm. (Chudinov 2001, 103)

As these commentators recognized, language influenced perceptions of reality as much as reality influenced language. The media projection of

---

13. Bernaskoni (2001, 26) describes the phenomenon more simply in the now familiar discourse of "linguistic citizenship," writing that, "when street cursing is put into circulation, sounding from various tribunals, it acquires something of a right to citizenship."

shifting norms in everyday language and life may also have influenced real behavior, linguistic and otherwise, as was indeed happening from the late 1980s onward.

Imidzh—Voucher—Killer

On the surface, the case of loanwords seems quite distinct from that of profanity and criminal argot. One is clearly "alien," but not necessarily taboo or even substandard; the other two are more organically "Russian," but often far more taboo. Despite these apparent differences, the three are quite often lumped together as a triumvirate of threats to the native tongue and motherland. Underlying functional affinities suggest there may be good reason for the linkage.

First of all, as I pointed out earlier, loanwords, like profanity and argot, are often quite useful—if not the only—means of articulating changing realities and even transformed identities. It is difficult to imagine a post-Soviet democracy and market economy without loans such as *parlament, ministr, demokratiia, pliuralizm,* and *privatizatsiia.* One would be hard pressed to call them "cathartic" in the manner that profanity and criminal slang can be viewed as a form of psychological and even physiological release, but there is, nevertheless, a similarly liberating aspect of loanwords, for instance, in the new options and forms of identity they may provide in personal life or in the business world. Such was certainly the case for the reader of the popular youth journal *Ptiuch,* for whom youth slang and loanwords represented a source of mystery and a means of growth, new opportunity, and empowerment:

> Привет Птючу и всем тем, кто работает над этим классным журналом!
>
> Знаете, что в первый раз ПТЮЧ мне купил папа. В первую очередь меня привлекло это таинственное название «птюч». А потом, как открыла, так и сидела, за один раз перечитав ваш журнал, но не весь.
>
> Я стала совершенно другим человеком: примерно через неделю после покупки вашего журнала мне предложили работать манекенщицей. Выгляжу я на 16 лет, хотя мне

немного меньше, и разговор, запас слов—тоже на 16 или
больше. И все это благодаря вам. Я стала действительно
взрослой, ве щи называю своими именами. Спасибо вам!
    Пока! I LOVE YOU, ПТЮЧ!
    Марселина[14]

[Greetings Ptiuch and all those who work on this classy magazine!

You know, it was my dad who bought me Ptiuch for the first time. First
off I was attracted by the mysterious name "Ptiuch." Then, once I opened
it, I sat down and in one sitting read through your magazine, though not
all of it.

I became a completely different person: about a week after buying your
magazine I was offered a job as a model. I look 16, even though I'm a little
younger, and my conversation, my vocabulary, are also around 16 or more.
And all this is thanks to you. I have become really grown up; I call things
by their real names. Thank you!

So long! I LOVE YOU, PTIuCh!

Marselina]

Second, although they may not be seen as "authentic" in the same organic sense as *mat,* loanwords, in the late 1980s and early 1990s, did enjoy a
heightened degree of status and influence owing to the clear contrast they
provided to the discredited language of the Soviet state. Where *mat* gained
authority through its authenticity, loans did so through their exoticism and
their association with a world and lifestyle of freedom and opportunity.

Finally, like the terms *mat* and *argot,* loanwords were capable of infus-
ing contemporary language culture with a degree of aggression and even
violence that easily turned them into a source of metalinguistic resentment
and attack. Especially when overused or simply invoked to describe some
of the seedier sides of new post-Soviet life, loanwords, also known in Russian as "barbarisms," quite crudely and blatantly symbolized a new barbar-
ity that most Russians had come to resent, if not loathe.

On closer examination of the list of loans most mentioned in metalinguistic discourse of the day, one is struck by the collective portrait of

---

14. *Ptiuch* 8 (1997): 5. Published from 1994 to 2003 under the editorship of Igor' Shulinskii,
Ptiuch was among the first, trendier, and more offbeat youth glossies to appear during this period.

negative influences they project. In many of the most prominent cases the signifiers ruffle feathers not only because of their foreign origins or stylistic markings, but also because of the very phenomena that they signify. The world described by the list of leading offenders, such as *privatizatsiia* (privatization), *monetizatsiia* (monetization), *devaluatsiia* (devaluation) and *defolt* (default), was truly one that was anathema to traditional Russian linguistic economies and ideologies. Consider, for example, three of the most highly mentioned culprits: *imidzh* (image), *voucher* (voucher), and *killer* (hired assassin).

Often critics of the word *imidzh* would complain that Russian had a perfectly good word for this—*obraz*—a faulty assumption that failed to recognize the aspect of the loan word that is so contrary to *obraz* and the cultural values that underlay it. *Obraz* can mean "image," but it is largely limited to the image one sees when one looks in the mirror, at an icon, and into the symbolic meaning of a literary hero. Quite prominent in the semantic range of the word is a certain sense of depth that is lacking in the English term.

Imidzh is more often than not that which is projected on the surface for external consumption and often bears little correspondence to the more substantive subject that lies beneath that surface. A politician or movie star "polishes" his or her image so as to get elected or sell more films. Literary and even lofty as it, *obraz* cannot capture the idea of manufacturing a fake persona for personal or commercial gain. In fact, to a large extent, it, together with the related concept of *piar* (PR) or *pablik rileishens* (public relations), works at complete cross-purposes with the more spiritual idea of *obraz*.

Voucher lends itself less to such philosophical analysis. It simply has the dubious distinction of being the main lexical indicator of what was formally called the "privatization check" (*privatizatsionnyi chek*) and what most Russians view as the major con job that Yeltsin and his economics advisors Yegor Gaidar and Anatolii Chubais pulled on the Russian nation and national economy, resulting in the rise of the much-despised oligarch class, the collapse of the Russian economy in 1998, and the disappearance during that crisis of people's life savings. Even though one evidently reform-minded couple from Ekaterinburg apparently used the term to name their newborn son, "voucher" became something of a keyword for the economic woes and political corruption commonly associated with the 1990s (Dulichenko 1999, 261). In a plenary speech at a conference dedicated to the "Year of the Russian Language" (which 2007 was declared by presidential decree), the Russian Orthodox-minded writer Nikolai Koniaev offered an interesting (and somewhat paranoid) metalinguistic narrative of how the words themselves and those who introduced them into the Russian public sphere bore the brunt of responsibility for the disastrous economic reforms:

> И понятно, что для проведения такого реформирования экономики, такой чубайсовской приватизации в нашей стране помимо введения гибкого и податливого законодательства, необходимо было и соответствующее языковое обеспечение.
>
> Едва ли нынешним олигархам и чиновникам, превратившимся в олигархов, удалось бы так лихо «Едва кинуть» всю Россию, если бы не придумали они свои загадочные «ваучеры,» если бы не переименовали знакомые и привычные русскому уху слова в «маркетинги» и «консалтинги.» …
>
> Действительно, слова «киллер» и «рэкетир» не так сильно резали слух, как «убийца» или «вымогатель».…И слова эти были необходимы тем реформам, которые проведены в нашей стране, так же, как слово «ваучер.» (Koniaev 2007)[15]

[It's understandable that conducting such a reform of the economy, such Chubais-style privatization in our country, in addition to flexible and compliant legislation, corresponding linguistic support was absolutely necessary.

Today's oligarchs and bureaucrats who turned into oligarchs would hardly have been able to so slickly "scam" all of Russia if they hadn't thought up their magical "vouchers," if they hadn't renamed words familiar and habitual to the Russian ear with "marketings" and "consultings."…

The words "killer" and "racketeer" really did not grate on their ear as much as *ubiitsa* and *vymogatel'* [the Russian words for "killer" and "racketeer"—MSG].…And these words were as essential as the word "voucher" to the reforms that were introduced in our country.]

In *killer* we have a fascinating case of a loanword that apparently pushes out a relatively close Russian equivalent in *naemnyi ubiitsa*. In part, one could attribute the word's wide circulation to its economy of form; as in

---

15. In a similar rhetorical tack, a 1991 *Sovetskaia Rossiia* commentary identifies *konsensus* as one of the keywords of the Gorbachev era, a strange non-Russian word used to effect the wholesale destruction of the USSR (Dulinchenko 1999, 219).

the case of many loans (e.g., *komp'iuter*), it is better because it is shorter. But there is more to it than just that, as the preceding passage suggests. A pair of sociologists writing on the detrimental effect of *chernukha* on children argued that the use of a foreign term such as *killer* to replace a negative Russian one killed two birds with one stone—introducing an element of exoticism *and* releasing Russian culture from the moral responsibility for the concept (and the underlying reality it describes) (Medvedeva and Shishova, 1997).[16] Zoia Zhuravleva echoed this sentiment when she wrote about *killer:* "Our language has unconditionally accepted it—or rather, taken it—and has done so exclusively because it did not want to assume the responsibility for this despicable profession, synonyms for which do not exist in Russian" (Zhuravleva 1996, 3).

Early post-Soviet television advertising constituted something of a foreign import on the generic level, being both alien and aggressive to the Russian public eye when it first appeared in the early to mid-1990s. The aggression manifested itself on nearly every level (including intonational, lexical, stylistic, generic), and the matter was made far worse by the fact that the bulk of products advertised lay outside the range of affordability for the average viewer. As one analyst put it, "The rise in the number of advertising publications and places occupied by them in the mass media (and) the dissonance between the advertised objects and the real financial capabilities of people have led to a situation where an advertisement is often perceived to be something alien (*chuzhdoe*), annoying (*razdrazhaiush-chee*), and therefore aggressive" (Amirov 1997, 106).

Given the overall negative effect that the referents of these terms had on the Russian population, it is not surprising that emanating from the criticism of these words—to almost the same degree one sees it in the criticism of *mat* and criminal slang—was a strong strain of ethical disdain for the linguistic assault on the language, along with the social or cultural assault by the type of society that the words themselves had come to signify. As another critic of the new ad culture noted, foreign ads were not just affecting language, but also the lifestyle of an entire generation: "Today's children understand brilliantly what "Snickers" and "Pampers" and "Bounties"

---

16. Later President Vladimir Putin would use this distancing technique to defend Russia (and, by extension, his own administration) against claims of rampant organized crime, noting patriotically that "'mafia' was not a Russian word" (Putin 2001a).

are, but they do not know *miatlik* (bulbous bluegrass), *lisokhvost* (meadow foxtail), *timofeevka* (Timothy), *l'nianka* (toadflax), *drema* (Melandrium), *ivan-da-mar'ia (Melampyrum nemorosum)*, *tavolga* (dropwort): the common grasses and flowers of our meadows are unfamiliar, uninteresting" (Ganina 2001, 250). While to a certain degree historically grounded, linguistically necessary, and even physically therapeutic, as their use increased in frequency and the negative phenomena they described grew more acute, nonstandard speech categories assumed the status of verbal scapegoats, shameful lexical reminders of the degree to which public life had become alien, vulgar, barbarous, criminalized, and removed from a more authentic "Russian" core.

From Freedom of Speech to Linguistic Lawlessness

Zhel'vis argues that the rise in profanity partly resulted from a kind of "testing of the boundaries of freedom, an attempt to...see how far one can go in the violation of generally accepted taboos" (Zhel'vis 1997, 195). If one accepts that argument, then at some point in the middle of the 1990s that boundary was crossed decisively; in an associated process, the positive discourse on language as free speech, democracy, liberation, and Westernization ceded cultural authority to the negative language on barbarization, vulgarization, and criminalization. Celebration of "freedom of speech" (*svoboda slova*) ceded authority to laments about "linguistic lawlessness" or *iazykovoi bespredel* (cf. Elistratov 2001; Ryazanova-Clark 2006).

Despite the big boost it had received from Yeltsin and like-minded democrats, the concept of "freedom of speech" does not really have a long or rich history in Russia. Unlike glasnost, *svoboda slova* has never truly occupied a place in the common popular lexicon, and when it has, it has largely been restricted to Western-oriented intellectuals and formalistic phrases in national constitutions. One of the hallmarks of liberalism and democracy, the term has its origins in the English Bill of Rights (1689), the French Declaration of Human Rights and Citizenship (1789), and the writings of John Stuart Mill (1806–1873), among others. In Russia, where traditions of liberal democracies were far less developed, the term never acquired wide circulation in public discourse. In his 1882 dictionary Vladimir Dal' included it under the general headword *svoboda,* but the definition of the latter nicely illustrates the word's perceived potential for doing harm to the moral fabric of society: "Freedom is a relative term; it can refer to a partial, limited expanse, to a known issue, to various degrees of that expanse, or to full, unbridled arbitrariness (*proizvol*) or self-will" (Dal' 1882, 151).[17] More recently, the linguist Anna Wiezbiska has argued that, while the English word "freedom" is closely linked to notions of individual freedom, the Russian *svoboda* connotes breaking free *from* some greater force and is dependant more on the complicity of others. And while she takes issue with claims that the word is synonymous with "disorder or the opportunity to indulge with impunity in some kind of antisocial or dangerous behavior," Wiezbiska notes that it may have undergone "a semantic turn" during the Soviet period that gave it more "'anarchic' implications" (Wiezbiska 2001, 233–41). Although the concept did appear in Soviet constitutions, it did not enjoy much linguistic capital, and pragmatically was more likely to be used in a negative context in association with the bourgeois ideologies of the West, which pretended to offer this entity to the masses in order to deprive them of actual freedom.

Though the atmosphere was not so ideologically charged, it is these more ambivalent, if not negative, associations one sees with rising frequency over the latter part of the 1990s. A 1997 commentary on the dire state of public discourse, particularly in the print media, argued that, in spite of hopes that the arrival of freedom of speech would give rise to the drive to speak and write in a truthful and free language, the predominant trend had increasingly become what the author called "discursive unruliness" *(slovesnaia raznuzdannost')* akin to public graffiti (Vainonen 1997, 38). The philologist Vladimir Kolesov likewise interpreted the term *svoboda* in a manner that underscored the ethical conditions attached to it, in particular the link between "freedom" and "responsibility" (Kolesov 2004a, 108–9).

So when *svoboda slova* emerged as a dominant phrase of the perestroika and early Yeltsin years, it did so, for all practical purposes, as a calque from

---

17. In the original, "Свобода понятие сравнительное; она может относиться до простора частного, ограниченного, к известному делу относящемуся, или к разным степеням этого простора, и наконец к полному, необузданному произволу или самовольству."

the West. This was unproblematic at the peak of perestroika, when public opinion supported more radical interpretations of glasnost. But when the floodgates of freedom—verbal and otherwise—opened wide in the early 1990s, the precarious grounding of the term began to show.

Some critics derided the term for giving rise to "high-handedness or self-will (*svoevolie*) among journalists," which had led to the "criminalization of public consciousness" (Grachev 2001, 67–68). Others mocked it for having grand pretensions that, in reality, boiled down to little more than a license to swear in public: "Today *mat* is protected no worse than the 'White House,'" the Russian parliament building that served as the focal point for popular resistance during the failed 1991 coup: "People have united around it, legalizing its status in literature, armed with golden quills. Barricades have been constructed out of brave and weighty formulas" (Potapov 1991).

Some dismissed it as a preoccupation only of journalists and the marginalized intelligentsia ("Who, other than the producers of words, seriously wants freedom of speech? The wishy-washy, grumbling, and thinking reed—and that's it" [Radzikhovskii 2008]). Still others linked the word in conceptual association with keywords such as "black PR" or *kompromat* (compromising evidence), which had come to symbolize the cheapening of the social and ethical fabric of the new Russian society. One of the more interesting of these was the notion of *iazykovoi bespredel* (linguistic lawlessness). According to Valerii Mokienko, the word *bespredel* itself was not new, dating back to the youth slang of the 1960s, where it signified "lawlessness," "some action carried out beyond all normal limits," or even "a crowd of young people," and before that to thieves' argot, where it denoted "lawlessness," but "not in the official judicial sense—as a violation of legal norms of the state, but rather as the absolute failure to follow the unwritten law, the norms of behavior, accepted in the thieves' world" (a point quite interesting in and of itself, given contemporary discussions over Russians' dismissive attitudes toward the "rule of law") (Mokienko 1994, 156; cf. Borenstein 2008, 197–205).

But *bespredel* has deeper roots in the notion of *proizvol,* or "arbitrariness," which dates back at least to the era of the Great Reforms. In the context of linguistic debates during political transition, it conveyed a sense of freedom of action dependent solely on the will of the individual and unconstrained by any wider social responsibility.[18] Clearly a negative term, *proizvol* marked a sharp contrast to the more positive "freedom of speech." An opinion piece in *Delovye liudi* in 2000 succinctly defined the opposition between *svoboda slova* and *volia/proizvol:*

> In general, *svoboda* is somehow not a Russian word. They say it comes naked, they say it is chosen, but few have looked it in the eyes or know what one is supposed to eat it with. *Volia* is more appropriate and comprehensible. When used in reference to the media—*proizvol*. We have no freedom of speech. We have plenty of discursive arbitrariness *(proizvol slova).* ("Perekoshennye khari," 2000)[19]

So where does this leave us? How do we account for the different metaphors and symbolic associations linked to vulgarity and criminal argot— from freedom and liberation, to prosthesis and catharsis, to irresponsibility and lawlessness? Although to a certain extent they represent discourses that coexisted throughout the late- and post-Soviet era, one can clearly detect a shift in the cultural capital between the two at a point in the mid-late 1990s, when the language culture, in the eyes and ears of a critical mass, crossed over into the realm of *bespredel.* By 1997 or so, the dynamic had changed and the specter of the clichéd, wooden discourse of Soviet newspeak had faded, with new threats, both of foreign origin and internal collapse, coming to the fore. Add to this the nationwide identity crisis embodied in efforts to compose new anthems and sketch national ideas, and you have a language culture less inclined to celebrate the liberation of discourse and more inclined to seek out root causes of existing pain, as well as

---

18. Dal' gives the following string of attributes: "The deed is given over to his whim, as he wishes. In his actions one can see total whim, self-will, unbridledness or despotism; there is nothing that causes him to restrain his will."

19. In the original, "Вообще 'свобода' какое-то не русское слово. Говорят, приходит нагая, говорят, ее выбирают, но в глаза мало кто видел, и с чем едят ее тоже не известно. Годнее и понятнее воля. В применении к СМИ—произвол. Свободы слова у нас нет. Произвола слова сколько угодно." V. N. Shaposhnikov corroborates the symbolic link between freedom and lawlessness in his own study of the language of the 1990s, where he argues that among the key antonym pairs that have emerged in contemporary discourse are *svoboda* versus *ravenstvo* (equality), *svoboda* versus *poriadok* (order), and *svoboda* versus *spravedlivost'* (fairness), on the one hand, and *bespredel* versus *poriadok* and *zakonnost'* (lawfulness), on the other (Shaposhnikov 1998, 160–209).

positive forces of stability and pride to counteract it. And it is at this point that a more or less free-form celebration of *mat* ceded symbolic authority to discussions of "linguistic constants" *(iazykovye konstanty)* and "linguistic mentality" *(iazykovaia mental'nost'* or *mentalitet)*—language-based efforts to identify those more "organic" and authentic expressions of Russianness that ought to serve as the ethical keywords and guideposts for the speech culture of the new era.

In Defense of the National Tongue

Guardians, Legislators, and Monitors of the Norm

"In language, that which is conservative is progressive."
—Mikhail Panov

The dynamics examined in chapters 2 and 3—first the battle over glasnost then the reframing of "freedom of speech"—tend to feature instrumental attitudes toward language, views of language as a tool for bringing about either reform or revolution in a positive light, or anarchy or lawlessness in a negative one. When the debates tend in the direction of excess and lawlessness, they likewise places greater focus on language's "organic" or essential bond with the individual, society, and nation, and the threats to this bond from "impure," "contaminating," and "perverse" forces—both external and internal alike.[1] Metaphors of unruliness, aggression, and alienation, as argued in the preceding discussion of the economies of profanity, are part of a time-honored discourse of linguistic "protectionism"

---

1. My use of the term "perverse" and "perversion" is based on the Russian *iskazhennyi/iskazhenie,* which are also commonly translated as "distorted/distortion," "corrupted/corruption." Although all three definitions are apt in the context of the language debates, "per-verse" best conveys the Russian word's link to notions of discourse and narrative (iz-SKAZ[zh]-enie).

that dates back in Russian history at least to the early nineteenth century and the debates between the so-called archaists and innovators over the proper place of (largely French) loanwords and Slavonicisms in the contemporary language (Zhivov 1996; Lotman and Uspenskii 1975). Both then and in subsequent manifestations of this preservationist orientation, debates about language frequently served as thinly veiled arguments about the state and fate of Russian national identity itself. Its traces can be found even in the earliest days of glasnost, but it acquired significant cultural capital only with the increasing concern over linguistic and social lawlessness, documented in chapter 3. Within the discourse we see a relatively broad range of ideological positions, ranging from the xenophobic purist to the enlightened traditionalist. We also see a range of linguistic practices, from the penning of lectures, speeches, sermons, and editorials, to the production of guidebooks, laws, and popular shows designed to ensure some modicum of stability in the contemporary language culture. This chapter examines these varieties of linguistic preservation, legislation, and monitoring; it documents both the rise and the contours of their symbolic authority at the turn of the twenty-first century.

Varieties of Linguistic Purism

The most colorful and vituperative form of defense against perceived slights to the mother tongue comes in the form of "purism," which I understand here as the broadest sense of a language ideology marked not only by the "scrupulous or exaggerated observance of or insistence on traditional rules or structures," as the *American Heritage Dictionary* defines it, but also by an underlying moral or political assumption that violations of those rules or structures pose a threat to and distortion of national identity itself. In his seminal study on language culture, Vinokur (1929, 85–114) described language purism as a kind of mood or disposition (*nastroenie*) most often grounded in a dogma or a (frequently false) sense of tradition, and directed against any sort of novelty in language form. Three of the more prominent discourses of purism found in post-Soviet discourse on language are particularly emblematic of the shift from instrumental to organic metaphors of language—"language identity" (*iazykovaia lichnost'*), "language ecology" (*ekologiia iazyka*), and "linguistic taste" (*iazykovoi vkus*)—and all three recognize a direct link between language and national identity. More precisely, all three presume an essentialist notion of language and identity, the idea that Russianness is a marker that is both biologically determined and rooted in some commonly recognized and immutable history.[2]

The notion of "language identity" first appeared on the contemporary verbal landscape as the subject of a 1987 monograph by Iurii Karaulov of the Academy of Sciences Russian Language Institute. "Language identity" is, in essence, a mark of national distinction, though it is more complicated than that. "The national (*natsional'noe*)," Karaulov wrote, "permeates all levels of organization of language identity, on all of which it assumes a distinctive form of embodiment (*voploshchenie*)" (Karaulov 1987, 42). The notion reemerged in a more openly russified form in the pedagogical discussions from the early 1990s, when language methodologists used it to advocate for the promotion of "a vocabulary of value to Russian Studies" (*rossievedcheski-tsennaia leksika*) and entire conferences were dedicated to the formation of language identity among students and even Russian-language teachers. The organic or essential (as opposed to constructed) nature of Russianness stood out in one author's comment that: "In the words of Russian there dwells not only the purely communicative-informational possibilities of forms and meanings, not only the rules for combining the two…[but also] the past and the present of the Russian people, their everyday life, traditions, customs, [and] morals" (Denisova 1993, 68, 74, 71).[3]

The need to look at language study in terms of the rediscovery and preservation of a national identity took on more urgent tones in the metaphor of "language ecology" (*ekologiia iazyka*), most clearly articulated in a series of 1994 articles by the same Lev Skvortsov involved in the early years of the "speech culture" movement, who three decades later had become rector of the Gorky Literary Institute. For Skvortsov, language, like one's natural surroundings, has an essentially "pure" and "clean" original state, which must be preserved against contaminating forces: "Just as nature has upper

---

2. The fundamental problems of this essentialist conception of identity have been brought to light in a growing body of literature that has emphasized the constructed or invented nature of all perceived markers of identity—be they biological, historical, social, or economic (Hall 1990; Hall 1996).

3. For a report on the Fourth International Conference on "Issues in the Formation of the Language Identity of Teachers of Russian in Foreign and Domestic Schools," see Blokhina 1993.

limits on levels of radiation, the gaseousness of the atmosphere, the pollution (poisoning) of the aquatic environment, above which the irreversible processes of destruction will begin, so too does language contain limits to its perversion, coarsening, [and] the violation of semantic, stylistic, and grammatical norms....Our environment—language environment included— must be healthy, cleansed of pernicious admixtures, and suitable for self-revival and renewal" (Skvortsov 1994b, 105).[4]

Beyond its status as a natural resource, language is perhaps the most valuable national resource, as it is the primary "embodiment of historical memory." Processes contributing to the "uprooting" of the national language also lead to the "destruction of the genetic code" of that historical memory. To the extent that language is a natural and national resource, then, its preservation and destruction each carries profound moral implications ("such losses tear the link of times and generations and lead in the end to the fall of morality"). Abuse or perversion of one's native tongue is tantamount to the wanton disregard of patriotic duty and proper behavior in a civilized society. Constant scrutiny and care, in contrast, will ensure that everyday language would not only begin "to revive and enrich itself, and support people's moral experience," but also protect Russia from all threats of "denationalization in the face of...economic and political changes, even cataclysms" (Skvortsov 1994a, 83, 85).[5]

As is frequently the case with discourses of identity, the negative image of the sources of pollution commanded a strong presence throughout Skvortsov's ecological and genetic model of language, bringing it close in function to the tradition of the purism more familiar in the history of the Russian language. Metaphors for verbal contamination abounded—the

---

4. It has been suggested more recently that Skvortsov's use of the term "language ecology" is conceptually linked to the notion of *noosfera,* a neologism that in English might be expressed as "gnososphere" or "knowosphere," advanced by V. I. Vernadskii and others, designating an "area of interaction between nature and society within which the rational activity of humans becomes a main factor in development, a kind of 'thinking' membrane surrounding the earth, the world of ideas, that is, language in all its manifestations" (Reznichenko 1997, 110).

5. See also the interview with Skvortsov in Morozov 1997. Under the rubric "Conversations about Russian" that appeared on occasion in the journal *Moskva,* Valerii Kharitonov took the genetic metaphor one step further by claiming that "in a moral and religious-mystical fashion, language carries within it those same genes that are almost burned up on the biological level" (Kharitonov 1994, 118). Along similar lines, Nikolai Skatov (1996, 154) wrote that "an excommunication (*otluchenie*) from language is more terrible than any economic collapses, financial punctures, or deficiencies in defense. For us it is the equivalent of an excommunication from history."

passages cited here alone include notions of "perversion" (*iskazhenie*), "coarsening" (*ogrublenie*), "impoverishment" (*obednenie*), and "violation" (*narushenie*). When used in conjunction with language, all functioned as broader moral and ideological signifiers, indicators of a certain dynamic of power and authority. If a language was impure, contaminated, perverted, impoverished, or violated, someone, or some group, was most likely perceived as the source of the contamination, and thereby the logical target for "cleansing" or "purification."[6] Skvortsov pointed to two sources of linguistic perversion—a general degradation of language fuelled from within Russian society (largely from contemporary youth culture), and the equally pernicious influx of loanwords in the language of politics, commerce, and popular culture. Both trends were exacerbated by an increasingly dilettantish and reckless mass media and a powerful faction of pseudo-democratic forces, as discussed in chapter 3, that operated according to the slogan "Bring on democracy and glasnost, and down with shame!" (Skvortsov 1994c, 104).[7] In a separate essay he wrote, "In our age...of mass commercial culture it is easy to give in to general fashion (*moda*) and not notice the alienation from that which is native [and] national—in language among other things. Our everyday language itself to a significant degree is losing its face and its image (*obraz*)" (Skvortsov 1994b, 104).

Given his views on the impending threat of linguistic alienation and deformation—literally, the "obliteration" of Russian national identity—Skvortsov was unapologetic about the purist tone of his analysis. Defending himself from imagined critics who would scold him for acting as though Russia were in the midst of a foreign invasion, he bluntly remarked: "Do our cities not resemble cities subjugated by alien countries, their streets made gaudy by foreign-language advertisements and signs, not infrequently appearing in Latin letters?" He was equally disdainful of attempts to interpret the language changes as a process of linguistic democratization: "Such deliberate coarsening of speech, of course, has no direct relationship to the normal democratizing processes of a literary language, but rather serves as a reflection and indicator of an insufficiently

---

6. I make a similar point (Gorham 2000) with regard to the language purification of the 1920s and 1930s encouraged by the likes of Maxim Gorky.

7. Making a similar link between proper speech and shame, Kharchenko (1997, 97) wrote, "The more shame one has [before the word], the better one's speech is." This sentiment was shared by at least some representatives of the press itself (cf. Vainonen 1997).

high level of both speech and general culture among speakers and writers, the absence of language taste (*otsutstvie iazykovogo vkusa*)" (1994b, 100; 1994a, 84). Laying down clear lines of authority, he declared that the chief "regulators" of language should be writers, linguists, and educators (such as himself) (Skvortsov 1988, 6).

Like identity and ecology, the notion of "taste" assumed national proportions when coupled with language in the contemporary didactic discussions. For Vitalii Kostomarov, former rector of the Pushkin Institute of Russian Language and author of *Iazykovoi vkus epokhi* (*Language Taste of an Epoch*, 1994), taste was a quality that was "nurtured" over years, even generations, and depended largely on such essential traits as "intuition," "feeling" (*chuvstvo*), and "instinct" (*chut'ie*) in being able to ascertain the appropriate measure of "correctness" (*pravil'nost*), "propriety" (*umestnost'*), and "aesthetics" in verbal expression (Kostomarov 1994, 21). While not so biologically grounded as to be inscribed in the Russian genetic code, this nurtured intuition was nevertheless susceptible to "viruses"—in particular, the excessive linguistic innovation and democratization born in the passion of the early perestroika years: "Human interaction and Russian language use nowadays are characterized by a primary emphasis on freedom, attended in our case by an elemental indulgence, a revelry of will (I get what I want), a carelessness, unfetteredness, and obliviousness to the fact that without subordination [freedom] is chaos" (Kostomarov 1994, 30).

This fetish for freedom represented for Kostomarov taste turned sour, spoiled by the more selfish and fleeting fancies of what he, like Skvortsov, derogatorily termed "fashion" (*moda*). Unlike "linguistic taste," "linguistic fashion" had no organic link to national speech traits or traditions and was, in his opinion, the predominant source of the current linguistic "debauchery" and "chaos": "It is currently fashionable," Kostomarov complained, "to play at being discontent, original, to somehow 'switch the furniture around' in order to change the surroundings, and just simply to play the hooligan. Journalists, especially in newspapers for youth, want 'to tease [and] irritate everybody,' and cultivate a coarsened Russian language'" (Kostomarov 1994, 25, 30).[8]

---

8. In an article critical of what he called the "surrogate" language currently dominating the public sphere in Russia, Vladimir Vasil'ev (1993, 237) employed the metaphor of "taste" in a manner that underscored both its biological beginnings and its essential link to national identity:

Linguistic Purification and Identity Politics in Practice

If one takes seriously the flood of scholarship in recent decades examining the manner in which power and authority are established and maintained within various social institutions, the central role of language in that process, and the growing concern in all spheres with issues of identity, then one would need at least to recognize that commentaries such as those summarized here are themselves important factors in what may be understood as an ongoing negotiation of meaning within the (vaguely contoured) institution of "language studies."[9] Even if one is not prepared to reject altogether the existence of some national tradition in the history of the Russian language, which has forged over time more naturalized models of speaking and writing, one must nevertheless admit that those who act publicly as guardians in the name of preservation are to a large extent themselves negotiators of power in a language culture constantly in flux. As arbiters of taste (more specifically, of that which is tasteful or refined and that which is tasteless), they set down markers of distinction and, as a result, of difference between those with taste (or "refined" taste) and those who are "tasteless." "Tastes," writes Bourdieu (1984, 56), "are perhaps first and foremost distastes, disgust provoked by horror or visceral intolerance ... of the tastes of others."

Notions of *lichnost'*, *obraz*, and obliteration, of ecological preservation and contamination, and of taste and fancy appear throughout the linguistic practice of the language professionals. In a simple amalgamation of nation and language, for example, one methodologist organizes her "speech studies" class around the topic "the image of Russia" (*obraz Rossii*), and sets for herself two goals: "(1) the formation of a figurative-emotional (*obrazno-emotsional'noe*) impression of Russia—the motherland; (2) the nurturing of a language identity." Discussion questions include: "Why, for the majority of you, does the image of Russia have a feminine face (*lik*)? ... Has Russia awoken? ... Who will wake (save) Russia?" (Mishatina 1996, 41, 42–43).

"Surrogates spoil the natural physical taste of the user, newspeak alters the nature of the human mind: it removes man from his customary historical and national environment and turns him into a forgetful and ahistorical creature."

9. Among the numerous titles that address the issue, those that have most influenced my readings of language culture in modem Russia include Hall (1990; 1996), Bakhtin (1986), Bourdieu (1991), and Cameron (1995).

By integrating these themes into a Russian language class, the practice of speech development became at once an exploration of national identity. Talking about nation promoted the nationalization of talk.[10]

In the subdiscipline of lexicology, attention shifted from the legitimation of the language of perestroika and the critical reassessment of the official public discourse of the Stalin and Brezhnev years to a more critical assessment of contemporary language phenomena—in particular, the growing vulgarization of public discourse (especially among youth) and the "invasion" of unnecessary loanwords. Quite often, as seen in chapter 3, the purist discourse was pitted directly against the language of democracy brought about by perestroika. "In an effort to emancipate our language," wrote one critic of excess innovation, "we have wound up in the prison of certain complicated (*zamyslovatyi*) word combinations, at times even difficult to translate into Russian" (Liuboshits 1991, 69). Even more neutral discussions of word histories functioned as an authoritative filter for the national language, determining, by virtue of the linguist's professional status, which words deserved "the right to citizenship" (*pravo grazhdanstva*), and which did not; which discourses were "conditional" (*uslovnye*), and which were not; which structures simply constituted *iazyk perestroiki* ("the language of perestroika/restructuring") and which represented a more detrimental *perestroika iazyka* ("the restructuring of language") (Saliaev 1996; Saliaev 1995; Petukhov 1992). A 1992 article, for instance, lambasted the ubiquitous *imidzh* (discussed in chapter 3), which the author argued was entirely unnecessary because of the perfectly suitable Russian equivalent, *obraz* (Starkova 1992, 61–62).

A second form of lexical purification appeared in efforts to revive vocabulary perceived to have been unjustly exiled from the literary language—the language of Russian Orthodoxy and Christianity being the most obvious example. Pedagogical journals published guidelines on basic spelling rules for religious terms ("How Is It Written: 'God' or 'god'?") and the proper use of biblical terms and phrases ("Evangel'skii tekst...." 1995; "Iz Shestodneva Ioanna Ekzarkha Bolgarskogo" 1998; Chel'tsova 1991;

---

10. In its more extreme manifestations, this national discourse on language becomes unabashedly nationalist, such as in one author's complaint about the overwhelming predominance of Jewish writers represented in the word glosses of a recently published dictionary of the Russian literary language (Shapovalov 1991, 272–81).

Granovskaia 1998; Ivanova 1998). The effort in part spoke to a growing need in the post-perestroika years for basic information about the Russian Orthodox tradition on the part of those in search of new faith, yet it also frequently served as a means of promoting linguistic purification and cleansing (which in this context tended to go hand in hand with moral cleansing) (Rodnianskaia 1997; Miroshnichenko 1996).[11] Indicative of the link between language purity and Orthodoxy was the May 1994 conference entitled "In Defense of the Russian Language," hosted by the Russian Orthodox Church and the World Russian Council (*Vsemirnii russkii sobor*) at St. Daniil's Monastery in Moscow, with a keynote speech by Patriarch Alexii II himself. The conference also featured addresses from the well-known writers Vasilii Belov ("We Save Russia By Saving the Language") and Vladimir Maksimov ("To Defend from Violence"), Father Aleksii (Ostaev) ("He Who Is Not Foul Shall Not Be Defiled"), and Vladimir Krupin ("Russia Speaks Russian").[12] In his own speech to conference participants, Valerii Ganichev, cochair of the council and chair of the Russian Writers' Union, placed the burden of preservation on all guardians of the word, making it clear that it was likewise a battle for the preservation of "authentic" Russian national identity:

> It is up to members of the younger generation whether they master the authentic Russian language or become subservient to a foreign-born and alien speech (*chuzherodnaia i chuzhezemnaia rech'*), [caught] in the net of foul-mouthed language (*skvernoslovie*) and the vocabulary of criminals. Without their exploits in the nurturing of love for the Russian word, for our great national literature and history, the Russian people will not be reborn and true freedom, harmony, and peace among our people will not become firmly established....
>
> In the Russian folktale about Ivan the Wordless (*Ivan Besslovesnyi*), the national hero, having lost the gift of speech, was on the verge of perishing. Only the living water of his motherland restored his speech and

---

11. A study by Bennett (2011) provides the most comprehensive analysis to date of the various dimensions and symbolic meaning of the post-Soviet rival of Russian Orthodoxy in general and the Church Slavonic orthography in particular.

12. Excerpts from these and other addresses can be found in "Zashchitu rodnogo slova" 1994. Also noteworthy is the 1998 conference on "The Language of the Church," sponsored by the St. Filaret Orthodox High School of Moscow and the journals *Kontinent, Vestnik RKhD*, and *Russkaia rech'* (summarized in Kolymagin 1998).

returned [to him] a full-blooded life. We hope that the live, popular participation in the fate of the native language, the attention and reverence for it from leaders, and the interest of all society, all Russian people, can completely revive the strength and Spirit of Russia! ("Zashchitu rodnogo slova" 1994, 148–49)

As with the ecological and biological metaphors, this part-religious, part-folkloric framing of the problem synthesized morally charged notions of language ("foul" versus "authentic") with those of Russianness ("alien" versus "full-blooded"). Only a nation actively respectful of both the purity and the fate of its language could hope to revive its strength and spirit, a concern that must manifest itself in a society-wide struggle against blind servitude to foreign and foul tongues.

Perhaps the most utopian (and in linguistic-historical terms, "Shishkovian") effort at reviving lost language came from Aleksandr Solzhenitsyn, author of the 1990 *Russian Dictionary of Language Expansion,* a 270-page compilation of words and expressions that had disappeared "prematurely" from the "living language" and that, in the words of the compiler, "still deserve[d] the right to live." In addition to a "loss of feel" for the Russian language, especially among youth, Solzhenitsyn blamed the invasion of needless foreign words for its current "wasting impoverishment": "If we permit into the Russian language without impediment such insufferable words as *uikend* (weekend), *brifing* (briefing), *isteblishment* (establishment), and even *isteblishmentskii* (*verkhoustavyi? verkhoupravnyi?*) (establishment [with Slavonic variants suggested parenthetically]) [and] *imidzh*—then we might as well pay our last respects to our native tongue altogether" (Solzhenitsyn 1990, 3).[13]

Most of the entries in Solzhenitsyn's compendium came from the nineteenth-century four-volume dictionary of Vladimir Dal'—the same collection that the Soviet-era Ushakov (1935) dictionary had been meant to replace on the basis of quite a different "purifying" rationale. If the Ushakov compendium had sought to marginalize regionalisms, archaisms, and Slavonicisms, Solzhenitsyn's effort attempted to rehabilitate them—and

---

13. In a more elaborate explanation he wrote, "Collected here are words in no way deserving of a premature death, still entirely flexible and concealing a rich movement, but which have nevertheless been almost abandoned, existing too close to the edge of our worn out, narrow usage— in an area of desired and realizable language expansion" (4).

did so in many cases without bothering to provide definitions—"for greater freedom in use [and] scope of expression," as he explained (1990, 4). Among the words and expressions included without any notes or definitions: *dugobokii, dumno, duplet', kruchinit', kryl'ia nosa, kuroladets, otlapok, otmoklyl, oshershavet', parsh', perevekovat', peredokuka (peredokuchlivyi), razmiaklyi, raskudlatit', svorob (sverbota, sverb), szhivchivyi, skorokrady, slovobitnia.* While to the native ear many of these might well have sounded familiar, or "sensible," the idea of using words purely for their expressive qualities, potentially impervious to any concrete signifieds, seems a form of purism even more extreme than that of the "Shishkovites," who at least provided definitions for the more Slavic sounding neologisms. The idea, however, was that once actively reinstated into the literary language, these words, almost regardless of how they were used, would help rescue that language (and its speakers) from its current impoverished state. And in this sense, this most recent chapter of Russian purism—like its predecessors in the eighteenth, nineteenth, and early twentieth centuries—was as innovative as it was reactionary, not only rejecting the language of the emerging sources of authority but also projecting a vision of an ideal language culture based on the memory of a mythical lexicon of national ideals. Writing in the journal *Molodaia gvardiia,* the literary critic Vladimir Vasil'ev (1993) justified Solzhenitsyn's efforts by noting the perverse priorities of the publishing industry, which in recent years had rushed to put out dozens of dictionaries dedicated to Russian slang of the streets, prisons, and camps, while ignoring and even stopping midstream the publication of multivolume dictionaries of Old Russian and the Russian language of the eighteenth century—a fact that threatened the viability not only of the culture but also of the history and consciousness of the nation itself (cf. Shvetsova 1996).

   That Russian vulgarity had itself been embraced as an organic part of Russianness in many of those dictionaries, of course, went unnoted by the purists, but attested to the conditional nature of their essentialist claims. The ambiguity of the Russian purist's claimed "authenticity" was further exposed by the variety of ways Church Slavonic was usurped and promoted for causes unrelated at best to the Church's mission. The post-Soviet commercial market swiftly commodified the language and alphabet of the sacred realm by attaching it to a range of products—including banks, beer, business newspapers, cigarettes, theater troupes, and pop music stands—that had little or nothing to do with religiosity (Kara-Murza 2001; Priadko 2001; Ageev 1995). Entire graphic systems of "faux-Slavonic" emerged to satisfy the demand for lettering that gave products an old Russian, if not sacred, feel (Bennett 2011, 91–92).

New Russian capitalists were not the only ones to commandeer sacred language to serve profane goals; the language and symbolism figured centrally in the spread of Russian nationalist movements, as well, where dozens of newspapers and magazines emerged featuring the Slavonic script (Bennett 2011, 104–7). Indeed, quite the purist voice itself crossed the border into nationalism, invoking a mish-mash of historical, ecological, biological, and ethical metaphors to form a potent, but unseemly, form of linguistic xenophobia—as in the following 1996 diatribe against the pernicious effect of contemporary radio and television:

Всё замечательно: нет цензуры, нет худсоветов и, к сожалению, нет профессиональной чести. Зато есть сатанизация эфирного пространства. Черная энергия эфирных вибраций, злая, отрицательная энергия словесных заклинаний превращается в живую психическую энергию, духовно уродующую незащищённых людей. Нельзя сказать, что вся Россия во мгле, но с появлением «свободы слова» (мата в театрах и с экрана кино), теле- и эфирной разнузданности, признанием воровского жаргона парламентским языком—по окраинам России от Владивостока до Приднестровья идет постоянное проявление зла. Это и четыре подряд взрыва складов с боеприпасами, наводнения, землетрясения, аварии газопроводов, Таджикистан, Карабах, Азербайджан, Грузия, Абхазия, ГКЧП, штурм телевидения и «Белого дома,» Чечня и т.д. Злоба порождает зло. (Makarov 1996, 249)

[Everything's just great: no censorship, no art-soviets, and, unfortunately, no professional honesty. To make up for it, there is the satanization of ethereal space. The black energy of ethereal vibrations, the evil, negative energy of verbal incantations turns into living, psychic energy, which spiritually mutilates defenseless people. One cannot say that all of Russia is in darkness, but with the appearance of the "freedom of speech" (obscenity in the theater and on the movie screen) of tele- and ethereal unruliness, of the recognition of thieves' jargon in parliamentary language—a constant manifestation of evil has spread through the distant lands of Russia, from Vladivostok to Pridnestrov'e. This and four explosions of munitions storage units in a row, floods, earthquakes, gas line fires, Tajikistan, Karabakh, Azerbaijan, Georgia, Abkhazia, GKChP, the storming of the TV station and White House, Chechnia, etc. Malice begets misfortune.]

While the Russian term *efir* (literally, "ether") is ordinarily the unmarked word designating "airwaves," its use here leaves little doubt as to the potency implied by its classical origins. Modern technology permitted tainted language to spread like a diabolic infection throughout the physical and spiritual terrain of the national landscape, threatening that landscape's integrity by giving rise to the most terrible of natural and man-made disasters—all because of this new state of linguistic affairs—vulgar and criminal language draped in the shrouds of "free speech." The distorted nature of the nationalist rhetoric itself, however, largely undermined its claims to organic purity.

Language as a Window to Mentality

Early twenty-first century scholarship would institutionalize the search for the essence of Russianness in language in a more measured and academically grounded subdiscipline that might be called "mentality studies." Seifrid (2005) documented this tradition within Russian philosophical and theological writing, which viewed the centrality of language and logos in the formation and articulation of the "self." It has found more recent philological manifestations in the work of the Academy of Science scholar Aleksei Shmelev, son of the esteemed Soviet linguist and one of the founding fathers of the "speech culture" movement, Dmitrii Shmelev. Shmelev the younger argued as early as 1996 that "the analysis of the Russian lexicon allows us to draw conclusions about the particularities of the Russian vision of the world . . . and to give an objective base to arguments about the 'Russian mentality,'" and went on to parse a handful of words that for him are quintessentially Russian—*pravda—istina, dolg—obiazannost', svoboda—volia, dobro—blago; sud'ba, dusha, zhalost', toska, udal '*, and even such particles and exclamations as *avos', nebos',* and *zaodno.*[14]

The movement linking language to a national "mentality" gathered steam in Putin-era Russia, with bookstore sections, conference schedules, and television programming dedicated to the study of the Russian language as a window onto national identity, *lichnost', mental'nost',* or *mentalitet.* As one scholar of language and mentality put it, "Language also embodies national character and the national idea, and the national ideals that in a completed form can be represented in the traditional symbols of a given culture. In the Russian tradition, the broad concept of 'mentality' had its term: spirituality" (Kolesov 2004b, 74). The rhetorical link between "the way Russian is" and "the way Russians are (and long have been)" also emerged from explanations of Russians' inability to express more objective, rational thought:

> In Russian it is nearly impossible to express oneself precisely, objectively, in a terminological fashion: you immediately get buried in an environment of evaluations, emotions, and passions. For this reason, when one needs to express oneself in a nonjudgmental fashion, it is necessary to borrow wholesale from foreign languages.... This language gave us a great literature that has reflected and expressed moral searches and the agony of the most feverous passion. But it is a language that is not oriented toward objective truth *(istina).* More precisely, it is oriented toward the search for and expression of *pravda*, not *istina,* toward the ideal and compliance to the ideal, but not reality. (Graudina et al. 1995, 78–79)

Just as the plethora of dictionaries of *mat* proliferated in the 1990s, the 2000s witnessed an emerging cottage industry of popular scholarly works dedicated to identifying and parsing the "constants" of Russian language and/or national identity—a kind of representative "lexicon of Russianness" that, taken together, projected a certain ideology

---

14. The first four pairs are synonyms, the closest English approximations for which are "truth," "duty/obligation," "freedom/will," and "goodness/kindness"; after these pairs—"fate," "soul," "pity," "longing," "daring," "perhaps," "I dare say," "at the same time" (Shmelev 1996, 83–84, 86–87, 89; cf. Denisova 1997, 87–93; Shmelev 1998, 48–55).

or clusters of ideologies of language.[15] Stepanov (2004) did this on the level of concept, including essays on terms such as *svoi—chuzhie* (self—others), *rodnaia zemlia* (native land), *iazyk* (language), *slovo* (word), *vera* (faith), *pravda* and *istina* (near synonyms for "truth"), and *dusha* (Soul). Vladimir Kolesov made a similarly ambitious attempt at indexing and analyzing lexical constants in Russian in no fewer than three hefty volumes (Kolesov 2001, 2004a, 2004b), defining the very term *mental'nost'* in a manner that presumed a Whorfian view of language as a reflection of national identity, calling it "a world view in the categories and forms of the native language, in the process of perceiving the unifying intellectual, spiritual, and volitional qualities of national character in its typical manifestations" (Kolesov 2004b, 15). Taken at face value, the definition echoed the sort of justification for close etymological study one finds in the field of "history of concepts" (*Begriffsgeschichte*) as practiced by Koselleck (2002) and others. At the very least, it was a powerful metalinguistic assumption about the way language worked that was shared by many in the preservationist camp and was the source of a productive industry of scholarship that attempted to look for clues about national identity through quintessentially *Russian* terms. Kolesov singled out the following as some of the keywords of Russian linguistic identity, many of which overlapped with concepts examined by Stepanov and others: *dusha i lichnost'* (soul and personality/identity), *liubov' i svoboda* (love and freedom), *chest' i sovest'* (honor and conscience), *pravda-istina* (truth), *sud'ba i schast'e* (fate and happiness), *uzhas i gnev* (horror and rage) *smex i gore* (laughter and grief). His chapter on the dominant linguistically relevant traits of Russian mentality featured the centrality of concrete deeds over facts and ideas; the moral dimension commonly attributed to deeds, thoughts, and words; a belief that "beauty is more important than utility" (*krasota vazhnee pol'zy*); a common disdain for philistine practicality and scholarly positivism; the primacy of spirituality over mercantile sensibilities; and the sort of ambivalent attitude toward the spoken word seen in examples of language ideologies discussed in my introduction:

---

15. Interestingly, in size and quality this industry approaches the competing, or at least parallel, industry of dictionaries of "alien" language such as profanity, thieves' slang, and loanwords.

The Russian word as an embodiment of thought does not permit superfluities in form, excessively rhetorical phrases and figures, embellishments and prolixity.... Laconism of form together with substantiveness in thought— that is what is important, and the one who speaks intelligently and briefly is valued, speaking to the word of the other, not to the echoing emptiness caused by the absence of human life (*bezliud'e*). The monologue offends; it leads to *grief*. The Russian utterance is the prophetic phrase, summoned to convince of its *pravda,* rather than prove abstract *istina*.... (Kolesov 2004a, 32–33, 76)

Legislating Language: State Efforts at Policing Proper Usage

Efforts by the Academy and Church to rein in linguistic excess and preserve the purity of the national tongue can be traced back to the very beginning of the post-Soviet reform era, although during this earlier period these efforts tended to go largely unnoticed outside of the walls of these institutions, their journals, and conferences. Church-sponsored conferences on the fate of the Russian language could not compete with American, Mexican, and Brazilian soaps that glamorized violence and adultery. Dostoevsky and Berdiaev were no match for Stallone, Schwarzenegger, and Willis. Punk rock and rappers drowned out traditional folk tunes and Church liturgy. With the growing perception later in the 1990s of a language culture run amok, however, they began to find support among the broader public, buttressed by growing critical attention to national politicians and the main perpetrators of the excess, the media themselves. Calls for legislation designed to protect and cleanse the Russian language of loanwords and vulgarity can be seen with particular frequency on the pages of *Literary Russia* and *The Literary Gazette* throughout the latter part of the 1990s (e.g., Rudnitskii et al. 1996; Anishkin 1997; "V zashchitu very i dukha naroda!" 1997; Ramenskii 1998). Indeed, it is no accident that within months of Yeltsin's 1995 challenge to the Russian people to articulate a new national ideology he also decreed into existence the President's Russian Language Council. A body made up of distinguished writers, philologists, university administrators, and state officials, it was assigned with the task of discussing and reporting to the President on "issues relating to the support and development of the Russian language." ("Sovet po russkomu iazyku...." 1996). In a January 1997 preliminary report the Council recommended, among other things, the regulation of public discourse through legislation (by establishing, for instance, language standards for advertising and the mass media); the production of popular Russian language lessons for television and radio; and the monitoring of the language practices of key problem areas—the business world, the mass media, the movie industry, and advertising—to provide them with "practical recommendations" for the "elevation of speech culture" ("O federal 'noi tselevoi programme...." 1997).[16] While there is some evidence of popular support for the creation of legislation that would defend and preserve the Russian language, the Russian Language Council under Yeltsin did not enjoy nearly the same degree of public recognition and moral authority as the French counterpart that served largely as its inspiration. In fact, during Yeltsin's presidency none of the Council's goals or recommendations made it beyond this preliminary report, and the Council itself was shut down in 1998 by Prime Minister Kirienko owing to lack of funding (Vorotnikov 2002).[17] Yeltsin likewise approved the Russian legislature's "Comprehensive Program for the Russian Language, 1996–2001," but this too was starved for funds and nothing was accomplished (only 0.5 percent of the allotted funds were actually distributed [Vorotnikov 2002]).

The government's involvement in language policy increased significantly during Vladimir Putin's first two terms as President, though with mixed success. In January 2000, Putin revived the Russian Language Council, this time giving it greater financial and symbolic support than it had enjoyed under Yeltsin. In contrast to its first-generation counterpart, the new Council acted swiftly to bring issues of language closer to both political and popular consciousness, with projects such as the Internet portal "Russkii iazyk" (www.gramota.ru), a virtual mediator of language-related issues and resources, including official documents and decisions, scholarly papers, national contests, conference announcements and reports, informal

---

16. Part of the Council's problem also seems to have stemmed from a lack of publicity—an inability to draw the attention of the very media it sought to purify (see Parnakh 1997).

17. The Council's "quiet burial" was noted by Kostomarov (himself a member of the group) in a 1999 speech on the state of the Russian language (Kostomarov 1999).

chat forums, and an extensive catalogue of online resources. In July 2001 the government approved the "Comprehensive Program on the Russian Language for 2002–2005," with an allotted budget of 80 million rubles and a broad range of plans that include the development of a new code of usage rules, a new generation of textbooks, technology-based methods and materials for teaching and learning, and a series of TV and radio programs "propagandizing Russian language and culture" ("O federal 'noi tselevoi programme...." 2002).

In 2002 Putin signed a law making Cyrillic the official alphabet of the Russian Federation and in 2005, after several years of contentious debate, the Russian parliament passed a law "On the State Language" (*O gosudarstvennom iazyke*), which sought to restrict loanwords, vulgarity, and other nonstandard verbal practices in all government business, as well as to establish Russian as the official language of state. Almost immediately the law was berated for its glaring loopholes and lack of teeth in the way of enforcement. Nevertheless, it still stood out symbolically as a declaration of the bounds of purity and the rightful place of Russian (as the first among equals) in a multiethnic, multilingual nation. According to article 1, paragraph 5 of the law: "The defense and support of Russian as the state language of the Russian Federation enables the increase and mutual enrichment of the spiritual culture of the peoples of the Russian Federation."[18]

Although largely symbolic, these efforts—particularly those designed to use the mass media and Internet to bring language issues to the attention of the general public—were significant in that they brought new legislative- and media-based impetus to issues that had largely been restricted to the pages of professional journals, conferences, roundtables, and commissions. Beginning in the late 1990s, purists began to make inroads into the very media they hoped to rein in—radio, television, the print media, and the Internet. These mass-oriented venues held greater potential for influencing the popular linguistic consciousness, creating space for what Cameron (1999) calls "folk linguistics"—opinionated nonspecialists engaging in discussions about their mother tongue in public.

---

18. For a copy of the law in its entirety and scholarly discussions of its history and efficacy, see *International Forum* 2006.

We Speak Russian: Mass Media as Norm Negotiator

Although still outnumbered by the relatively unmediated influx of violators of linguistic norms (or promulgators of linguistic innovation, depending on one's perspective), language protectors were at least and at last waging their campaign for normalization on the same playing field. Television proved too pricey a venue for popular language programs, but radio came to host a number of shows, including *We Speak Russian* (*Govorim po-russkii,* 1998–present) on the station Echo of Moscow *(Ekho Moskvy)*; *The Grammarian (Gramotei,* 2003–2007) on Radio-Beacon and Voice of Russia *(Radio-Maiak* and *Golos Rossii); Erasing Illiteracy (Likbez,* 2001–2008 [a stump compound of *likvidatsiia bezgrammotnosti,* which arose during earlier Soviet literacy campaigns]), hosted by Russian News Service *(Russkaia sluzhba novostei); and From Russian to Russian* (*S russkogo na russkii*) and *How Is That In Russian? (Kak eto po-russki?)* on Radio Russia *(Radio Rossiia)* (cf. Ryazanova-Clarke 2006). They did so in a manner that engaged the listening public, introducing a more effective, even democratic, mode of interaction that promoted popular expression of opinions on language and negotiations of normative boundaries.

As one of the longest running and most successful of the lot, *We Speak Russian*[19] serves as a particularly appropriate case study in the shape and impact of norm negotiation and folk linguistics in the age of mass and new media, as well as some of the dominant trends in public discussions of language since the turn of the twenty-first century. The show began in December 1998 as a weekly broadcast featuring comments, analyses, and etymologies by the cohosts and trained philologists Marina Koroleva and Ol'ga Severskaia. Then the only such program on the air, it quickly grew popular and expanded to include a shorter daily rubric, *What's Correct?* (*Kak pravil'no?*), hosted by Koroleva, and dedicated specifically to issues of usage. At the request of station producers, they soon expanded again, moving to an hour-long live broadcast on Sunday mornings that included guests, games, prizes, and live interaction with the listening audience

---

19. The Russian title for the program contains a play on words that gets lost in English translation; it not only implies the declarative "We speak Russian!" but also carries the hortative connotation of "Let's speak Russian!"—dual modalities that nicely reflect the multiple functions of the program.

(Koroleva 2003, 3–4). To this day, one may tune in Sunday mornings and listen to what has become something of a variety show about language, usually hosted by Koroleva, Severskaia, and the Echo of Moscow journalist (and graduate of the GITIS theater school) Kseniia Larina.

According to Severskaia, the *We Speak Russian* listening audience differs little from that of Echo of Moscow as a whole, "since issues of language are of interest to everyone, without exception." Based on calls received, the most active participants are "those with a higher education between the ages of thirty and forty-five, and the number of male, white-collar professionals seems on the rise." The reach of the broadcast, Severskaia notes, extends beyond the live and virtual communities and into Russian classrooms: "Shows about Russian are in demand among teachers—both school teachers and teachers of Russian as a foreign language; they are recorded and used as learning materials in classes. They also serve as a means of monitoring the media and the public sphere...and resisting the onslaught of illiterate usage."[20]

The structure of the show has evolved over time—no small reason being the need to keep listeners engaged and ratings up—and has expanded into other media spheres as well, turning what was once just a radio show into something of a multimedia institution.[21] Both Koroleva and Severskaia have authored regular language columns in print venues—Koroleva in the eponymous column "We Speak Russian" for *Rossiiskaia gazeta* from 2003 to the present and Severskaia in *Vremia MN,* under the headings of "Word for Word" (*Slovo za slovo* 2003), "We Speak Russian" in *Rodnaia gazeta* (2006–2007), and "Speech Culture" (*Kul'tura rechi*) and "You Asked? We Answer!" ("Sprashivali? Otvechaem!") in *Russkii iazyk.*[22] Each has published a book based on material from the show (Koroleva 2003; Severskaia 2004). They debuted on the Internet with a discussion forum linked to the site, which exists to this day but has taken on a life largely independent

---

20. Personal correspondence with the author, 8 September 2008. Subsequent quotes from Severskaia are from this correspondence.

21. On the ratings-driven need to devise new ways of attracting and keeping listeners, Severskaia writes "the infamous 'rating' and 'share,' as they begin to fall, force us to quickly change the conception of the show."

22. Koroleva's columns for *Rossiiskaia gazeta* are available online at "Kolonka Mariny Korolevoi," *RG.RU,* http://www.rg.ru/plus/koroleva (accessed 8 August 2012).

of the show.[23] More recently they have integrated text messaging, blitz polling, and blogs to create additional ways of engaging folk linguists in the debates.

A closer look at the format of the show suggests that much of its success stems from a winning mix of enlightenment, engagement, and entertainment. It offers a host of informational rubrics, background on various aspects of the history of the language, language-related resources, and reports on matters of language policy. It provides nuts-and-bolts explanations of usage issues, sometimes spontaneously, sometimes in the form of set rubrics such as the previously mentioned *What's Correct?, The Reference Desk (Spravochnoe biuro)*, and *Radio Almanac*. At least in its later manifestations, the show has also involved a considerable amount of give-and-take through the discussion forums and listener and reader comments and questions submitted by phone, email, text message, or blog. Its interactive component also comes in the form of play—on-air quiz questions and games that occupy nearly one-half of the broadcast in its more recent form and give listeners the chance to test their language skills and win some sort of edifying prize. The current title of the program, *We Speak Russian: Game Show (peredacha-Igra)*, underscores the notion of metalanguage as entertainment.

Varieties of Norm Negotiation

A closer look at the show's content reveals two basic types of norm negotiation. "Authoritative" norm negotiation features more "top-down" metalinguistic practices such as clarifying, articulating, and generating rules, laws, or guidelines about what is right and wrong, proper and improper. Here, the negotiation takes place essentially on unequal turf, between the authoritative hosts or guests, on the one hand, and on the other hand, one of two types of audience—either users in search of answers (in advice mode), or the perpetrators of linguistic violations (in policing or monitoring mode).[24] "Democratic" norm negotiation features more inter-

23. The *We Speak Russian* forum archive contains entries dating back to 1 October 1999 (http://zbook.ru/book.cgi?GPR-forum [accessed 12 July 2013]).

24. One may well question the status of this sort of activity as "negotiation"; I retain the term, qualified by inclusion in quotes, to acknowledge the listener's ability, even in this more

active, give-and-take, discussion and debate between hosts and listeners or readers. Here the negotiation more actively includes parties on all sides, although it is clear that the views of the hosts hold more sway (they are still the specialists, choose the themes, direct discussion, and often select user input). In many cases, it should be added, the two modes of negotiation can and often do overlap.

Authoritative norm negotiation more closely resembles the traditional practice of "speech culture," where there are relatively clear lines between "specialist" and everyday language user, and the latter more often than not is expected to abide by the professional pronouncements of the former. Despite the traditional nature of the practice, however, its transposition into a weekly interactive radio show instills the old practice with new vibrancy. This comes in part from the energy and spontaneity that the live format brings to discussions of even the oldest of timeworn issues. The regularity of the broadcasts also brings a degree of relevance often untenable for published books—a piece on the lexicon of balls and dancing at New Year celebrations (1 January 2003), one on the origin of crib notes (*shpargalki*) during university entrance exams (18 June 2000), a discussion of Putinisms in the wake of the former President's final press conference (17 February 2008), or a piece on "the language of top managers (*top-menedzhery*)" in the winter of 2006 (5 February 2006), when the popular novels about the new Russian bourgeoisie by Sergei Minaev, Oksana Robski, and others were in wide circulation.[25] Finally, the show injects traditional speech culture practices with new life by offering an entertaining mix of subgenres that strike the right balance between sparkle and substance.

One such subgenre is a revival of the speech culture tradition's "linguistic first-aid," a quick-response mechanism designed to help listeners (and Internet readers) solve their usage problems (e.g., Which is it—*kUkhonnyi* or *kukhOnnyi* [kitchen (adj.)]? How about *odnovrEmennyi* vs. *odnovremEnnyi* [simultaneous]? [29 April 2007]). A related practice comes in the form of what might be called "linguistic self-help"—concrete advice to listeners geared toward maneuvering through practical everyday situations. For listeners concerned about job-related speech etiquette, for

---

top-down form of attempted inculcation, to react—be it in the form of adoption, modified personalization, or rejection.

25. All cited shows are listed by the date on which the show aired, based on audio files and transcripts posted at http://www.echo.msk.ru/programs/speakrus/ (accessed 19 August 2012).

instance, the 8 January 2006 broadcast discussed the use of *ty* versus *vy* in the workplace, and two months later the hosts reached out to job-seeking listeners by discussing appropriate and inappropriate language for interviews (12 March 2006). A 21 November 2004 show cast its net wider to all those interested in improving their speech skills by tackling the question, Is it possible to teach someone how to speak attractively and correctly? (*Mozhno li nauchit' krasivo i pravil'no govorit'?*) and inviting two guest specialists from the speech department of the Shchukin Theater Institute to offer their views (which were unsurprisingly optimistic about the prospects, given that they had just written a book titled *104 Exercises in Diction and Pronunciation for Independent Work*) (Brusser and Ossovskaia, 2005).

Another productive type of authoritative norm negotiation comes in the form of linguistic enlightenment—commentaries and rubrics dedicated to educating listeners on a variety of language topics, from set pieces on archaisms ("Forgotten Words" [*Zabytye slova*]); loanwords ("Foreigners in Russian" [*Inostrantsy v russkom*]); and vulgarisms ("Rude words" [*Sil'nye slovechki*]), to forays into the history of the Russian language designed to offer listeners glimpses of Russian's linguistic past.[26]

A third productive authoritative practice falls into the category of "language monitoring" or "policing." Again, it is a time-honored practice by language specialists, but here the frequency and the interactive nature allow the hosts of *We Speak Russian* to do it in a more engaging, more immediately relevant, and more sustained manner. In December 2003–February 2004, for instance, they dedicated a "miniseries" to the language of advertising. Later that same year they addressed the rampant use of the parasitic (*slovo-parazit*) phrase "in reality" (*na samom dele*), suggesting that it functioned as something of a verbal antidote to the ubiquitous "seemingly" (*kak by*)—itself, they argued, a phraseological indicator of the profound uncertainty that colored Russian perspectives through the 1990s (6 November 2005).

---

26. Such as the decade-by-decade survey of the linguistic highlights and lowlights of the Soviet era that aired during the summer of 2000 (including the Ushakov dictionary for the 1940s and the origins and proper usage of the phrase "traitor of the Motherland" [*izmennik Rodiny*] for the 1950s). The entertaining presentation of the "history of the language, popularizing knowledge about language, and the achievements of national and international Russian studies" rank high in Severskaia's own list of goals for the program—along with "showing [listeners] the place of language in the life of contemporary society."

Other subgenres of more authoritative norm negotiation include reports on contemporary Russian language policy and legislation, such as the 2000 draft legislation "On the Russian language as the state language of the RF" (22 November 2000), the status of Russian in countries of the "near abroad" (featuring one country per show, November–December 2002), and a proposed initiative requiring upper-level bureaucrats to pass a Russian language proficiency test (21 April 2004).

The show's producers also integrate metalinguistic public relations in the form of book reviews and guest specialists, in effect killing two birds with one stone—getting synopses of the content on language issues out while enhancing the linguistic capital of the experts and resources in question. On 22 November 2000, for example, *We Speak Russian* hosts discussed the launch of the new government-backed language "portal" *Russkii iazyk* (www.gramota.ru). The rubric "Our Kindergarten" (*Nash detskii sad*) appeared later in the same broadcast, and was based on *From Two to Five* (*Ot dvukh do piati*), the classic book on children's language by the Soviet author Kornei Chukovskii. For an extended period in 2001 the hosts integrated the notorious mangling of Russian by leading Russian politicians collected in *Itogi* magazine's regular rubric "Interjections" (*Mezhdometiia*, e.g., 31 January 2001), thus extending the scope and shelf life of this jocular form of public, metalinguistic shaming.

Folk-Linguistic Practices

While many of the above-mentioned practices resemble the traditional spheres of influence of language specialists, nearly all can be rescripted as more democratic practices by drawing on the interactive interfaces accessible to the various branches of the *We Speak Russian* project. Severskaia, in fact, sees the hosts' function not so much as edifiers as of interlocutors sensitive to the needs and interests of listeners: "We study our listeners and offer them that which is essential to them at the moment. We do not preach (*My ne pouchaem*), but rather reason together with them." Take the practice of language monitoring as a case in point. Rather than penning a description of or diatribe against neologisms that have entered or "distorted" the contemporary mass media, the *We Speak Russian* hosts enlist listeners to offer their own discoveries, then publish the collective labor in the form of a "List of Disgusting Neologisms" (*Spisok otvratitel'nykh neologiz-mov*) on the program's website in the form of an "Internet event" (*internet-aktsiia*).[27] They have orchestrated a similar "event" dedicated to "Hated Forms of Address" (*Eti nenavistnye obrashcheniia!*)[28] and on 30 June 2006 organized a "popular monitoring" (*narodnyi monitoring*) of the mass media called "On the Air Today—In Your Apartment Tomorrow?" (*Segodnia v efire—zavtra v vashei kvartire?*), in which listeners were instructed to collect mistakes they heard on the air and send them in to *We Speak Russian*. The "gotcha" nature of the last event and the charged language of the first two ("disgusting," "hated") clearly tip the hand of the hosts; folk linguists are expected to share in their distaste. But rather than being preached at, they are enlisted as co-monitors, a kind of civic language patrol. It is noteworthy that the hosts on several occasions point to the "Russian Language Service" (*Sluzhba russkogo iazyka*), a citizen-based language police initiated by residents of the city of Voronezh, as a laudatory model of popular linguistic action (1 November 2009).

Another democratic format introduced by the hosts in earlier 2008 is the blitz survey conducted live on air by having listeners call in to cast votes for one of two positions on an issue (e.g., dial one number for "yes," another for "no"). Some of the issues they have polled listeners on: whether or not they find the colorful language of Vladimir Putin appealing (20 percent "yes," 80 percent "no"), whether the language of Russian Orthodox Church services should be translated from Old Church Slavonic to modern Russian (57 percent "yes," 43 percent "no"), and "for" or "against" the rehabilitation of the word "comrade" (*tovarishch'*) as a form of address (43 percent "for," 57 percent "against").

Inevitably, integrating more democratic forms of folk linguistics into a forum traditionally reserved for authoritative declarations leads to metalinguistic tension and conflict, particularly in instances where both

---

27. http://www.echo.msk.ru/doc/152.html (accessed 21 January 2009). Among the more frequently mentioned words: *kreativ* (*kreativnost'*, *kreativnyi*), *glamur*, *vau* (wow), *gotichnyi* (gothic), *vintazh* (*vintazhnyi*) (vintage [adj.]), *kazhul'nyi—elitnyi* (casual—elite [adjs.]), *piar* (*piarshchik* [PR-man], *otpiarit'*, *propiarit'* [variants of "to promote"]), *merchendaizer* (merchandiser), *otnosheniia* (relationships), *koroche* (in short), *messedzh* (message), and *trend* (trend).

28. http://www.echo.msk.ru/programs/words/42037 (accessed 21 January 2009). The five most hated turned out to be *zhenshchina* (woman), *dama/damochka* (lady/little lady), *brat/bratan/bratello* (variants of criminal slang for "brother"), *sudarynia* (madam), and *tovarishch'*.

opinions and sources of authority become contested. Listeners witnessed just such a clash in norm negotiation in the 18 May 2008 episode, which centered on the very issue of norms and featured a guest specialist in pronunciation (in Russian, *orfoepiia*), Maria Kalenchuk.[29] A closer look at the transcript of the conversation gives a better sense of the nature of the tension between "folk" and "specialist," and the heightened urgency it assumes in the context of a live broadcast that invites real-time contributions from listeners. Ol′ga Severskaia opens the show by introducing the guest, underscoring in the process the long list of titles that give her authority to offer pronouncements on pronunciation and norms:

O. Severskaia:	Our guest is the main authority on pronunciation, assistant director of the Academy Institute of Russian Language, chair of the phonetics commission of the Russian Academy of Sciences, doctor of philology, Professor Mariia Kalenchuk. I have listed only a selection of her titles. If I were to continue it would take too long.

Almost immediately, however, the show's other host, Kseniia Larina, complicates the situation by bringing up a proposition from an online contributor essentially questioning the real authority of the specialists: are they not, in essence, simply beholden to the dominant usage practices of the speaking population?

K. Larina:	Before we begin our conversation, I would like to recall a meeting that I have already mentioned....Mikhail Kazakov laments, "Now you'll see—after some time dictionaries will record the word "zvOnit"—that's the way 70 percent of the Russian population speaks."[30] He was convinced that that was the way it happened. If the populace insists, then scholars will, in the end, have to correct some word stress in the dictionaries, right?

---

29. Both an audio recording and a transcript of the complete broadcast can be found at http://www.echo.msk.ru/programs/speakrus/514670-echo (accessed 21 January 2009).

30. The third-person singular, present tense form of *zvonit′* (to call), *zvonit,* when stressed on the first rather than second syllable, as required by all Russian grammars, is among the biggest bugaboos of Russian language mavens—precisely because the mispronunciation has become so prevalent in colloquial Russian.

Larina's position as the only nonphilologist among the three regular hosts turns out to be quite interesting and important from the perspective of folk linguistics, as she ends up more often than not articulating the sorts of questions and opinions one might more readily associate with the nonspecialist—that is, either a more populist position with regard to language practices or, in other instances, a viscerally patriotic one. In this episode, as suggested by the passage above, we see her in the former role.

Telling in this exchange, however, is the degree to which the authority relies quite heavily and at times entirely on her status as specialist (as well as that of authorities who preceded her) in establishing normative boundaries. Her opening response to Larina's provocative challenge is itself laden with weighty loanwords and technical terms:

M. Kalenchuk: Good morning! It doesn't quite work that way, thank God. The thing is, not everything that the natural (*stikhiinyi*) flow of speech presents to us (and this is an unbelievable variety of living variants) becomes a norm. To understand this, we have to clarify what we mean by "norm": pronunciation norms, orthoepic norms are typically understood as those pronunciation features that are characteristic of educated people, pronunciation features that are codified in special dictionaries and guides. For this reason, the question is what of real speech flow (or "usage," as linguists call it) becomes a norm and by what criteria does one or another pronunciation variety acquires the status of norm. This is an extraordinarily complicated issue.

I should say that there are certain predetermined criteria. First of all, there's no question that the literary language is the language of culture and it is extremely important that the link between eras not be broken, and for this reason we cannot allow our norms to change chaotically and very quickly. If this happens then we will very soon be unable to read Pushkin, Lev Tolstoy. If the language begins to develop very quickly..., then tradition will be broken off and the language of centuries gone by will become an alien language for us and no longer will be able to provide us with such esthetic pleasure. You know,

I very much like the expression of our great linguist Evgenii Dmitrievich Polivanov, who said that "one of the laws of development of any literary language is that it develops less and less." Or, as Mikhail Viktorovich Panov, another one of our great linguists, said, "In language, that which is conservative is progressive." For this reason we are obliged to a certain extent to pull at the bridle, preventing norms from developing very quickly and replacing one another. At the same time, in addition to this, we must be selective in choosing what constitutes a norm. This is done by those who codify and officially fix norms in dictionaries, guides, and other manuals. As a matter of fact, those with a mastery of the literary language do this intuitively. We must fix only that which abides by the internal laws of language.

In the invocation of "complex" technical explanations, quotes from a "who's who" of linguistic icons, and references to "predetermined criteria" and "internal laws," we find a clear invocation of linguistic power that would have us believe that we are saved from total linguistic "chaos" (a state in which we could no longer even understand one another, let alone the literary classics) by those select "educated people" who intuitively use the "right" form and those linguists who lock that proper usage into dictionaries and guidebooks and thereby "bridle" language's dangerous potential to get out of hand. Additional authority is recruited through quotes of various patriarchs of language (here Polivanov and Panov) who attest to the essentially conservative nature of language change (a point that seems to undermine Kalenchuk's warnings of unbridled linguistic chaos).

After running through a laundry list of some of the more contentious normative issues (*zvonIt* versus *zvOnit,* the gender of *kofe,* etc.) Larina steps back and asks a broader question on behalf of the multiple folk linguists of the listening audience who are sending in examples and counterexamples that bring into question the very validity or "lawfulness" (*pravomernost'*) of norms in the first place. She does not really get a direct answer at first—just a reiteration of the orthodox pronunciation. When pressed, the specialist suggests that, in part, it is up to specialists and, in part, it is a matter of a "social contract." Larina's skepticism is underscored when she catches Kalenchuk herself using a normatively questionable term:

K. Larina:	In general, how valid are debates about stress? Because for every one of your norms our listeners have put forward 225,000 arguments against those norms, ... for example: "What about the word *rog* (horn)? Where's the voiced ending there?" Or just the opposite, such as the word *bog* [pronounced *bokh*] (god), which many pronounce as [*bog*].
M. Kalanchuk:	It can only be pronounced [*bokh*].
K. Larina:	Of course. Or, for instance, they are writing about [*zvOnit*] (calls) and [*zvonIt*].
M. Kalenchuk:	You have already vocalized (*ozvuchili*) one question; give me a chance to answer it.
K. Larina:	Is it proper to say "vocalize a question?"
M. Kalenchuk:	I don't like it, to be honest. But nowadays they often say "vocalize an issue," for example, in television speech. That, of course, seems to me to be a violation of speech culture.
K. Larina:	Then the question is simple: to what extent are these conversations debatable?
M. Kalenchuk:	They are debatable, as they should be, because a norm to a certain extent is our social contract. And there is no 100 percent instrument that would allow us to say that this way is right, that way is wrong. It is the professional specialists, specialists first and foremost in pronunciation, who analyze each concrete instance, taking into consideration, no doubt, the frequency of dissemination of variants as well.

Paying little attention to the underlying contradiction between the claim that norms are a "social contract" and thus debatable among everyday users and the assertion that their validity is determined by the detailed analyses of "professional specialists," Larina (again speaking on behalf of the listening audience) presses on:

K. Larina:	Here's a whole list for you: Dima writes, "I'm not a big supporter of those who *zvOnit* (phone) and *lOzhit* (lies). But how do you explain to me that [the third-person

singular form of] *khodit'* (to walk) is *khOdit* (walks), *brodit'* (to wander) is *brOdit, stonat'* (to moan) is *stOnet* (moans), *mochit'—mOchit* (to soak—soaks), *tochit'—tOchit* (to sharpen—sharpens), *pisat'—pIshet* (to write—writes), but for some reason *zvonit'* (to call) is *zvonIt* (calls)?"

Kalenchuk offers a long, technical answer that ends with a "reassurance" to concerned listeners that the situation really is not all that bad—that only 4 percent of words in Russian have shifting stress.

Meanwhile, the questions keep rolling in, this time articulated by Sever-skaia in regard to *obespechEnie—obespEchenie* ("provision"). Here, after a series of relatively authoritative declarations of a proper form, Kalenchuk deems both variants permissible—a liberalism that both surprises and distresses Larina:

O. Severskaia:	Now we have more questions from the SMS feed. It's hard not to take advantage of the chance to hear an authoritative opinion: *obespEchenie* or *obespechEnie?*
M. Kalenchuk:	Both.
K. Larina:	Why? There used to be just one variant.
M. Kalenchuk:	The thing is that it simply corresponds to a specific tendency.
K. Larina:	When did the second norm appear? When Vladimir Vladimirovich Putin began to speak that way?
M. Kalenchuk:	Nothing of the sort! Of course not! This norm has long been fixed in orthoepic dictionaries. First the second version was the less preferred of the two, but now they appear as absolute equals....
K. Larina:	And *mYshlenie* (thinking)?
M. Kalenchuk:	For me, *mYshlenie* is an incorrectly colored word. What's more, it is colored socially. Nevertheless, it is heard more and more often from very authoritative lips (*iz ochen' avtoritetnykh ust*), which still does not give us the opportunity to consider it a norm.
O. Severskaia:	*v sEti* [on the web] or *v setI?*
M. Kalenchuk:	Both.
K. Larina:	Always both.
M. Kalenchuk:	No, not always both. In the current case only.
K. Larina:	Still—which is better, more correct?

Again Larina as a representative of folk linguists shows an equal measure of deference to the specialist and her role in dictating norms, and frustration over the specialist's apparent equivocation, suggesting in a half-joking way that, as in other spheres, phoneticians take their cues from political leaders when establishing the ground rules for proper speech. What good are linguistic authorities, she essentially asks, if they cannot provide clarity to murky aspects of language usage?

As the discussion about the need for norms continues, Larina attempts to negotiate with Kalenchuk, suggesting that a variant qualifies as a norm when 70 percent of the speaking population use it:

> K. *Larina:*   Wait a minute! I still want to understand why, then, we
>   need strict norms, if they can change so quickly.
> M. *Kalenchuk:*   First of all, they are not at all quick.
> K. *Larina:*   With the help of those people who can bend the norms
>   as they see fit. Then let's count the percentage content, ah
>   yes, 70 percent say it this way—then let's accommodate it
>   (*davaite togda poidem navstrechu*).

But the specialist will have nothing to do with such accommodation, returning to her favorite theme of "internal laws of language," which in this case relegate the fashionable term *imidzh,* because of its violation of the natural law of devoiced consonants in word-ending positions (pronounced with the Anglicized [*imidzh*] rather than according to Russian devoicing rules [*imitsh*]), to the bone pile of "aggressive Anglicisms":

> M. *Kalenchuk:*   No, it doesn't work that way. I've noted on more than one
>   occasion today, using various examples, that the fact that
>   70 percent of people say something a certain way does not
>   mean that it is a norm. You can only consider 70 percent
>   usage of a certain variant grounds for attributing norma-
>   tive status to a form when at the same time certain other
>   conditions of cultural tradition are met. The most impor-
>   tant is the conformity with the internal laws of language.
>   For instance, I've said today that the vast majority of the
>   younger generation will say [*imidzh*] because they are all
>   aggressively English-language oriented. But there isn't the
>   slightest hint that this is normative pronunciation. Only

when we combine various reasons and various conditions
of the functioning of variants can we draw conclusions
about the future and prospects. Not everything we hear
around us is a norm.

After another series of inquiries, Larina tries another tack—this one
exposing the vulnerability, frustration, and doubt felt by many who have
had to struggle to abide by the norms handed down from on high:

K. Larina:	So why is speaking incorrectly more comfortable?
M. Kalenchuk:	How so? Excuse me, but it depends for whom it's more comfortable!
O. Severskaia:	Is it more comfortable for you to say [*sredstvA* (means)]?
K. Larina:	No.

Kalenchuk's automatic comeback (*smotria komu, prostite, udobnee*) makes
it clear that, in the end, norms are essentially a mark of distinction that
some by dint of their birthright or education have acquired effortlessly,
while others, who have not felt compelled to struggle to master the established norms in order to make it, suffer from the repression of their own
socially acceptable standards.[31]
   It is for this reason as much as any that Larina and other folk linguists
express the simultaneous and somewhat contradictory desire to know
the rule and frustration over the complexity of the rules (or seeming lack
of rules), underscoring the notion that only a chosen few are able to ma-
neuver successfully through the minefield of norms. And yet try they
do; despite expressions of frustration and exasperation, they still proceed
to play the call-in game shows, testing their mastery (in this episode) of
pronunciation norms—such as the stress pattern in the oblique forms
of *den'gi* (money) and the proper pronunciation of *musoroprovOd* (gar-
bage chute). In this sense, even the give-and-take format of the *We Speak
Russian* project, as diverse as it can be in both form and content, not only
marks a new style of norm negotiation, but, in the end, constitutes an institution of normalization as well—and one arguably more effective than

---

31. For a discussion of language norms as markers of cultural distinction, see Bourdieu
(1991, 43–65).

purist moralizing or bureaucratic legislation by virtue of its messier, more democratic structure.

As easy as it is to mock purist projects for their essentialist and at times nationalist excesses, it would be wrong to underestimate either the power or the potential popular appeal for sanity from traditional institutions of linguistic authority. Ordinary citizens still attend schools and learn the rules as passed down by the philological classics; they still turn to dictionaries and other language references as authoritative sources; and some—perhaps in increasing numbers—even take public offense when they sense that their national language is being littered, their national identity obliterated, by "linguistic lawlessness." Indeed, as indicated in the discourse on freedom of speech in chapter 3, the balance of cultural authority shifted markedly in the latter half of the 1990s. Although the push for linguistic cleansing first manifested itself in narrower venues sponsored by the Academy and Church, on occasion buttressed by symbolic laws and pronouncements from the state, it eventually worked its way into mainstream mass media, where, with a larger captive audience and more subtle (and less moralistic) means of monitoring, it was able to draw more prominent attention to issues of proper speech culture. This more popular, vernacular form of monitoring had greater resonance among the reading and speaking population by virtue of its ability to entertain and engage them in matters of language usage in a nondogmatic manner. As it turns out, this popularizing trend corresponded to the emergence in the political realm of a leader who also came to be known for populist, even vulgar, rhetorical turns, a speaking style that in its own way brought a startling modicum of stability, if not normalization, to the language culture of the day.

5

Taking the Offensive

Language Culture and Policy under Putin

Мочить 1. Делать мокрым, влажным. 2. Держать в воде,
пропитывая влагой для придания каких-либо качеств. [*Soak*
1. To make wet, damp. 2. To hold in water, saturating with moisture for the
infusion of certain qualities.]

—*Novyi slovar' russkogo iazyka*

It may at first seem a contradiction to associate Vladimir Putin with the
notion of linguistic norms and proper usage. This, after all, is the man who
has been notorious for his colorful and at times crass turns of phrase. And
yet he was selective about his use of such turns and the contexts in which
he used them and, for the most part, distinguished himself—particularly
apart from his predecessor—as a master of bureaucratic competence. *We
Speak Russian* host Larina joked about Putin laying down the law on the
pronunciation of *obespechEnie,* but there is no question that by virtue of
their national stature and at times as spokesmen for the nation, prominent political leaders enjoy a significant degree of authority in establishing
keywords and marking boundaries for contemporary language culture. In
this chapter I examine Putin's verbal practices on a variety of levels and
suggest that, while he may not have become a model for proper speech,
his most memorable speech moments, his astute manipulation of language
technologies, and his support for promoting Russian internationally as a
tool for "soft power" all helped project a general sense of stability in the

contemporary language culture and bestow upon him personally a degree of rhetorical authority that Russian leaders had not enjoyed since the early days of perestroika.

Bumping Off Terrorists and Castrating Oligarchs

Before August 1999, the Russian word *mochit'*, if appearing in the public airways, would be as likely to refer to either of the two literal meanings proffered in the definitions above. Take the following usage from a 1997 article in *Komsomol'skaia pravda* on methods of preserving wild berries: "Many aficionados of preserving for some reason believe that only huckleberries are soaked (*mochat*). In fact, strawberries may also be soaked (*zamochit'*)" (Zelenkov 1997). Late in the summer of 1999, however, this all changed. At a televised press conference in Astana, Kazakhstan, Yeltsin's most recently appointed prime minister uttered a six-word phrase that would not only change the semantic balance of the word for the foreseeable future, but would also catapult its speaker, Vladimir Putin, into the national consciousness and pave the way for his eventual assumption of the Russian presidency a short four months later. In response to a question on a recent spate of terrorist attacks in Russia and continued insurgencies in the Northern Caucasus, Putin boldly declared, "We will follow the terrorists everywhere. If we catch them in the toilet, please pardon the expression, then we'll waste them (*zamochim*) in the outhouse once and for all. That's it. End of issue."[1]

The key phrase that filtered its way through the media, "we'll waste them in the outhouse," drew immediate national attention, and not only because of the new tough line on terrorism, implying that Russia would now proactively seek out potential insurgents, rather than waiting for them to act yet again. Arguably as seismic was the language Putin chose to communicate this new hard-line policy, combining the vulgar, substandard reference to the outhouse or the "loo" with the equally shocking

---

1. In the original, "Мы будем преследовать террористов везде. Значит, Вы же меня извините, в туалете поймаем, мы и в сортире их замочим в конце концов. Все. Вопрос закрыт окончательно." Transcribed by the author from a video recording of the comment in Hata et al. 2003.

mochit', slang from the criminal underworld meaning "to kill," "waste," or "bump off." Some journalists and commentators took the Prime Minister to task for perverting the Russian national tongue in a manner more fitting for a common criminal than for the second most powerful politician in the country.[2] But for the most part, the quote turned out to be enthusiastically received among the broader Russian electorate—those scheduled to elect representatives to the Russian Parliament in December of that same year, and then a successor to Yeltsin in the spring of 2000. One commentator described the expression as "an absolutely perfect campaign slogan," as it reflected the latent aggression in that electorate: "The cowardly aggression of the voter has finally, at least for a moment, received open encouragement and justification from a politician" (Radzikhovskii 1999). According to the pollster Yurii Levada, "with that comment [Putin] enchanted (*obaial*) the people, showed his decisiveness, his approachability. And many people believed that he would really be able to achieve what nobody else had been able to do thus far" (Ofitova 2000). Within months the phrase *mochit' v sortire* had earned a place in the common lexicon of public discourse. Other politicians, as one commentator put it, "Passed along the baton from hand to hand: 'They've declared war on me,' grumbles Boris Fedorov, 'they say that they'll waste me (*zamochat*), cover me with dirt....' 'It's all the same to me whom you waste (*kogo mochit'*)—the yellows, the greens, the reds or the blues,' joins in Aleksandr Nevzorov. Even Aleksei Podberezkin, forgetting about his own 'spiritual legacy,' pronounces: 'What can we rely on? On the tax cudgel. With its help we can "waste" (*mozhno "zamochit'"*) any single banker'" (Shchuplov 2002).[3]

Several commentators noted how the utterance jacked up the rhetoric of already volatile television talk-show hosts such as Dorenko, Leont'ev, and Nevzorov (Radzikhovskii 1999; Filippov 1999). Journalists and op-ed writers commonly invoked it not only in discussions of policies toward

---

2. See Filippov 1999, who notes ironically that "rudeness and aggression were always dear to the Russian man's heart."

3. Economist Boris Fedorov occupied several finance-related posts under Boris Yeltsin before moving into the private banking and finance sector in the 2000s; journalist Aleksandr Nevzorov co-produced the perestroika-era television news shows *Vzgliad* and *600 sekund* and later represented the Leningrad oblast' in the Russian State Duma; Aleksei Podberezkin was the founder of the movement "Spiritual Legacy" and a regular fixture in Russian politics since the Gorbachev era.

Chechnya and terror, but in broader contexts as well, such as in characterizing Putin's electoral reforms of September 2004 ("They've wasted the
governors in the outhouse" [Tirmast 2004]). As a sign of true codification, it
took on a life of its own beyond politics. A 1999 article on aggressive advertising strategies in *Delovoi Peterburg* appeared under the title "Advertiser
Will Waste Consumer Even on the Bus and in the Outhouse"; the title of
a 2000 *Literaturnaia gazeta* article uncovering local government corruption
in Sochi announced, "Poor Pensioner is 'Wasted in the Outhouse' by Sochi
authorities."[4] Russian readers actually saw the rhetorical gesture brought
to life in Aleksandr Ol'bik's action-adventure novel, *Prezident,* which features Putin as President, secretly joining a division of special forces to root
out Chechen leaders in a remote mountain hideaway in the Caucasus. The
book's climax describes the President face-to-face with one of the leading
Chechen warlords, Garaev, in the very room he invoked in his 1999 threat:

> Swiftly retreating along the corridor, he adjusted the barrel of his sub-
> machine gun and "inscribed" a large portion of its contents into Garaev's stom-
> ach. Garaev was not able to grab onto the ringlet with his teeth, as he had no
> more strength left for the extraction of a pin. He took several steps, his mud-
> dled consciousness leading him to the side, into an open doorway where he
> fell to his knees and, losing his balance, collapsed face forward, stretched
> out, exhaled a mix of air with bloody ichor, and froze in perpetuity.
>
> When the President stepped through doorway of the room, he realized
> that he had come upon a bathroom. (Ol'bik 2002, 427)

Russia's age-old love for and pride in her national tongue is axiomatic,
and the late 1990s, as documented in chapter 4, witnessed a growing backlash against manifestations of linguistic lawlessness. So why is it, then, that
in the Russia of 1999, rhetoric that could have been uttered by a common
thug or craven boor should enjoy such popular appeal?

As seen in chapter 3, the process of linguistic democratization that characterized the language culture of the 1990s brought along with it a concurrent process of "vulgarization." A quick look at the entry for the word

---

4. *Delovoi Peterburg* 136 (13 December 1999); *Literaturnaia gazeta* 24 (14 June 2000). The
phrase has also predictably provided fodder for neo-Nazi, nationalist groups who see in Putin an
ally (e.g., "Mochi ikh, Putin! Sait v podderzhku Prezidenta," http://suicide.lenin.ru/putin/ [re-
trieved 9 November 2005]).

"vulgar" in a standard English-language dictionary suggests that there is little reason for surprise at this, and that, in fact, the link is etymologically embedded in the term itself. Looking in the *American Heritage Dictionary*, we find, as the first two definitions, associations most commonly held today: "1. Crudely indecent. 2a. Deficient in taste, delicacy, or refinement. b. Marked by a lack of good breeding; boorish. See synonyms at 'common.'" The third and fourth definition, however, reveal the history of the term and its original, less negatively charged meaning: "3. Spoken by or expressed in language spoken by the common people; vernacular: *the technical and vulgar names for an animal species*. 4. Of or associated with the great masses of people; common."

If "democratization" involves giving more voice to the people, then that likely means accepting some degree of "vulgarization" as public discourse becomes more "common," closer to the "vernacular." It also means it will have a tendency of becoming, at least in the perception of some, more boorish and crude, tasteless and unrefined. In her essay on the criminalized state of the Russian language, Bernaskoni (2001) linked crude language and democratic language when she explained the contemporary vulgate as a reaction to the inflated rhetoric of the Soviet state: "If we use Lomonosov's delineation of 'styles,' then today linguistic taste is governed by the lower style, strongly seasoned by nasty little jargon words. It has arisen as a protest against the Soviet order and its cant, the soaring rhetoric of party meetings, lead articles, and slogans."

There is no doubt that, especially in its early stages, the phenomenon was somewhat reactive in nature. But this oversimplifies the new Russian vulgate. This initial "reaction" was compounded by a process of democratization that gave broader, unfiltered access to a wider variety of voices and views, a process of Westernization that led to an inundation of loanwords, and the perception that both of these processes unfolded in an excessive, distorted, perverted, corrupt, or criminal manner, leading, by the late 1990s, to a culture commonly characterized by terms such as *proizvol* (arbitrariness) and *bespredel* (lawlessness).

Which brings us back to Mr. Putin and his *sortir*. For all the flak that he took from language mavens for his *mochit'* clause and several others subsequently, Putin reflected rhetorically the general sense of desperation that had come to dominate Russian society, while at once demonstrating a willingness to use it to do battle against the very sources seen as the prime perpetrators of corruption and instability. Whether or not this language was part of Putin's personal vocabulary from the start, by using it he tapped into an ever-rising flood of verbal discontent among the "common people," and elevated that common boorishness to a level of prominence hitherto unknown.[5] He also tapped into a language ideology, discussed in the introduction, that was already firmly part of the Russian tradition— the Gogolian view of Russians speakers as a people who "express themselves strongly."

In fact, the greater part of Putin's speech style can actually be described as the drone of a competent technocrat.[6] But when he did slip into the spicier "low-style" vulgate, his listeners took note. And the two most likely contexts in which Putin invoked the new Russian vulgate, particularly during his first term in office, happened to be the two most common sources of popular anxiety, resentment, and blame for the criminalization of Russian life—terrorism and oligarch wealth. His second most notorious comment in connection to the conflict in Chechnya was actually directed toward a journalist (and a foreign one at that) who asked an unpleasant question about Russia's apparent indiscriminant use of landmines and their impact on the innocent Chechen population. After a long excursus outlining the harsh exclusionary perspectives of Islamic fundamentalists, Putin concluded his reply,

Если вы хотите совсем уж стать исламским радикалом и пойти на то, чтобы сделать себе обрезание, то я вас приглашаю в Москву. У нас многоконфессиональная страна, у нас есть специалисты и по этому «вопросу,» и я рекомендую сделать эту операцию таким образом, чтобы у вас уже больше ничего не выросло.[7]

[If you want to completely become an Islamic radical and take the step of getting yourself circumcised, then I invite you to Moscow. We have a

---

5. Some (e.g., Krongauz 2005) have insisted that Putin employed the *mochit'* expression quite consciously.

6. For a complete analysis of the speech styles of Vladimir Putin, see Gorham 2013.

7. Quoted in *Putinki* (2004, 49) from a Brussels press conference following a Russia-EU summit. The official transcript of this press conference at www.president.ru omits Putin's closing "recommendation."

multifaith country and have specialists on that "issue," and I recommend you have that operation in such a way that nothing more grows.]

Curiously, a similar castration theme echoed in Putin's response to Mikhail Khodorkovskii's belated offer to pay back taxes:

Вот сейчас ему предъявили конкретное обвинение. Он говорит: «Ну ладно, согласен, давайте сейчас заплачу.» Вот такая торговля, такой сговор, он недопустим. Все должны раз и навсегда для себя понять: надо исполнять закон всегда, а не только тогда, когда схватили за одно место. ("Interv'iu ital'ianskim informatsionnomu agentstvu ANSA," 2003)

[So now they've finally brought concrete charges against him. He says, "Well okay, I agree, how about if I pay up now." This kind of trade, this sort of collusion, is impermissible. Everyone needs to understand once and for all: you have to obey the law all the time, and not just when they've got you by the balls.]

Numerous other vulgar or violent rhetorical moments stand out from Putin's otherwise nondescript speech, including the verbal realization of rude, nonverbal gestures ([On turning Kaliningrad over to Germany to pay back foreign loans:] "You know, that is a completely unexpected formulation of the issue. I would really like to give the finger straight into the camera to everyone wishing such an outcome, but I cannot on account of my upbringing" ["Vystuplenie i otvety...." 2002]), and expressions of what he would feel or say were he (1) not entirely in control of his emotions ("When you look at it [violent criminal acts—MSG] then you feel like strangling them with your own hands—but that's just emotion"),[8] (2) not being broadcast on television ("I have other definitions [for Osama Bin Laden—MSG], but I cannot use them in the mass media" ["Vstrecha s shef-korrespondentami...." 2001]), or (3) bargaining like a New Russian ("'Put up 250,000 dollars and you won't hear another bad word during the election campaign'").[9] Another, perhaps more adolescent strategy is

---

8. Quoted in ibid., 149, from a conference on judicial and legal reforms, ITAR-TASS (9 July 2001).

9. Vladimir Putin, Kremlin press conference, 24 June 2002.

simple name-calling. Terrorists and Chechen rebels commonly receive derogatory, dehumanizing labels such as "bandits," "fanatics," "mercenaries," and "rats," who must be "rooted out of their caves and destroyed" ("Stenogramma 'Priamoi linii' 2002"; "Mochit' v peshchere" 2006; *Putinki* 2004, 167). Oligarchs are also frequently likened to bandits and thieves, not to mention such subhuman creatures as leeches and fish (Kremlin press conference 2001; "Interv'iu Prezidenta Rossii telekanalu RTR...." 2000; *Putinki* 2004, 119).

Ascribing to Mr. Putin a mastery of this "low" style, of course, does not necessarily mean that Putin himself is a product of this new Russian vulgate. Far too many of his public pronouncements feature the dry bureaucratese of a polished technocrat to conclude that the Russian people have chosen a leader cut from the same vulgar cloth. And he can be exceedingly diplomatic when he wants. Instead, while Putin may well be earnest and relatively spontaneous in his deployment of these juicy phrases, he uses them more as "special effects" than as the only available option under the circumstances (which, of course, differentiates him from the classes and voices, whence the new vulgate originated) (cf. Bourdieu 1991). Trained originally "as a specialist in human relations" (his own self-description [Putin 2000, 44]), Putin is a master at engaging his interlocutor, as well as his national viewing and listening audience, in their own terms, even when it is the source of those terms he seeks to eradicate. In fact, over the first two terms of his presidency, Putin and his political team invented what could be considered an original genre of public-relations event—"The Direct Line with the President of the Russian Federation"—designed to take advantage of his locutionary prowess and advanced television technology to transmit a more cohesive vision of the Russian nation and more authoritative image of its supreme leader.

Staging the Russian Nation

From Marshall McLuhan to Jean Baudrillard, numerous scholars have noted the critical role played by the mass media in giving shape to perceptions of reality. While some may balk at Baudrillard's assertion of a "hyperreality" that entirely supplants the original, a simulation that "threatens the difference between 'true' and 'false,' between 'real' and 'imaginary,'" it is less difficult to accept the idea that more abstract notions such as "nation" and "national identity" are essentially discursive constructs and therefore natural fodder for the ethereal world of mediation (Baudrillard 1983, 5). From their very conception, as Ernest Gellner (1983, 6) argues, "Nations, like states, are a contingency, and not a universal necessity." If Gellner underscores the importance of language, culture, and education for shaping and preserving perceptions of national identity, Benedict Anderson in his study of nineteenth-century nation building singles out the print media—newspapers in particular—for their role in creating forms of "mass ceremony" and "imagined community." Readers, though they consume it in private, are vividly aware of the contemporaneous act being performed by others like them: "The newspaper reader, observing exact replicas of his own paper being consumed by his subway, barbershop, or residential neighbors, is continually reassured that the imagined world is visibly rooted in everyday life....Fiction seeps quietly and continuously into reality, creating that remarkable confidence of community in anonymity which is the hallmark of modern nations" (Anderson 1983, 39–40). While newspapers still play an important role in shaping public perception at the turn of the third millennium, that function to a greater proportion has fallen to television and other more recent forms of electronic media, most particularly the Internet.

With the advent of relatively democratic forms of authority, the post-perestroika political climate created a greater need for the development and use of what has come to be known in Russia as "political technology." Not unlike the ethically challenged Western "spin doctor," the political technologist generates the events themselves and uses them as a means of "programming" the political landscape, promoting the agendas of their backers, and even staging pseudo-fictitious parties and events through the art of what Wilson (2005) called *dramaturgia*. Though Yeltsin's supporters first brought such technologies into prominent play in the political arena (using it to win him re-election in 1996), Putin and his handlers became masters at the art of media manipulation. Putin well understood the power of the media in telling stories and forging images. As indicated by his famous promise to bump off terrorists, he used choice words, press conferences, and photo-ops right from the start to solidify his image as a tough guy (Goscilo 2013; Cassiday and Johnson 2013).

One of the most curious forms of political technology has come in the form of his annual televised meeting with Russian citizens, known in its first six editions (2001–2003, 2005–2007) as the "Direct Line with the

President of the Russian Federation" (*Priamaia liniia s prezidentom RF*). A multimedia extravaganza usually staged in the final weeks of the year, the "Direct Line" attempted not only to instill a "confidence of community," to use Anderson's term, but also to project, through language and images, a coherent and appealing collective identity, or "cognitive map," of the Russian nation as a whole.[10] If Soviet citizens held only a hazy and incomplete mental picture of the contours and boundaries of the USSR (Neidhart 2003), collective images of the post-Soviet Russian nation, while filled in substantially by open borders and new access to information, nevertheless assumed a largely fractured form as a result of the collapse of the Soviet Union and the growing economic, demographic, and ethnic problems that dominated the 1990s (Medvedev 1995; Guseinov 2005; Parthé 1997). Through the adept use of multiple technologies, the "Direct Line" offered some of the clearest and most coherent portraits of Putin's vision for a new Russia in all its vastness, diversity, unity, and might. It did so by employing multiple layers of framing—technological, geographic, historical, demographic, and linguistic—in order transmit an imagined community that was (1) historically rich, geographically expansive, and demographically diverse; (2) actively and democratically engaged in the political process; and (3) reverential toward its President, looking to him as to a merciful tsar.[11]

The "Direct Line" was always staged as a modern high-tech performance, but even more so in the later editions from Putin's second term.[12] The 2006 and 2007 events were carried live by the two largest television

---

10. Originally introduced by Lynch (1960) as a way of describing the mental maps citizens create of cities (and the ease or difficulty with which the landscape and planning of a city allows for such mapping), "cognitive mapping" was recontextualized with a more ideological footing by Jameson ([1984] 1991), among others. As Hardt and Weeks (2000, 22) describe it, "Cognitive mapping involves a series of aesthetic practices, theoretical projects, and even political activities that produce the sense of orientation that a map provides. A cognitive map is a necessarily partial and incomplete rendering of the multidimensional and constantly changing totality that serves as a kind of navigational aid."

11. For an incisive discourse analysis of the 2007 episode of the "Direct Line," see Ryazanova-Clarke (2008), where attention is likewise devoted to the event as a "discursive construction of national identity."

12. This discussion focuses on the six editions of the event that were staged during Putin's first two presidential terms, which took place on 24 December 2001, 19 December 2002, 18 December 2003, 27 September 2005, 25 October 2006, and 18 October 2007. He continued the annual tradition during his tenure as prime minister, with a slightly pared-down format, under the name "Conversations with Vladimir Putin."

channels, *Rossiia* and *Channel One,* and by *Radio Rossiia* and *Beacon (Maiak)*. For citizens less fortunate than those present in the audiences of the regional field studios (explained below), questioners had the option of sending questions via Internet, phone, and text messaging. The structure of the event changed little over the course of its implementation. One of the show's two anchors would always begin by asking Putin for his general assessment of progress made over the past year ("How are things going?") in an open-ended manner that essentially gave him the ability to establish an opening frame for his portrait of the state of the nation. Using his full repertoire of technocratic jargon, he would take the opportunity to run through a list of favorable economic indicators that drove home his main talking point—that the country was becoming economically more stable and sound. The middle segment of the broadcasts is the longest, structured in the 2003–2007 episodes of the "Direct Line" around direct satellite TV uplinks to regional field studios staged in town squares of ten to twelve preselected cities and towns, where citizens from local audiences asked Putin questions live on the air (see table 5.1). A team of prominent journalist-broadcasters served as hosts for this central section, with two main anchors, Sergei Brilev (*RTR/Rossiia*) and Ekaterina Andreeva (*ORT/ Channel One*), sitting with Putin in Moscow and making contact with field correspondents at each of the regional sites. Brilev and Andreeva were assisted by a team of tech specialists and telephone workers vetting the onslaught of questions received by the program's "call center" (*koll-tsentr*— whose lines were open beginning five days in advance of the event itself).[13] According to the Kremlin, Putin answered 55 questions in just less than three hours in the 2006 episode and received approximately 2.2 million questions by phone and another 100,000 via the Internet. In 2007 the show received 5,000 calls per minute ("Statisticheskie dannye...." 2006).

Despite the projected impression of communicative spontaneity, participants at all levels engaged in some form of preparation prior to the event. Putin himself attested to spending upward of three days perusing the hundreds of thousands of questions submitted in advance and gathering together vital facts and figures, yet assured viewers of the unscreened nature

---

13. Selection for phone operators to the event was itself a highly competitive process ("New Putin's Dialogue...." 2007).

TABLE 5.1. Field studios for "Direct Line," 2003–2007

18 Dec. 2003	27 Sept. 2005	25 Oct. 2006	18 Oct. 2007
Komsomolsk-on-the-Amur	Iuzhno-Sakhalinsk	Nakhodka	Vladivostok
	Tomsk	Irkutsk	Novosibirsk
Berezovskii (Kemerov obl.)	Vorkuta	Kondopoga	Aktau, Kazakhstan
Krasnoiarsk	Izhevsk	Podgorodniaia Pokrovka	Ekaterinburg
Russian Airforce base in Kant, Kyrgyz Republic	Saratov	Naberezhnye Chelny	village of Podkolodnovka (Voronezh obl.)
	Groznyi		
East Surgurt oil field, drill rig no. 504, pad no. 504 (in Western Siberia)	Riga, Latvia	Kaspiisk	Plesetsk
	Gelendzhik	Tver'	
	Volgograd	Sevastopol', Ukraine	Botlikh (Republic of Dagestan)
Nal'chik (Northern Caucasus)	village of Golovchino (Belgorod obl.)	Briansk	Kazan'
Vologda		Baltiisk	Sochi
Novaia Derevnia (Stavropol region)			Krasnaia Poliana
Nizhnii Novgorod			Rzhev (Tver' obl.)
Michurinsk (Tambov obl.)			Kaliningrad
Vyborg			

of the submission process.[14] According to several reports, audiences also came to the events well prepared, receiving detailed instructions from local film crews on how to behave during the broadcast (including orders not to "drink, smoke, or chew"). Reports also suggested that questioners and the nature of their questions were prescreened ("Phone-in with Putin...." 2006; Abdullaev 2006).[15] The elaborate staging, or *dramaturgia,* of the event

---

14. All citations of and references to the "Direct Lines" come from transcripts originally posted at the Kremlin website, *Prezident Rossii,* now archived at "Stenogramma...." 2001, "Stenogramma...." 2002, "Stenogramma...." 2003, "Stenogramma...." 2005, "Stenogramma...." 2006, and "Stenogramma...." 2007. A separate site dedicated to the "Direct Line" alone ("Priamaia liniia...." 2006) provides direct access to all six editions and includes various data for each.

15. A *BBC Monitoring* report on the television coverage of the 2006 event cites claims by RenTV analysts that access to audiences in Tver' and Kondopoga was particularly limited, that

was captured nicely in one commentator's description of the operations behind the scenes:

> The logic of the staged performance presumes that questions are asked by all regions—from Vladivostok to Kaliningrad—and all layers of the population: the student, the soldier, the scientist, the mother, the villager, the doctor, the lathe operator. Everything as it should be. A worker at the call center, on the condition of anonymity, told a *Nasha versiia* reporter that all the calls were recorded somewhat in advance. From these, they then selected the ones that fell within the format of the "dialogue" (*obshchenie*) and finally ran them on the air. Television personnel also admitted to us that not everyone who wanted was permitted inside the fences [of the field studios— *MSG*]. Only by list and only screened people with thoroughly memorized questions. Plus, according to our information, the broadcast was transmitted with a slight delay in time (around forty seconds), just to be safe. (Kazumova and Fil'kina 2007)

A second critical commentator declared, "What was broadcast on the screen and shown in the 'roll captions' (*begushchaia stroka*) in no way resembled the citizens speaking with the President of their country. The tense faces (God forbid they should say something wrong), memorized questions, and totally indifferent reactions to the answers betrayed the rigid stage direction of the performance" (Andrusenko 2007). And in a radio interview a television critic called it "one of the most staged, most technological operations that has been organized, executed over recent years in television" ("Chelovek iz televizora" 2007).

Claims that central authorities carefully choreographed the "Direct Line" found substantiation in reports of the increased level of security surrounding the field sites and the secrecy in which their identities and locations were held by Kremlin officials up until the very last minute before broadcasts ("New Putin's Dialogue...." 2007). Despite such evidence of scripting, however, focus-group data from the Russian Public Opinion Foundation suggested that viewers for the most part did not perceive the questions as "planted." Television ratings for at least the last two episodes of Putin's second presidential term (2006–2007) ranked them the

---

audiences were coached in their behavior on the air, and that certain types of questions were deemed out of bounds ("Russian TV highlights...." 2006).

most viewed shows for the week in which they appeared ("V. Putin v priamom...." 2007).[16] Among the most frequent reasons given by viewers when asked to explain the appeal of the "Direct Line" was Putin's own rhetorical style, which viewers saw as sincere, articulate, knowledgeable, and direct ("V. Putin: 'priamaia liniia'" 2007). Enthusiasts from the village of Kishkino went so far as to stage their own "Direct Line," using a life-sized doll of Putin and recordings of his voice downloaded from the Internet.[17] Even if viewers did recognize it as the public relations stunt that it was, many bought into the notion of a televised summit between the President and the people and tuned in to see how both the conversation and the nation were taking shape.

A variety of structural and rhetorical levels contributed to this multi-layered image of a country that was as vast as it was united in its ethnic, demographic, and geographical diversity—a country that shared the patriotic sentiments of its President, revered that leader, and looked to him as a "final authority" (*posledniaia instantsiia*) when all other venues for grievances had been exhausted. On the level of choreography, the overall orchestration by the central and field correspondents—particularly their segues from site to site and introduction of regional studios—played a critical role in defining the various demographic, geographical, historical, and geopolitical markers of the Russian nation. They promoted the fiction of the all-inclusive nature of the event metonymically by referring to regional studio audiences by city and the national audience by country, as in a 2005 segue from the site correspondent in Tomsk ("Hello! Tomsk greets the President of the country and all those who live in Russia"), or a 2003 transition from Siberia to the Northern Caucasus executed in the following exchange between the central hosts Brilev and Andreeva:

---

16. According to the All-Russian Center for the Study of Public Opinion (VTsIOM), the 2006 ratings were even higher compared with 2005, increasing from 66 percent to 72 percent, a number supported by different polling data from the Fond "Obshchestvennogo mneniia," which put the audience size at 67 percent of those surveyed. Later evidence suggests the popularity of the event declined, but the fact that the ratings remained in the 60–70 percentage range suggests that the event remained highly popular among viewers—a notion that received additional support by focus-group polling data as well ("V. Putin v priamom teleefire...." 2006; "V. Putin v priamom efire...." 2006; "V. Putin v priamom teleefire...." 2007).

17. "After the bread-and-salt ritual came the questions: Senior cow milker of the village: 'When will we have good roads in our village so my cow and I don't break our legs?' Only the people of Kishkino did not receive concrete answers to their questions; he [Putin] only advised them to look at their problems 'without rose-colored glasses'" (Grigor'eva 2007).

Brilev: So, thank you Western Siberia. Katia, which city do we
               have next in line (*na pokhode*)?
Andreeva: We march along to the Northern Caucasus, to the capital
               of Kabardino-Balkariia. Our correspondent Vladimir
               Solov'ev is working in Nal'chik. Take it away, Vladimir.

Regular updates from the call center, and the number of questions
received over the various types of media involved, underscored both the
popular and high-tech nature of the national conversation. In one 2005
replica, for instance, the call-center coordinator emphasized the active engagement of SMS users and Russian youth (not without coincidence, during the first episode broadcast since the Orange Revolution in Ukraine,
which first put new media technology on the Kremlin's radar screen as a
tool for oppositional mobilization):

N. Semenikhina: It's hot over this way. A few minutes ago we passed the
                   million marker and over 130,000 phone calls have been
                   fielded during the broadcast itself. One thing that's nice
                   to see is that college and school children have been very
                   active today. As for SMS questions, there have been
                   100,000 of those already.... Thanks so much to the oper-
                   ators who have been on the line with all of Russia for five
                   days now.

Call-center updates also provided an opportunity to fill in more obscure
corners of the national map, as when the 2007 coordinator noted, "Now I
know that in our enormous country there is, for instance, the village Old
Turnip (*Staraia Repa*)—it's in the Irkutsk oblast'; in Udmurtiia there is the
hamlet of Game (*Igra*); and in Amur oblast'—Freedom (*Svoboda*)." Segues
between regions accentuated the vastness and diversity of Russia herself.
Far East cities—Komsomolsk-on-the-Amur (2003), Iuzhno-Sakhalinsk
(2005), Nakhodka (2006), and Vladivostok (2007)—served as the starting
point for each of the four broadcasts to feature regional studios, and in each
case the locale provided the chance to celebrate the idea of "expansiveness"
(prostor) that had always served as a keyword for Russian national identity
(Pesmen 2000). The same can be said about remote or border towns such
as Michurinsk (2003), Vorkuta (2005), Baltiisk (2006), and Plesetsk (2007).
The Nakhodka site correspondent invoked dual metaphors that played on

time and geopolitics: "Evening Nakhodka is now on the line with midday Moscow. The city is seven time zones from the capital, which absolutely qualifies it as Russia's eastern maritime gateway to Asia" (2006). Putin himself invoked the theme in his response to a question about the lack of roads leading from the Far East to what the questioner referred to as the "Big Land" (*Bol'shaia zemlia*), pointing out the misnomer of Japan as the "Land of the Rising Sun":

> The correspondent working there mentioned that, when it's morning here in Moscow, you've got evening in the Far East. This speaks to the huge territory of our country. By the way, everyone calls Japan the "Land of the Rising Sun," meaning that it is an Eastern country, but New Zealand is farther east and our Chukotka is farther east than New Zealand. So if you want to be precise, the Land of the Rising Sun is Russia.[18]

The segue to the Irkutsk studio added a historical dimension to the expansiveness, invoking at once the Angara River and Alexander III: "It's already 5 p.m. here and our stage is the bank of the Angara River, near the monument of Alexander III, whose gaze is aimed to the east of Russia, and we are all looking to the East of our country and are ready from here, from Siberia, to ask questions" (2006). And the 2006 introductory segment from Baltiisk added a military dimension to the geographical and historical markers:

> Hello, Moscow. We now have Baltiisk, the westernmost city of Russia today. Its history is a chronicle of the glory of Russian armaments. Peter I studied artillery here and by the beginning of the eighteenth century an entire flotilla of ships stood by the wharf wall under the Russian flag. It was Russian enlisted men and officers who liberated the city from Napoleon's troops.[19]

In 2005 the village of Golovchino provided the westernmost frame, even sporting a signpost at the edge of town (as viewers learned from the local field correspondent) reading "Russia begins here" (*Zdes' nachinaetsia*

---

18. The eastward expansion of the Russian nation is underscored in the 2007 broadcast with Putin's mention of plans to build a bridge linking Vladivostok to the island of Russkii in preparation for an upcoming Asian-Pacific Economic Council summit.

19. Cf. introductory remarks from Rzhev in 2007 linking that city to both the historical importance of the Volga River and its central role in the USSR's victory in WWII.

Rossiia). Border towns such as Golovchino also allow the President to address in the most concrete and humanized terms possible the more abstract political issue of the status of Russians living in the "near-abroad," and Ukraine in particular. In this case, he is given that opportunity by a local grandmother who complains of the regular trial she endures trying to deliver potatoes to her children and grandchildren living across the border in Ukraine—particularly since the onset of what she calls the "orange muddle" (*oranzhevaia nerazberikha*):

L. Murakhovskaia:	Hello, Vladimir Vladimirovich. I am Murakhovskaia, Liudmila Aleksandrovna. My husband and I live by the Ukrainian border. Our daughter lives in Kharkhov. It's very inconvenient to visit one another by train, because the train goes only once a day. If you go by car, you have to take this really long route on account of the "orange muddle"—more than 120 kilometers instead of 60 because you have to cross the central border crossing and pay for entry into Russia. And car insurance is very expensive. Conditions for crossing the border are getting stricter. For this reason we can't even take our children a single sack of potatoes. And it was not at all long ago that, almost every weekend, hearing the sound of the car horn on the street, we would greet our grandchildren with joy. And they would jump for joy, too, when they saw their grandpa and grandma. We're afraid we'll soon be deprived of this joy. Even worse, if some misfortune like the funeral of a relative were to happen, how would we get there?
V. Putin:	I understand your pain and concern and share it entirely. Entirely! This is absolutely unacceptable, with two peoples who are ethnically and historically close in a cultural sense, the closest of relatives in the spiritual and the literal, full-blooded sense of the word, wind up divided. And this fracture, it seems to be growing wider all the time as a result of the muddle that you refer to. (2005)

In fact, the Putin team regularly crossed Russian borders physically, as well as rhetorically, during the national "conversations" by including non-Russian cities in the broadcast—the Kyrgyz Republic in 2003, Riga (Latvia) in 2005, Sevastopol' (Ukraine) in 2006, and Aktau (Kazakhstan) in 2007—as if to underscore the fact that Russia, at least in an ethnic and cultural sense, extended beyond the borders of the Russian Federation. Brilev did this quite consciously in his 2006 introduction to the Sevastopol' site, making full use of the key semantic distinction between *rossiiskii* (the adjective used to refer to someone or something "of the Russian Federation") and *russkii* (the adjective to denote cultural or ethnic identity): "We have next up not the Russian (*rossiiskii*) but the Russian (*russkii*) city of Sevastopol'." And the first questioner of the same segment echoes the geographic ambiguity, noting, "we have a saying here that 'we're located in alien (*chuzhaia*) territory, but on our own (*svoia*) land.'" The same Sevastopol' segment featured a labor-union representative of a local shipbuilding factory who saw fit to assure Putin of the region's national allegiances: "Over 26,000 citizens of Ukraine work for the [Russian] Black Sea Fleet. In case you may have doubts, these are patriots of Russia. We were forced to become citizens of Ukraine." While often showing empathy to such charged questions and comments, Putin usually refrained from taking the nationalistic bait—in this case, by pointing out that the Crimea was now Ukrainian sovereign territory. Rhetorically, of course, he did not need to, the patriotic chord already having been struck by the common people themselves, allowing Putin, in the process, to maintain a modicum of diplomatic neutrality. One sees a similar strategy with regard to the Riga audience in the 2005 episode, where local correspondents performed the role of popular tough talkers on the issue of language and citizenship, making light of ethnic Russians' status as "noncitizens" (*negrazhdane*).

As the focus shifted to communities well within Russia's borders, the framing of the Russian nation took on a different rhetorical accentuation, underscoring Russia's internal strength and cohesion—in all its diversity. The majority of the nonborder and extraterritorial communities selected for inclusion in the "Direct Line" fit one of four roughly delineated profiles: (1) cities with deep historic roots (e.g., Nizhnii Novgorod and Vologda in 2003, Saratov and Volgograd in 2005, Briansk and Tver' in 2006, Krasnaia Poliana, and Rzhev in 2007); (2) towns and villages that highlighted Russia's rural, peasant core (e.g., Novaia Derevniia in 2003, Golovchino in 2005, Podgorodnaia Pokrovka in 2006, and Podkolodnovka in 2007);

(3) sites linked to Russia's military-industrial complex (e.g., Berezovskii [2003], Izhevsk [2005], Vorkuta [2005], Vyborg [2003], Ekaterinburg and Plesetsk [2007], and even the "East Surgurt oil field, drill rig no. 504, pad no. 504" [2003]); and (4) regions that either consisted of largely non-Russian ethnic groups (Kaspiisk, Dagestan [2006]; Naberezhnye Chelny, Tatarstan [2006 and 2007]) or had been hot spots for ethnic conflict (e.g., Nal'chik [2003], Groznyi [2005], Kondopoga [2006], and Botlikh [2007]). Historical and rural points of interest quite often made populist light of their authentic Russian roots:

Local correspondent:	The city of Vologda is an ancient Russian city, beautiful in its, you know, domestic, cozy beauty, completely Russian beauty, famous, of course for its Vologda butter [and] without doubt for its Vologda lace.... (2003)
Local correspondent:	Yes, it's really Briansk. It's a small city, but very rich in history. As the historians themselves say, it's even more ancient than Moscow. (2006)
S. Brilev:	We are transferred from the Northern Caucasus to the banks of the Volga—Tatarstan Respublikasy, as they say there. After Kazan's one thousandth anniversary the title of "Eastern Capital of Russia" has been attached to it. (2007)

Relatively younger military and industrial centers invoked the discourse of exploration, discovery, invention, and economic might:

Local correspondent:	Good afternoon! Greetings to you from Vorkuta— the largest city beyond the Arctic Circle and the center of Northern Russia's coal industry. (2005)
Local correspondent:	Greetings from the capital of Udmurtiia, Izhevsk— a city famous for many names, such as the legendary firearms designer, Mikhail Timofeevich Kalashnikov.... (2005)

Links to military bases and industrial complexes also highlighted Putin's role as commander in chief, perhaps no more blatantly (and bizarrely) than in the 2007 episode when a colonel Sokolov used the occasion to give his boss a report in fluent military argot:

Sokolov: Comrade Commander in Chief of the Armed Forces of the Rus-
             sian Federation! Commanding Officer of the 33rd independent
             motorized infantry brigade "Mountain," colonel Sokolov. Good
             day![20]
V. Putin: Good afternoon!
Sokolov: Comrade Commander in Chief! In accordance with your direc-
             tive from 30 June 2006, the 33rd independent motorized infantry
             brigade "Mountain" has been formed in the Northern Caucasus
             military district in the Republic of Dagestan in the Botlikh re-
             gion. At the present time the brigade has been provided with
             arms, military technology, and stores of material resources in a
             volume that permits the fulfillment of the tasks entrusted to it.
             The entire infrastructure has been created. A general education
             high school and kindergarten have been open since 1 September.
                 Comrade Commander in Chief! Colonel Sokolov has finished
             his report. (2007; cf. Ryazanova-Clarke 2008, 326–27)

Non-Russian ethnic regions and hotspots of ethnic conflict created the greatest potential for awkward moments and national embarrassment. Broadcasts from these areas typically used a handful of strategies to lessen the blow. In some cases, they conspicuously ignored issues of ethnicity and conflict altogether, asking the sorts of questions about housing, employment, pensions, and education heard from other, calmer regions. In others, the source of tension (past or present) was addressed directly, but with the specific purpose of projecting calm. The 2006 broadcast from Kondopoga, the site of ethnically motivated murders and riots earlier that year, actually set up two different mobile studios to demonstrate to viewers nationwide that peaceful relations had been reestablished. The 2007 link to Botlikh, Dagestan, recast the formerly war-torn region into a moral and spiritual center as a result of its dramatic transformation to peace (largely due to the transformation the region had undergone since Putin took office; he was last in Botlikh in 1999):

Essentially we are in the mountains at an elevation that can probably be described as follows: we are on the level of the clouds, you can stand here at a

---

20. *Zdraviia zhelaiu* (literally, "I wish you health") is a formal and arcane form of address dating back to imperial Russia and still commonly used in the military.

height equal to that of the clouds. It's a sensation impossible to communicate; the beauty is indescribable here. In Dagestan they say that Botlikh is not a geographic name, it's a moral category.

Where they could, questioners addressed conflict in a manner that made it clear that they were allied with the President, addressing him with friendly questions that gave him a chance to reiterate his stance on a particular ongoing problem. In the 2006 broadcast from Naberezhnye Chelny, for instance, a Dagestani elder asked Putin to comment on tensions between Russia and Georgia:

I'm offended and displeased to watch a situation in which our day-to-day relations with Georgia worsen—not so much with Georgia as with its leadership. It's offensive that Saakashvili is only dragging out the situation with his behavior. We Dagestanis are by no means disinterested in this matter, and so I have for you a concrete question: What more or less rational measures may be taken to improve the situation and live with them as we have lived for many centuries—as good neighbors? (2006)[21]

While their traditional dress and heavy Russian accents communicated strong links to a non-Russian regional and ethnic identity, the Dagestanis posed questions that signaled, for all intents and purposes, that they were rank-and-file Russian Federation (*rossiiskie*) citizens who just wanted everyone to get along as in the good old days. If anything, their "centuries-old" good neighborly relations gave them greater rhetorical clout in making the case against unilateral Georgian belligerence. In a similar fashion, non-Russian sites that have enjoyed peaceful coexistence with their Russian brethren were celebrated as models of religious and cultural diversity. In his introductory remarks to the Kazan'-based audience in 2007, Putin basked in the glow of brotherly love:

I always come to Kazan', to Tatarstan, with a special feeling. I like it not just because it's pretty, but also because it's a very good example of the coexistence—not only peaceful, but also brotherly—the coexistence of

---

21. The 2006 "Direct Line" featured several questions concerning tensions with Georgia, all of which were unabashedly pro-Kremlin. The others pertained to the issue of deporting illegal immigrants and the idea of Abkhaziia seceding to the Russian Federation. This last idea—of bringing both Abkhaziia and Northern Ossetiia into Russia—was proposed by a 2003 questioner from Nal'chik, as well.

different cultures and religions. Take what the correspondent there just said—that we're next to a mosque and nearby is an Orthodox church erected back in the days of Ivan the Terrible. The leadership, you see, had the option of taking down the church and building a mosque in its place. But they did it differently, both preserving the church and building the mosque. (2007)

Petitioning the Benevolent Tsar

Beyond projecting an image of a Russia robust by virtue of its geographical breadth, historical depth, ethnic diversity, economic strength, and national unity, the "Direct Line" genre provided maximum opportunity for Putin to cast himself in the role of the strong leader empathetic to the needs of his people ("I understand, Sabir, your anxiety and concern. There's no need to worry about this matter" [2006]) and endowed with the power and authority to act so as to improve their lot. It also perpetuated the long-held Russian view of the Kremlin as the source of goodness and justice—standing above and apart from the evil and corruption that may be rampant at other, lower levels of official bureaucracy ("Dear Evgeniia Ivanovna and other residents of the Saratov oblast' who find themselves in this situation: the abuse of power on the part of your bureaucrats, if what is written here is true, knows no bounds...." [2005]).[22] A caller from Naberezhnye Chelny expressed the dynamic quite directly in the form of a conspiracy-laced question: "Is Vladimir Vladimirovich sure that all of his orders are being fulfilled in a quality way and that in the country today there's no sort of sabotage by bureaucrats, by various levels of power?" (2005). Again, in contrast to the suspicious citizen, Putin strikes a more restrained tone (answering negatively to the first part of the question, but rejecting the idea of sabotage), but the exchange has served its purpose of invoking the popular issue of corrupt local bureaucrats in a manner that inoculates the head of state (who, it could be argued, is doubly inoculated by the fact that it is the Prime Minister, not the President, who is the head of government in Russia).

---

22. As Babich (2006) explained the dynamic, "This eternal good [in the Kremlin] can be surrounded by a host of evil advisers, heartless bureaucrats, greedy business lobbyists and so on. So, the trick is to find a way to communicate with this good directly, without any intermediaries. Internet, television, and radio provided this rare opportunity and more than 1 million people listened to their old instinct."

The projection of a tsar-like image is one of the more potent functions of the "Direct Line" and is far more pronounced here than in any of the other mediated genres that contribute to Putin's public persona. Particularly in the final part of the extravaganza, where the President offers rapid-fire responses to questions that he himself has preselected, we see Putin playing the role of benefactor, not only giving audience to his people, but also providing immediate positive responses to petitioners on personal matters they are unable to resolve on the local level. The following exchange from the first 2001 episode nicely illustrates the discourse of desperate petitioner and benevolent tsar:

Questioner:	I, Rzhanova Antonina Emel'ianovna, a participant in the war, receive a pension of 1,000 rubles. Help me, please. I was in the active army. I was in the active army, but for some reason I only have a pension of 1,000 rubles. I was in Kalmykia, was in Poland....
Correspondent:	Antonina Emal'ianovna, your question is clear. Thank you.
V. Putin:	I get it, Antonina Emal'ianovna. Thank you for the question. It is a bit strange to me to hear it, since the average pension nationally has exceeded the indicators that we established as goals at the beginning of the year....I hope they have your telephone number in the studio—they will it give to us and I promise you that this issue will be resolved. (2001)

These exchanges often feature performative speech acts on Putin's part—promises, for the most part, but at times even outright presidential declarations (Austin 1962). Those more marked in terms of cultivating national pride include:

- His promise of Russian citizenship to a decorated hero of the Afghan War: "If a Hero of Russia wants to become a citizen of Russia and cannot do so, then of course it is intolerable. In accordance with the law on citizenship and in accordance with the Constitution of the Russian Federation, the President has special authority in this area and I promise you that, in the course of the next week, this issue will be resolved once and for all" (2002).

- His promise of material compensation to the family of a soldier who died in Chechnya: "I can promise you that I will definitely find you and we will definitely resolve the problems that you mention. You can be sure of it" (2003).
- His promise to a tenth grader from Moscow that he will not be excluded for consideration for service in the elite Kremlin military division because of his non-Slavic facial features (2005).

Several others are significant more for the manner in which they help project a relationship between a benevolent and all-powerful president-tsar and his meager and oppressed people, such as in the case of Putin's 2005 promise of close-captioning for all television broadcasts in response to a deaf citizen of Sverdlovsk (who astutely frames his request in his desire to better follow the activities of the President when he appears in the news), or the case of the Orel double amputee who seeks Putin's intervention in a cruel bureaucratic tangle that required him to provide medical confirmation of his continued state of leglessness upon each attempted purchase of a new prosthesis. Follow-up reports to the latter case confirmed that the Prime Minister and government actually did right the wrong: "To Putin's credit, it is worth noting that he kept his word: three weeks following the 'Direct Line,' Premier Zubkov was already reporting to the President that he has relieved the disabled 'from unnecessary missions'" Andrusenko 2007). In response to a written submission from a person reporting harassment from local authorities who did not appreciate the person complaining to the President about local problems in a previous year's broadcast of the "Direct Line," Putin finds himself in his element as a former agent of the KGB:

(question, as read by Putin):	"People are persecuting me for a call I made to you during last year. Local authorities are not allowing me to get a job. When will this stop?"
(Putin's response):	I won't name the person who's asking this question or give the address. I just want to tell you that your appeal has been received and there will be an appropriate reaction. We will be in touch with you. (2003)

The final series of Putin-selected questions in the 2006 broadcast alone results in a spade of tsar-like assurances:

- a pay raise for a certain category of public school teacher ("I'm sure that it will all be done and I'll definitely keep an eye on it");
- a promise of increased attention to drug-dealing problems in the town of Bor ("I will definitely instruct [*poruchu*] the leadership of this service to look into both the oblast' and your town");
- assurance that a "patriotic club" in Ekaterinburg will not be closed by local authorities ("I promise you that the administration and the presidential representative in the region will definitely take up the issue");
- attention from the General Prosecutor's office in a case of inmate abuse by local Perm correctional authorities ("I can simply promise you that all the issues that have been brought up here will be examined by the General Prosecutor in a thorough manner"); and,
- a promise for funds to preserve a St. Petersburg residence for a retired veteran actors' guild ("We will allocate money from the budget, I promise you").

An exchange with an Ekaterinburg caller in 2007 magnifies the relationship between almighty tsar and worshiping follower to a nearly absurd level by suggesting that ultimate solace comes finally and simply through the direct, unmediated confirmation of the divine ruler's presence: after establishing that it is truly Putin with whom she is speaking, she thanks him in the name of God and hangs up ("Oh, Lord, thank you so much for everything, thank you so, so much!" [2007]).[23]

One may wonder why Putin and his political technologists would even bother staging such a complicated media extravaganza, given their near total control not only over the frequency of access to more conventional modes of political PR, such as news broadcasts, interviews, and press conferences, but also over the content and presentation of the material that goes to those outlets itself.[24] The "Direct Line" offered them three main advantages over these more traditional forms of media manipulation. First, it provided a carefully controlled, high-tech means of projecting

---

23. For a detailed analysis of this exchange, see Ryazanova-Clarke (2008, 329–30).

24. For an excellent discussion of the political technologies used to create "Tele-Putin," see Baraulina 2006.

a coherent cognitive map of a Russian nation strengthened by its geographical breadth, its historical depth, and its geopolitical might. Second, it allowed them to transmit a portrait of Russians united and strengthened by the various dimensions of diversity and strength.[25] And, finally, the genre provided a means of buttressing the public image of Putin as a president of the people in the long-standing Russian tradition of *batiuskha-tsar*. All together, these strengths communicated in a unique and potent manner the imagined community espoused by the Putin administration. It also articulated, on the abstract policy level, notions of "vertical of power" (*vertikal vlasti*), "sovereign democracy," and "managed democracy" (*upravliaemaia demokratsiia*), with heavier emphasis on "sovereign" and "managed" than on "democracy."[26] And it is precisely this ability to use the full power of the mass media to construct rhetorically a national and presidential image of continuity between the glory of the past, stability of the present, and promises of the future—all overshadowing the linguistic and ideological disarray that came to characterize the 1990s—that largely accounted for Putin's extraordinary, at times perplexing, popularity over the course of his first two terms as President.

Exporting Russian: Language as "Soft Power"

Vladimir Putin's drive to consolidate the Russian nation both literally and figuratively took a markedly international turn in November 2006, and the Russian language stood at the symbolic forefront of the effort. On the fourth of November, Russia's National Unity Day (*Den' narodnogo edinstva*), he announced that 2007 would be the "Year of the Russian Language," making it clear that the initiative would be as international as it was national, designed to extend the nation's symbolic borders beyond the geographic. "Russia is open," he declared in the announcement, "to all who identify themselves with its fate" (Putin 2006). Most of the sponsored activities, in fact, took place outside of Russia to promote the language and

---

25. Ryazanova-Clarke (2008, 312–13) rightly characterizes the event as a "co-operative polylogue" in which members of the participating audience are "co-constructors," with Putin, of a discourse of nation.

26. The definitive articulation of this doctrine comes from the pen of one of Putin's closest political advisors at the time, his deputy chief of staff, Vladislav Surkov (cf. Surkov 2006).

culture in the so-called near- and far-abroad, in part to bring about what one document referred to as "a strengthening of the positive image of Russia" (*ukreplenie pozitivnogo imidzha [sic!] Rossii*).

Putin had made efforts to reach out to Russians living abroad early in his presidency. In 2000, on a trip to Paris, he made a special point to visit the graves of well-known Russian émigrés at Sainte-Geneviève-des-Bois (Bogomolov 2000). In October of 2001, Putin sent members of the Russian Language Council to meet with members of the French International Organization of Francophonie to discuss that group's experience and ways in which it might be adopted to promote "rusophonia" (Vorotnikov 2002; Gorham 2011). That year Putin addressed the Congress of Compatriots (*Kongress Sootechestvennikov*), declaring that "the concept of the 'Russian world' (*russkii mir*) has for time immemorial extended far beyond the geographical borders of Russia and even far beyond the borders of the Russian ethnos" (Putin 2001b). Curiously, Putin also suggested that the strength of the Russian diaspora depended on the strength of the Russian state itself ("A truly strong diaspora can only exist—I have no doubt about this whatsoever—in connection to a strong state" [Putin 2001b]). It was Putin's philologist wife, Liudmila, who first made the direct link between transnational language ties and Russia's national interests. At a conference devoted to "The Russian Language on the Boundary of Millennia" in October 2000, she remarked that "the confirmation of the borders of the Russian world is also the assertion and strengthening of Russia's national interests. The Russian language unifies the people of the Russian world— the aggregate of those who speak and think in that language. The borders of the Russian world extend along the borders of Russian-language usage" (Kantor 2000, 2).

Rather than the relatively recent notion of "rusophonia," Putin opted throughout his presidency for the notion of *russkii mir*, or "Russian world," to refer to the Russian-speaking population residing beyond the borders of the Russian Federation, although arguably the two terms carried the same ambiguities that instilled them with both flexibility (for advocates) and danger (for skeptics). In the case of *russkii mir*, one finds clear symbolic links to the positive aspects of Russian spiritual and cultural heritage, however vaguely defined (e.g., Enikeeva 1996). Even in cases where the *russkii mir* was perceived as somehow vulnerable, it was, at its core, something spiritual (e.g., "It is not just the social system that is changing, but the entire spiritual composition of the Russian world as well. Material interest, the real, reality, are being made the ideal" [Zolotusskii 1998]).

At least by the 1990s the term *russkii mir* had become a mantle for the "patriotic" red-brown opposition, a convenient marker of that which had been demolished by the collapse of the Soviet Union, the rise of Western-oriented reform policies, or some other moral or spiritual calamity (Kozhemiako 1995; Ioann 1995). One author writing in response to Yeltsin's call for a Russian "national idea," for example, debunked the liberal, post-ideological stance, arguing that ideology was immanent and proposing the placement of "the traditional values of the Russian world" at "the foundation of the state ideology" as a means of helping Russia "restore the lost meaning of its public and state existence" (Stepanov 1997). Common also was the link to Eurasianism: "By virtue of its own past, which determines the movement of any civilization, Russia cannot help but move toward Orthodoxy, toward Slavic, Eurasian unity. All of these three beginnings were and still are present in the Russian world" (Davydov 1998). After equating *russkii mir* with "Eurasia" and the "former territory of the USSR," a 1996 Communist Party campaign document singled out the Russian language in particular as "the ideal field for developing the theme of 'spirituality' in the campaign," "the only thing that truly unites citizens of the Russian Federation (*rossiiane*) regardless of their social status, their economic well-being, their faith, their gender, their age, and even their political passions" ("Iz ust reformatora" 1996). Less blatant political uses of the term in nationalist-patriotic news outlets still assumed an exceptionalist stance with regard to Russia's spiritual and historical underpinnings (e.g. "[Pushkin] understood equally well the most treasured of secrets of the Russian world and the general features of the life of humanity" [Reshetov 1999]).

Evidence of the term's symbolic authority could be found even within the very reformist, market-oriented wing of the political spectrum demonized by communists and patriots alike. In 2000 the political philosopher Petr Shchedrovitskii published a conceptual piece on *russkii mir* in a number of high-profile venues that triggered a wide debate in the press through the remainder of that year and had a clear impact on, at least, the former prime minister Sergei Kirienko, who was then serving as governor of the Privolzhskii Federal Administrative District (Kalashnikova 2000; Pinsker 2000). More economic than spiritual in orientation, Shchedrovitskii's twenty-first century vision of "Russian world" included a "networked structure of large and small communities thinking and speaking in Russian," "transregional unions," and "global diasporas" dedicated to modernization and technological innovation that would enhance Russia's ability to compete within an increasingly globalized political and economic framework (Shchedrovitskii 2000a). "In our view," he wrote in terms anticipating Dmitrii Medvedev's 2009–2011 mantra of "modernization," "the strategy of forming postnational statehood in Russia can be realized with the support of the resources of the Russian World, professional and transprofessional schools and networks, traditions of innovative thinking and action shaped in the engineering and the social-humanities—by and large competitive and on occasion the leading educational technologies" (Shchedrovitskii 2000b).[27]

As it turns out, then, *russkii mir* was a protean concept with little baggage from the past, but having a store of symbolic potential that could be used to justify cultural patriotic visions of "Russianness," more exclusionary, nationalistic notions, and even more liberal, economic, and transnational sentiments. While the potential of all three meanings may well have proven useful to Vladimir Putin in 2001, who by then had already demonstrated a knack for appropriating and employing in less threatening tones the discourse of his opponents, what one can see in his use of the term at that time is the centrality of the notion of "consolidation" ("all this work will…become a real investment in the consolidation of the diaspora, in the strengthening of its ties with Russia") and the primacy of linguistic and spiritual markers of identity over political or geographical ones: "In the world today it is not one's geographical residence that is important; what is important is the state of one's soul (*dushevnoe sostoianie*), one's aspiration, and, as I have already mentioned, one's self-determination. Where one is going to spend the majority of time in a year—Moscow, Petersburg, London, Paris, Tel-Aviv—is no longer of fundamental significance. What's important is the result of collaborative efforts" (Putin 2001b). Underlying this outreach initiative, of course, was an essential paradox less readily

---

27. While clearly a minority use of the concept, Shchedrovitskii's *russkii mir*, particularly its emphasis on modernization and recognition of the economic and political potential of the international Russian-speaking community, bears a striking resemblance to the rhetoric coming out of the Medvedev Kremlin in 2009–2011.

acknowledged, namely, the promotion of an idea that was, on the surface, transnational for the nationalist aims of the state.

It is at once logical and ironic that language should serve as one of the primary means of strengthening Russia's image, especially regionally. Logical, because language as a vehicle for cultural expression and affiliation enjoyed more cultural capital than most things "Russian" at the time, as well as constituting an important symbolic bridge for the millions of "accidental émigrés" who, after the sudden collapse of the Soviet Union in 1991, found themselves detached from their original homeland and members of an ethnic and linguistic minority in another country.[28] Ironic, at least at first glance, since the Russian language—billed throughout the Soviet era as the language of international and interethnic communication— had also served as one of the very first and most vulnerable symbolic targets by means of which newly independent states declared their independence from Soviet (and Russian-language) dominance in the late- and post-perestroika era. As the historian of nationalities M. N. Guboglo put it, "Language reform became the first test case for the true liberation of the periphery from the force (*zasilie*) of the center" (Guboglo 1998, 165; see also Bilaniuk 2005, 71–121). By 1993, all fourteen of the non-Russian Republics or newly independent states had approved state language policies (only two—Belarus and Kyrgyzstan—gave Russian the status of either "state language" or "official language"), and by 2006 the official number of people in these countries who did not know Russian has risen from "zero" to 38 million over a fifteen-year period (and was projected to rise to 80 million by 2016) ("Russkii kak inostrannyi" 2006).[29] Be that as it may, from a post-Soviet Russian perspective, group identification through linguistic and cultural ties avoided more problematic national and ethnic forms of self-identification—the very forms that were deeply ingrained over years of Soviet nationalities policy and thus more likely to give rise to resistance

28. According to one source, around 12 million Russians were living in the non-Russian member states of the CIS as of 2000 (Zakhvatov 2000). For a discussion of the term "accidental diaspora," see Laruelle (2006, 196–97).

29. The specific language policies of each of the former Soviet republics vary widely, from exclusionary language in the Baltic States to recognition of Russian as an official state language in the two mentioned here. For an overview of the current status of Russian in the former Soviet republics, see Iatsenko, Kozievskaia, and Gavrilov (2008) and Gavrilov, Kozievskaia, and Iatsenko (2008).

among Russia's neighbors and accusations of neo-imperial aspirations. And while concrete evidence existed that this association of Russian with the language of colonial oppression persisted at least among those of older generations (Iatsenko, Kozievskaia, and Gavrilov 2008, 7–11), in the 2000s Russian authorities found themselves with greater economic leverage and a significant population of ethnic Russians living in the "near-abroad" who, they argue, were in need of defending because of their own post-Soviet status of oppressed language minority.

The Russian World Foundation

One of the more lasting institutional products of the aforementioned "Year of the Russian Language" was the creation, by presidential decree in June 2007, of The Russian World Foundation (*Fond Russkii mir*), perhaps the most concerted effort to date at conceptualizing a notion of "Russianness" (*russkost'*) that transcended ethnic bloodlines and geographical boundaries. A couple of things made this event more noteworthy than the formation of yet another presidential commission for the protection of Russian. First, it was a plan hatched very closely with, if not within, the Kremlin itself. The foundation's executive director was the political technologist Viacheslav Nikonov, who, since the onset of perestroika, served as presidential advisor to every sitting president from Gorbachev to Medvedev.[30] Second, the organization's trustees included ministers of education and foreign affairs, heads of major media organizations, representatives of the Russian Orthodox Church, university presidents, business leaders, and directors of charitable organizations.

Language and national identity lay at the foundation of the project, but clearly within the context of building Russia's image abroad and protecting and expanding its sphere of influence. According to the organization's stated "ideology,"

---

30. Nikonov also happens to be the grandson of the Stalin-era politician Viacheslav Molotov. In his youth he rose to a leadership position in the Komsomol and later served as head of the Central Committee's ideological department in the USSR. In 1993 he cofounded the political public relations firm Politika, where he is still president. He is president of the Unity in the Name of Russia Foundation (*Fond "Edinstvo vo imia Rossii"*) and a member (and former governing board member) of the Russian Federation Civic Chamber [*Obshchestvennaia palata*].

Russkii mir is not just Russians (*russkie*), not just citizens of the Russian Federation (*rossiiane*), not just compatriots (*sootechestvenniki*) in the countries of the near and far abroad, emigrants, natives of Russia and their descendants. It is also foreign citizens who speak Russian, who study or teach it, all those who are sincerely interested in Russia and who are concerned about its future.

All strata of the Russian world—polyethnic, multidenominational, socially and ideologically heterogeneous, multicultural, geographically segmented—are unified through the recognition of a sense of belonging to Russia.

By forming *Russkii mir* as a global project, Russia is discovering a new identity, new opportunities for effective collaboration with the rest of the world, and additional impulses for its own development ("O Fonde" 2011).

In his 2007 annual address to the Duma, where Putin first formally introduced the concept, he echoed Soviet language policy when he declared that "Russian is the language of a historic brotherhood of peoples, a language of truly international communication. It is not only the preserver of an entire stratum of truly global accomplishments, but also the vital space (*zhivoe prostranstvo*) for the many-millioned Russian world, which, of course, is significantly broader than Russia herself" (Putin 2007). Compared to Soviet language policy, however, which treated Russian as a "second native language" or "secondary native language" for non-Russians, as a source of enrichment for their own native tongues (Bruchis 1984, 110; Filin 1968), the Putin model reflected a less paternalistic attitude toward the non-Russian speakers of the former Soviet Union, viewing them more as potential kindred spirits sympathetic to the idea of a common, transnational Russian language space.

This being said, the political function of the language question did emerge, most visibly in cases where Russian-speaking populations were seen as victims of prejudicial language policies. In 2007, for example, the city of Simferopol'—regional capital of Russian-dominant Crimea (Ukraine)—hosted an international conference dedicated to "The Russian Language in a Multicultural World." Opening remarks by Anatolii Gritsenko, then Speaker of the Crimean parliament, framed the meeting around the anti-Russian policies of the Yushchenko-Timoshenko government—which not only failed to recognize Russian as an official language of a minority population, but also required Ukrainian as the language of legal proceedings, classroom instruction, and college entrance exams. Gritsenko described the term "Russian-language citizens" as one that referred to a "united community (*obshchnost'*) of people" that extended beyond political and geographical boundaries (Gritsenko 2007). A Crimea-based professor followed by proposing that that "community" be referred to as either "rusophonia" or a more russified variant of this, *Rusorechie,* and defined the concept as "a supra-state, supranational, supra-ethnic, supracultural, supraconfessional phenomenon, the geographic borders of which are defined by one factor alone—within those borders, the Russian language can be heard" (Rudniakov 2007, 15–16).[31]

One can find the same metaphorical mix of protection, consolidation, expansion, and repatriation—with language as the lynchpin for all—in a widely broadcasted list of Russian foreign policy principles published shortly after Medvedev became President in the spring of 2008:

> to defend rights and legal interests of Russian citizens and compatriots living overseas on the basis of international law and actual bilateral agreements, viewing the multimillion Russian diaspora—the Russian world—in terms of a partner, including in the matter of expanding and strengthening the space of Russian language and culture;
>
> to facilitate the consolidation of organizations of compatriots with the goal of more effectively guaranteeing them their rights in their countries of residence, the protection of the ethno-cultural identity (*samobytnost'*) of the Russian diaspora and its ties to its historical Motherland, consequently creating the conditions for promoting the voluntary relocation to the Russian Federation of those compatriots who would make such a choice; to facilitate the study and dissemination of the Russian language as an indispensible part of world culture and instrument of international communication ("Kontseptsiia vneshnei politiki" 2008).[32]

Elsewhere in Russian World Foundation formulations one finds the language of communion or communality, which evokes pre-Soviet notions of national unity and reunification that are targeted directly at the perceived verbal and social fracturing of the 1990s:

---

31. For an excellent discussion of language politics in postcommunist Ukraine, see Bilaniuk (2005).

32. It is noteworthy that these points appear under the subheading "International Humanitarian Collaboration and Human Rights."

Mir is a community. No matter how much terms like "communality" (*obshchnost'*), "conciliarity" (*sobornost'*), and "collectivism," are criticized, their historical presence was based on a certain social practice. The practice of the past ten years, in contrast, shows that one of the problems with Russia today is the disunity of society (*razobshchennost' obshchestva*), individualism, the breakdown of social networks. The task of building a civil society is unrealizable without their restoration, strengthening, without the creation of community, unification (*edinenie*) in space and time. All of these processes make up, in essence, the concept of "Russian World."[33]

Noteworthy in nearly all official invocations of *russkii mir* was the manner in which they downplayed new political boundaries that had emerged since 1991, focusing instead on more transnational boundaries marked by an amalgam of linguistic and affective allegiances. Linked to this new rusophonia was a notion of healing and reconciliation after decades of turmoil and disintegration. As one of the Russian World Foundation promotional videos put it, "*Russkii mir* is creating a new global informational and cultural space, because the Russian world is not just a unified people. It is a people living in the world with itself and with the rest of the world. The key word here is 'peace,' as in the absence of confrontation. The Russian world is Russian reconciliation, concord, Russian harmony, unity, the surmounted schisms of the twentieth century" ("Prezentatsionnyi rolik" n.d.).[34]

Particularly in his early years as national politician, Putin provided a rhetorical antidote for those disillusioned by the growing perceptions of disarray and lawlessness—political, social, economic, and linguistic—under Yeltsin. Language played a central role in shaping his reputation as a no-nonsense tough-talker capable of articulating the basic needs and fears of the people. Putin's recentralization of television media gave him a powerful platform for projecting an image of himself as benevolent tsar

---

33. The term *obshchnost'* had a prominent place within Soviet discourse as well (Azimov, Desheriev, and Filin 1972).

34. "Русский Мир создает новое глобальное информационное и культурное пространство, потому что Русский мир—это не только единый народ. Это народ, живущий в мире с собой и с остальным миром. Ключевое слово здесь— 'мир,' как отсутсвие вражды. Русский мир—это русское примирение, согласие, русский лад, единство, расколы 20-ого века." The word *mir* in Russian can mean both "world" and "peace."

and of Russia as a nation revived thanks to new-found stability, strength, and national pride. In the area of language culture this discourse of stabilization proved a natural partner to efforts among the language community—including the mass media itself—to rein in what came to be perceived as the linguistic lawlessness of the 1990s. Notions of "normalization" in both language and politics served institutional needs for reestablishing authority, but also found great resonance within the population at large. They also created a more stable foundation on which to promote the Russian language in a more positive way as a means of forging transnational unity and community among those who considered Russian their own. Instrumental to the new vision of Russian language as a tool for exporting and expanding Russian interests was the concurrent rise of the Internet. For, as the next chapter shows, with the growth of new media technologies in both Russia and abroad, new possibilities for international communication and community building emerged, and projects such as the Russian World Foundation sought to take full advantage of them. But the emergence of online and largely decentralized modes of communication and self-expression also posed serious challenges to Putin's ability to articulate realities of state and nation and restrict alternative discourses of authority.

"Cyber Curtain" or Glasnost 2.0?

Strategies for Web-based Communication in the New Media Age

> "In our time it is broadly true that political writing is bad writing. Where it
> is not true, it will generally be found that the writer is some kind of rebel,
> expressing his private opinions and not a 'party line.'"
>
> —George Orwell, "Politics and the English Language" (1946)

On 15 December 2011, then–Prime Minister Putin staged his tenth annual meeting with the Russian nation, newly dubbed "Conversation with Vladimir Putin." His first three meetings since assuming the premiership had largely followed the script of the earlier "Direct Lines": they too were marathon, multimedia displays of competence and supreme authority afforded by friendly journalists, prepared questions, and links to live audiences across the nation.[1] Viewers who tuned into the 2011 edition, however, witnessed something notably different. Superficially, the format looked similar, with a live audience in a Moscow studio, the "call center" logging questions by phone, texting, and the Internet, and field studios linked in via

---

1. In contrast to the presidential "Direct Lines," the "Conversations" with Putin as Prime Minister used fewer field studios and made little attempt to project a multidimensional cognitive map of the Russian nation, focusing instead on projecting the Premier as a man of action with concrete accomplishments and direct connections with the people and the participating communities. Toward this end, the events largely featured locales he had personally visited and even individuals or groups whom he had visited.

satellite. But the tone had changed, as had the topic of conversation. Rather than the obligatory opening assessment of the general state of affairs in Russia that had begun all preceding meetings, it was the issue of political protest that launched the 2011 edition. Staging the event just eleven days after the controversial 4 December parliamentary elections and five days after a demonstration that had seen upward of 120,000 citizens take to the streets in Moscow alone, producers of the "Conversation" permitted the problem of political unrest to trump Putin's usual summary of the year's economic highlights. The main host of the event, Ernest Matskiavichius, showed some deference to Putin by opening with an invitation for him to offer his reaction to events (a reaction the Russian population had yet to hear from the Premier), but proceeded to pose follow-up questions on the topic even as Putin expressed a clear desire to move on:

> В.Путин: Я уже сказал, что я думаю по поводу этих событий в целом. Мне кажется, что надо как-то уходить от этой темы. Наверняка, есть много других интересных вопросов.
>
> Э.Мацкявичюс: Я боюсь, что мы будем к ней все время возвращаться. ("Stenogramma programmy...." 2011)

> [V. Putin: I've already said what I think about these events on the whole. It seems to me we need to somehow move away from this topic. No doubt there are many other interesting questions.
>
> E. Matskiavichius: I'm afraid we'll be returning to it all the time.]

Putin acquiesced, but the more he spoke, the more he projected an image not of a benevolent tsar but rather of a defensive and defiant politician. Attempts at populist jokes and tough-talking turns of phrase, the standard fare of his earlier meetings, seemed to fall flat, with little or delayed and forced reaction from the live studio audience. Quips likening the white ribbons of protesters to used condoms bordered on the crass (if not outdated, white condoms being a deficit product of Soviet Russia), and comments equating protesters to Rudyard Kipling's foolish, chattering, and anarchic Bandar-logs served to alienate rather than unite.

Also adding to the change of tone was the fact that the studio audience contained participants sympathetic to the protesters—including the journalist and head of Echo Moscow, Aleksei Venediktov, who challenged Putin almost immediately on his choice of the term "opposition" to describe those who had turned out to demonstrate:

Вы говорите про оппозицию, но, поверьте мне, на Болотной площади была не только оппозиция. И Вы сейчас как бы даете ответ на то, что хочет оппозиция, но что Вы ответите тем новым раздраженным, новым обиженным, если хотите, несправедливостью—они считают, что у них украли голоса.... Я просил бы Вас сейчас этим людям ответить, а не оппозиции. ("Stenogramma programmy...." 2011)

[You talk about the opposition, but believe me it wasn't just the opposition on Bolotnaia Square. Your answer now is somehow phrased in terms of what the opposition wants, but how do you answer these new (citizens) who are irritated, insulted by the unfairness, if you will; they think that they have had their votes stolen.... I would ask that you answer these people, not the opposition.]

The very fact that Russian political discourse of the day distinguished between "systemic" and "nonsystemic" opposition was indicative of the rigged nature of Russian politics: "systemic" referred to members of minority parties officially recognized (and tacitly approved) by the state, "nonsystemic" referred to those groups and individuals not permitted or not opting to operate within the confines of the Putin-rigged system. Venediktov, however, argued that the protests went deeper and involved "ordinary" citizens who did not normally associate themselves with either state-approved opposition or state-demonized opposition. Echoing these sentiments, Anatolii Kucherena, a lawyer and member of the Russian Federation Public Chamber, described the problem in more basic terms—as a lack of communication between "society" and "the authorities" or "power" (the Russian term *vlast'* connoting both simultaneously):

Владимир Владимирович, если говорить о взаимоотношениях общества и государства, власти и гражданина, то Вы сами неоднократно видели, что в этой части мы никак не можем найти общий язык.... И люди ведь говорят об этом: мы хотим встретиться, мы хотим обсудить с главой города, мэром, хотим обсудить те или иные проблемы, мы хотим решить, где построить мост, мы хотим решить, где и что построить, но нам не должны навязывать. То есть получается, что мы живем по принципу "Для народа, но без народа,"—но мне кажется, что это недопустимо. Эти времена уже ушли в прошлое....Поэтому, мне кажется, наступило время все-таки изменить формат общения. ("Stenogramma programmy...." 2011)

[Speaking of the relationship between society and the state, the authorities (*vlast'*) and the citizen, Vladimir Vladimirovich, you have seen yourself how we just can't find a common language in this area....People are talking about it: we want to meet, we want to talk with the city chief, the mayor, we want to discuss certain issues, to decide where to build a bridge, where and what to build. We mustn't have these things forced on us. As it turns out, we are living according the principle "For the people, but without the people," and this seems unacceptable to me. These times have already receded into the past....This is why, I think, the time has come to change the format of communication.]

Kucherena tactfully excluded Putin from the group of bureaucrats guilty of ignoring the concerns of society, noting how actively as prime minister he had traveled and met with citizens, but the specter of a giant indifferent bureaucracy could not help but reflect poorly on the man who had been at its head, in one form or another, for the past twelve years. Though in all, the lion's share of participants followed a script similar to the "Conversations" and "Direct Lines" of the past, voices like Venediktov's and Kucherena's stood out as growingly frequent public rhetorical challenges to the political status quo. Clearly impromptu in a forum known for its high level of scripted staging, such utterances signaled a significant shift in the balance of power and the strength of reigning authority, or *vlast'*. And it was no accident that, just as in the era of glasnost, the very issues of speech and language were at the forefront of debate. Challenging the leader on the very terms of debate (it is rank-and-file citizens who are marching, not just the "opposition") and accusing *vlast'* in general of a failure to communicate struck at the very foundation of the political legitimacy of a state that on paper at least still called itself a democracy.

Compared to Gorbachev and Yeltsin, Putin was far less willing to open the public airwaves to such alternative voices, acquiescing to the questioning only grudgingly when he realized that considerable steam needed letting off. But, like Gorbachev, he found that once it opened up, the debate became far more difficult to control. For the first time in ten years of the "Direct Line," Putin came across as a ruler having to justify his legitimacy, and jokes that ordinarily helped spice up his speech and bring him closer to the masses came across as awkward and petty.[2]

How do we account for the transformation? No doubt, over time the novelty of the genre itself had dissipated. The dwindling ratings of the event in recent years suggest that the *dramaturgia* had lost all sense of drama. No doubt Putin's status as *only* prime minister (albeit one with considerable clout) also decreased the potency of the event as a meeting between national leader and his people. But the main reason was a combination of the dramatic change in the political landscape in the months leading up to the event and the substantive challenge that web-based communication posed to traditional forms of media in shaping perceptions and cognitive maps. With a citizenry increasingly connected to the Internet and relying on it for information and communication, Putin could no longer expect glowing results from his made-for-television PR event. With hundreds of thousands of voters taking to the streets, he no longer fully controlled the narrative and was forced into the defensive position of having to address real events beyond his control. True, he was still able to manipulate the medium to serve his needs, but his obvious discomfort and awkward jokes demonstrated that the communicative landscape had significantly changed. Largely without full recognition on the part of central authorities, a new era of glasnost had emerged, this time in spite of the talk of attained "stability" that still dominated political discourse at the top. It had originated in the relatively confined world of the Internet, but with the help of new media technologies had spilled out into the streets and then onto national television to seriously challenge Putin's long-vaunted veneer of order and stability.

---

2. The Kremlin's decision in November 2012 to skip the annual end-of-year event altogether led to wide speculation that Putin and handlers had decided that the genre had outlasted its usefulness. When the next episode of the "Direct Line" did take place in April 2013, the number of field studios had been scaled back and more questions delivered from a more conservative, hand-picked studio audience. Viewership ratings were markedly lower as well: 49 percent of Russians attested to watching at least some of the broadcast, compared to 65 percent in 2007—the last year the show was broadcast simultaneously over the two main, state-run television channels (Stanovaya 2013; Korchenkova and Samokhina 2013).

Glasnost 2.0?: Digital Protest Culture

If a revival of glasnost was far from Putin's top policy priorities in the run-up to the 2011 and 2012 elections, there was no question it was issue number one in the world of the Russian-language Internet, or Runet, as it has come to be known. Echoing sentiments voiced publicly by Venediktov and others, the opening line of the oppositional RosVybory website asked visitors, "How can you make sure that your vote in the elections is not brazenly stolen?" Recalling from chapter 2 that the Russian word for "vote" also means "voice" and comprises the root of the word "glasnost," or "openness," many of the events surrounding the 2011–2012 election cycle can be understood as a battle not only for fair elections but also for openness, for access to information, for the ability to speak out, to share one's opinion in public, no matter how critical that opinion was of ruling authorities. Given the central role the Internet played in allowing this debate to resurface in a very public way, one could argue that—with or without Putin's consent—Russia was witnessing something of a "glasnost 2.0."

But just as with the earlier glasnost, the exact nature and goal of the "openness" differed considerably among individuals and groups, depending on more general attitudes toward the current political state of affairs. For those closer to the center of authority, or *vlast'*, it tended to assume a more modest form of opening up the spigot of information enough to give the population a sense of "buy-in" over policy decisions that were still being shaped and made by those at the top. Kucherena's bureaucrats needed merely to open up a bit and listen to their constituents. For those on or beyond the margins of officialdom, glasnost took on a more radical form—an invitation to question, to opine, to protest in public, to use one's *vote* and *voice* to transform *vlast'* significantly. For them, United Russia Duma members who had won election as a result of vote rigging served illegitimately and needed to be replaced.

Closely linked to this tension were competing views of the proper role of the Internet in Russian politics—widely recognized as an increasingly influential technology of communication in Russia today. The view most dominant among Russian-language Internet, or "Runet," users saw the Internet as an outpost for activism and oppositional discourse, and one of the only remaining such outposts in a media environment otherwise dominated by Kremlin-friendly self-censorship. A second view assumed the rhetorical form of "direct Internet democracy," embraced most prominently by then-President Medvedev as a mechanism for bringing the state into sync with the opinions and needs of the population (Medvedev 2010). A third view of the political role of the Internet could be described as a kind of "sovereign Internet," where some effort was made to harness the more interactive capabilities of Web 2.0 technologies, but with a keen eye toward "information security" and promoting the interests of ruling authorities. As the following case studies show, the evolving models often rely on different types of public political communication and employ different technological and rhetorical strategies to promote their views—on glasnost, on public expression, and on the rightful place of the Internet in these processes. Particularly as the Russian Internet continues to grow and compete with mainstream broadcast media for the public eye, how public virtual space comes to be perceived and designed will have a considerable impact on the political language—and, indeed, the polity itself—in years to come.

Runet as Oppositional Space

Recent world events have shown that new media technologies are neither "democratic" nor "authoritarian" by "nature" or design. Depending on a variety of factors—cultural, political, and technological—they have the capacity to both aid and suppress revolution (Morozov 2010). That being said, Web 2.0 technologies such as blogs, social networking, and crowd-sourcing tools nearly always begin as alternative spaces and, as such, naturally attract oppositional voices. In the United States, political blogging grew out of a frustration with the mainstream coverage of television and print media for being (from either Left or Right) too "mainstream" (Rosenberg 2009). Such has especially been the case in Russia, where Vladimir Putin and associates have maintained tight control over print media and especially broadcast television (Schmidt and Teubener 2007; Oates 2013). If in its country of origin, the United States, LiveJournal served mainly as an outlet for earnest teens sharing their innermost thoughts and problems with the rest of the world, the Russian-language version (*Zhivoi Zhurnal,* or simply *ZheZhe*) has always had a strongly politicized orientation and to this day remains the home to the most influential political bloggers in Russia (Gorny 2007). In the early days of the Russian Internet's blossoming, the space was additionally marked as a technology that had been largely imported from the West (Schmidt and Teubener 2006). While the 2000s saw considerable nativization of the Russian Internet—tellingly referred to as "Our Runet" *(Nash Runet)*—American-born social networking platforms such as Facebook and Twitter still carried an air of exoticism that, for some, gave cause for suspicion. All of these communication platforms have become political game-changers in Russia on at least three different levels: sharing information, shaping public opinion, and organizing oppositional activities.

Runet as an Alternative Source of Information

As an alternative, more open source of information, the Internet has created a turbo-charged version of the more narrow definition of glasnost—sharing information with citizens about the policies and operations of the government. The big difference is that the decentralized architecture of Web 2.0 technology allows any citizen to assume the role of journalist and contribute to the open flow of information. It is this less hierarchical and more rhyzomatic communicative structure (Lévy 2001, 112) that gave rise to the phenomenon of Aleksei Navalny, a particularly well-qualified citizen-journalist thanks to his legal training and dogged pursuit of federal corruption. Navalny first made a name for himself through his investigative blog and net-based exposés of the embezzlement of billions of dollars of state funds in the Transneft oil pipeline construction project, efforts that ultimately forced Prime Minister Putin to launch a formal investigation (Kramer 2011).

With both the twenty-first century blogosphere and Gorbachev's glasnost in the late 1980s, authorities essentially ceded considerable authority over the flow of web-based information, and, by doing so, gave way to a torrent of news and information that radically changed the tone and content of the political debate. Gorbachev's main goal was to shake up an entrenched bureaucracy enough to bring about political and economic reform. Putin's motivations have been more self-serving in nature; as with other officially sanctioned oppositional outlets such as *Novaia gazeta, Lenta.ru,* and *Ekho Moskvy,* the Russian blogosphere has served as a useful mechanism for letting off steam within a minority group of more critical Russians, without threatening the generally accepting attitudes of the less digitally connected majority.

The calculation underlying these motivations proved faulty on two counts. It underestimated the entrepreneurial drive of Navalny and others to develop more stable and popularly accessible projects, and it underestimated the speed with which Runet would become a legitimate player in the arena of public opinion. The first of Navalny's citizen watchdog projects took the form of RosPil (www.rospil.info), an interactive site that allowed citizens to report official mismanagement of federal funds and track cases as they progressed through various stages of citizen and legal contestation. The second project, RosYama, was initiated later in 2011, and took on the more mundane but popular topic of the dilapidated state of Russia's roads. Both projects relied on Web 2.0 technology that enables end-using citizens to report cases of government mismanagement and trace progress and outcomes of ensuing investigations. The user merely needs to click on the "Report on a dubious [government] purchase" button and fill in the details, and the RosPil legal staff handles the case from there. One could monitor the case's status through the "State orders" button, check out the overall ruble amount that had been saved owing to reports on the site, and even make an online contribution to the project. RosYama worked in a similar fashion: those wanting to report the presence of a gaping pothole on their local streets followed a similar sequence of steps, reporting the location of the road problem and uploading a photograph to document the bureaucratic negligence. If after the legally allotted thirty-seven days the problem had not been fixed, informants could click on "send your complaint to the public prosecutor's office" to file a formal complaint.

Aside from the crowdsourcing technologies that provided a single common tool for citizens to voice and document their complaints locally, the projects offered potent symbolic fodder for antigovernment sentiments. The names of the projects themselves (RosPil, RosYama) enlisted the beloved bureaucratic stump-compound, pairing the common initial syllable for existing state agencies, *Ros* (cf. Rosatom, Rosnano), with a second component that introduced a parodic element to the formula (*pil* from the slang *pilit'*, meaning "to saw" or "to skim," and *yama* the Russian for "pothole"). When combined, they gave name to a general frustration shared by a large portion of the population—including many wired, middle-class white-collared workers—that the government was not serving the needs of the population and was, quite likely, lining its pockets generously in the process.

TABLE 6.1. Navalny's shadow government

Actual state agencies	Navalny's online projects
Rosatom (atomic energy)	RosAgit (agitational material)
Roskomnadzor (communications, information technology, and mass media)	RosMiting (information about demonstrations)
Roskosmos (space exploration)	RosPil (government corruption)
Rosmolodezh (youth affairs)	RosUznik (political prisoners)
Rosnano (nanotechnology)	RosVybory (elections violations)
Rosneft (oil)	RosYama (problems with roads)
Rosaftodor (roads)	RosZhKKh (problems with housing)
Rostelekom (telecommunications)	

At the same time they served as a surrogate, if not subversive, government that, in contrast to the legal government, was directly addressing those unmet needs (see table 6.1).

It is this deft ability to pinpoint issues of popular discontent, articulate them in coherent satirical language, and package them in web technologies that maximize the power of the Internet for decentralized aggregation of information that has made Navalny such a potent player in contemporary Russian politics. He has been so successful, in fact, that authorities have applied the full weight of the legal system, opening four different trumped criminal cases against Navalny at the time of this writing, the most advanced of which, the Kirovles affair, resulted in a conviction and five-year prison sentence that will make it impossible, by current Russian law, to run for public office (Sedakov 2013).

Runet as Mechanism for Shaping Public Opinion

In addition to aiding the swift, open, and decentralized dissemination of information, the Internet has changed the rules of the game in influencing public opinion. Its ability to make any political slogan viral was attested to by a number of web and even nonweb based "actions" conducted during the 2011–2012 campaign season. In a media environment where main outlets engaged in heavy self-censorship, the Internet provided a tool for bringing into wide circulation protest statements that before would have received little attention. Pedestrians had only a little over an hour, for instance, to lay eyes directly on the 145-square-meter "Putin Leave!" banner that activists managed to drape atop an office building facing the Kremlin in the early morning hours of 1 February, but thanks to the re-posting of images and online reports, news of the message reached a far greater portion of the population (Kozenko and Gruzdeva 2012; "Oppozitsionery...." 2012).

Many observers noted the high level of creativity invested in protest expressions, a sign of the relatively well-educated, urban demographic of the protesting population, but also an indication of their web savvy. Astute Runet users knew full well that entertaining content made it far more likely that a political statement would get any sort of sustained attention online. (If the total number of Internet users in Russia had reached close to 50 percent of the population by the end of 2011, a significantly smaller portion devoted attention while there to politics ["Chislo internet-pol'zovatelei...." 2011].) Navalny, for instance, launched an online musical video contest in September, offering 300,000 rubles in cash prizes for the best anti-United Russia song produced in the months running up to the December Duma elections (Navalny 2011a). The contest resulted in 116 entries, over five hours of content, and a top-ten list of YouTube videos that has received over 3 million hits since the contest launch ("Protiv PZhiV" 2012). First prize (of 100,000 rubles) went to the song "Our Crazy House Votes for Putin" (*Nash durdom golosuet za Putina*) by the well-established band Rabfak, who have since put out a series of anti-Putin tunes that have all gone viral (Navalny 2011b).

In the weeks just following the September announcement of Putin's plans to run for president and in conjunction with the Premier's fifty-ninth birthday, Russian Twitter users organized a flash mob around the hash tag "#испасибопутинузаэто" (#thankstoputinforthat), a satirical echo of the Soviet *chastushka,* "Winter has gone, summer has arrived, thanks to the party for that" (*Ushla zima, nastalo leto, spacibo partii za eto*). The battle for poetic creativity turned out to be as fierce as that for political irony, leading to such gems as the following and extending the life of the tag straight through the election season and well beyond:

Стабильность есть—свободы нету #спасибопутинузаэто (Mikhail Evstiunin @Fghtr5, 12 February 2012) [We have stability but there is no freedom #thankstoputinforthat]

Снова ночь....Мы ждем рассвета....#спасибопутинузаэто (Il′ia @jrf_cat, 13 February 2012) [It's night once again....We await the dawn....#thankstoputinforthat]

Путин В.В @Spasiboputin
    Воды в общаге утром нету #СПАСИБОПУТИНУЗАЭТО (Putin V.V @Spasiboputin, 14 February 2012) [There's no water in the dorm in the morning #thankstoputinforthat]

Aside from its potential for creative expression, the hash tag in general has become a potent alternative to centralized, more institutional forms of political communication. Searching it, following it, or adding it to one's Tweet will automatically connect one to like-minded Tweeters without having to "friend" or "join." It combines networking with political satire; the fact that one's tags appear alongside thousands of others offers confirmation that one's political sentiments are publically shared by citizens from all across Russia (and the world).

Russian citizens witnessed a similarly potent web-based articulation of popular sentiment in the spread of the Internet meme "The Party of Crooks and Thieves" (*Partiia zhulikov i vorov*), the pejorative nickname for the United Russia Party that went viral in the winter of 2011. The coining and codification of this term (and its acronym "*PZhiV*" [ПЖиВ]) has arguably been the single most potent blow to the authority of the party of power in Russia. Its birth is owed also to opposition leader Navalny, who first used it in passing during a February 2011 Internet radio interview ("Sukhoi ostatok" 2011a). The meme went viral early in part because United Russia defenders called out Navalny on his characterization and threatened legal action (Martyshchuk 2011). United Russia member and Duma representative Evgenii Fedorov agreed to debate Navalny three weeks later, on the same radio station, thereby ensuring further circulation of the term ("Sukhoi ostatok" 2011b). Fedorov certainly did not help

United Russia's cause, as Navalny spent much of the hour picking apart his vague defense and articulating a series of concrete incidents involving fraud and government negligence. Later that year United Russia member Vladimir Svirid sued Navalny for 1 million rubles as compensation for "moral harm" (*moral'nyi vred*), bringing further publicity to the term. Not only did the court find his accusations unfounded, but publicity from the case again served to boost the meme's legitimacy, providing it attention in the mainstream media as well as online ("Edinoros ne smog zasudit" 2011). Soon the term and its acronym served as the shorthand of choice for oppositional communication and inspired a host of more ambitions net-based initiatives. In addition to the song competition already mentioned, it became the favorite theme of antiestablishment campaign posters. If one typed the word "party" in Cyrillic into a Google search window, the "Party of Crooks and Thieves" would appear first in the list of suggested phrases. If one followed that top link, one would arrive at the actual United Russia website, which, however, still sported the Cyrillic URL http://партия-жуликов-и-воров.рф// (http://partiia-zhulikov-i-vorov.rf).

It would certainly be an overstatement to attribute United Russia's decline in popularity over the course of 2011 solely to Navalny and his meme; the party's actions (or inactions) deserved a fair bit of the credit. But the arrival of the meme and its viral spread across multiple layers of Internet technology provided a timely and expressive means of labeling that discontent. With its poetic rhyme scheme (two dactylic feet with a single anapest at the end [Baunov 2011]) and its nod to the time-honored vices of Russian officialdom, *PZhiV* succinctly articulated Russians' general skepticism toward ruling authorities (*vlast'*). The last link was even acknowledged by Putin himself, who felt compelled to allude to the moniker in the wake of United Russia's poor showing in the December elections:

> They say that the party of power (*partiia vlasti*) is a party linked to thievery, corruption. If we remember the Soviet years, who was in power then? They were all called thieves and corruptionists too. And in the 1990s? The same thing.... It is the stamp not of a concrete political force, it is the stamp of power (*shtamp vlasti*). (Latukhina 2011)

Given Putin's main strategy with regard to the "opposition," which traditionally had been to ignore it altogether in public, the mere fact of his explanation was noteworthy. It was not coincidental, then, that four months after the meme's presence in the public sphere, Putin announced the formation of the All-Russian People's Front (*Obshcherossiiskii narodnyi front* [ONF]), an umbrella movement whose stated purpose was to extend political authority to a broader coalition of pro-Putin forces. Through the entire election cycle it was the symbols of the People's Front, not those of United Russia, that adorned Putin's campaign materials.[3] Even well after the discord of protest and elections had died down, the Kremlin continued to promote the Front—with mixed results—as a new brand of pro-Putin popular support (Vinogradov 2013).

Runet as Organizational Tool

Perhaps the most well-covered aspect of the Internet's role in bringing about contemporary political change has been its function as an organizing tool—facilitating communication in its most basic form. Particularly the spread of mobile digital technologies has allowed citizens to both congregate and aggregate like never before. The Facebook group "Saturday on Bolotnaia Square," hastily set up in the days leading up to the 10 December demonstrations, had over eighteen thousand visitors declare their intention to attend, with seven thousand others expressing their intention on the equivalent site in Vkontakte (the Russian equivalent of Facebook) (Balmforth 2011). According to the Levada Center, nearly 60 percent of those who attended the 24 December 2011 demonstration on Sakharov Boulevard in Moscow found out about the event through the Internet (Trudoliubov 2012). Twitter hash tags directed protesters to important logistical information and provided onsite reporting for those not in attendance. The website RosMiting.ru ("The coordination portal for citizens who are not indifferent") aggregated within a single space information about all of the elections-related demonstrations scheduled across Russia and logistical details for participating in them. RosAgit.info allowed demonstrators to download their favorite "fair elections" or anti-Putin slogan for upcoming demonstrations or to watch promotional videos featuring TV personalities and common citizens encouraging viewers to serve as

---

3. The move itself, by some accounts, has led to a tension within the Putin political camp between the United Russia "old guard," who tend to advocate a stronger stance against the growing opposition and protest movement, and newer supporters having come into the fold by way of the People's Front, who are more inclined to seek compromise (Pavlov 2012).

election observers for the presidential elections on 4 March 2012 ("Ia idu nabliudatelem...." 2012).[4]

One of the more interesting and effective technologies was the crowd-sourcing platform Ushahidi, which added a global positioning dimension to technology of online community coordination and communication.[5] In the weeks leading up to the December 2011 parliamentary elections, the election watchdog organization Golos set up a "Map of Violations," which gave users the ability to report and document a variety of different forms of elections violations across the country—again using global position to map the location of the reported violation on the map.

In all these examples we see the degree to which technological advances dramatically improve the ability of antiestablishment voices to express themselves, to be heard, to organize, and to offer alternative narratives on both the party of power and the current state of political affairs in Russia. With over 70 million active Internet users at the time, it was no wonder that the December 2011 edition of Putin's "Direct Line" fell flat.

Bots, Bloggers, and Other Forms of Pro-Kremlin Pushback

The anti-Putin protest voice enjoyed broad web-based coverage in part because of the oppositional nature of Runet culture itself, in part because of the diverse technologies the movement has employed, and in part because of its rhetorical flair—its ability to imbed a sharply critical discourse of protest and opposition in contexts that garner mass appeal among Internet users and spillover into traditional mass media. Given this wave of publicity, Putin and supporters found it increasingly difficult to ignore it. So what strategies—technological and rhetorical—did they use to counter this insurgency? Putin himself is on record as having dismissed the Internet as consisting of 50 percent pornography and taking pride in the fact that he has never sent an email (Lastochkin 2010). But he does have a loyal web-savvy following, willing to serve as virtual advocates—essentially

---

4. In the first week after its launch, the site attracted over ten thousand volunteers (Dmitrienko 2012).

5. The first of these, called the "Help Map" (*Karta pomoshchi,* http://russian-fires.ru/), actually appeared as a grassroots reaction to the Russian government's inability to respond promptly to communities engulfed by raging wildfires in the summer of 2010.

attempting to counter the opposition on its own terms and turf. In July 2011 a Vkontakte group called "Putin's Army" posted a video featuring three attractive young women discussing their admiration for the Premier and deciding to express their support by sporting revealing blouses emblazoned with "I'll rip it for Putin" in lipstick on the front ("Por'vu za Putina!" 2011; Goscilo 2013). The video received over 2 million views over the period leading up to the March 2012 presidential elections. January 2012 marked the online arrival of a new anthem to Putin written by Vladimir Slepak, "Forward, Vladimir Putin," which in lofty tones reminiscent of a Soviet patriotic song draws a stark contrast between Putin as a man of action and hack politicians blathering from the rostrum: "Politicos edifyingly read speeches from the tribune.... We only believe in creation, not in the grandeur of plans" (*Politikany v nazidan'e/ S tribun chitaiut rechi nam.... / My verim tol'ko sozidan'iu,/ A ne velichiiu program,*" "Davai vpered, Vladimir Putin" 2012).[6] And in the wake of protests at which one of the dominant slogans was "Russia without Putin," his supporters produced a text entitled "Russia without Putin?: Apocalypse Tomorrow!" forecasting a doomsday scenario in which the various oppositional factions tear the country to shreds as they battle for power and wealth, allow the United States to take over the world, and let Russia slip back into a bleak historical mix of the economic chaos of the 1990s and the political turmoil of 1917 ("Rossiia bez Putina?" 2012).

Attempts to counter the negative impact of the *PZhiV* meme also assumed a variety of forms. The legal approach having backfired in terms of public relations, some prominent political figures tacitly acknowledged the underlying problem of bureaucratic corruption and demanded that it be vanquished at all costs. At a pro-Putin rally outside the walls of the Kremlin on 12 December 2011, the then-NATO envoy and patriot Dmitrii Rogozin declared that "the party of power must fight by the harshest means possible the crooks, thieves, and traitors, who, unfortunately, exist everywhere" (Rogozin 2011). A Facebook group calling itself "United Russia for Honest Elections," sponsored by a women's organization belonging to Putin's People's Front, called for "a serious purge from the party of thieves and swindlers,

---

6. One should note here that, while the song has received close to six hundred thousand views on YouTube, in voting, the "dislikes" outnumber the "likes" by two to one.

of indifferent careerists, of political marionettes, of ossified partocrats."[7] A clever attempt to defang the phrase on the eve of parliamentary elections came in the form of a campaign ad put out by United Russia member and youth activist Robert Shlegel', playfully extending the list of attributive nouns to underscore the inclusiveness and success of the party:

> Голосуй за партию жуликов и воров! За 10 лет экономического роста, за многократное увеличение зарплат и пенсий; за строительство дорог, школ и больниц; за национальный суверенитет и благосостояние; за тех, кто преодолел мировой экономический кризис; за тех, кто мало говорит и много делает, а не наоборот. За партию жуликов и воров, студентов и учителей, ученных и военных, врачей и безнесменов, за всех нас. За наше будущее! Как бы кто нас не называл, мы любим нашу страну и вместе работаем на ее благо. За Единую Россию! ("Edinoros opublikoval" 2011; "Golosui za partiiu" 2011)

> [Vote for the party of crooks and thieves! For ten years of economic growth, for multiple increases in salaries and pensions; for the construction of roads, schools, and hospitals; for national sovereignty and well-being; for those who overcame world economic crisis; for those who speak little but do much, and not the other way around. For the party of crooks and thieves, students and teachers, scientists and military personnel, doctors and businessmen— for all of us. For our future! No matter what we might be called, we love our country and work together for its well-being. For United Russia!"]

Like the "anthem" to Putin and like the more conservative apparatchiks who resisted Gorbachev's glasnost, the Shlegel' video promoted the primacy of concrete deeds over words without deeds, foregrounding a list of the many ways United Russia had improved the lives of everyday Russians during its years in power. Unlike its communist predecessor, however, Putin's party of power recognized that even a minority of articulate

---

7. In the original, "Нам надоело, что нас—честных и порядочных людей, членов партии—клеймят наши политические оппоненты при молчании наших руководителей. Мы—за серьезную чистку партии от воров и жуликов, от равнодушных карьеристов, от политических марионеток, от костных партократов. Присоединяйтесь все, кто хочет очищения «Единой России», кто хочет ее движения вперед!" (Kobzen 2011).

and well-positioned "blabbermouths" had the capacity to influence public opinion.

Particularly in the context of the Internet and new media, technological positioning in the rhetorical struggle became critical. The most blatant means of thwarting oppositional discourse would be to simply shut down its main channels of communication. In the days leading up to the December 2011 parliamentary elections, the main websites of key oppositional information sources went offline for extended periods as a result of crippling "distributed denial of service" or DDoS attacks. Executing such attacks required access to an army of "bots"—hacked computers programmed to act en masse to access the target site and, through their sheer numbers, cause the site to crash. According to one security analyst describing the nature and origin of the 4 December 2011 attack, "The attack is being conducted from a big botnet [a network of infected computers] distributed all around the world—a lot of attacking computers are located in the United States, China, and other countries. There are only a few Russian IP addresses" (Sidorenko 2011). Similar botnet attacks cluttered Twitter during the first postelection protests on Triumfal'naia Square ("Russian Twitter...." 2011).

Rhetorically, the DDoS attack served the new media equivalent to the old Soviet technique of using critical applause or "noise from the hall" to disrupt the speech of a speaker at the podium, or jamming shortwave radio signals from Voice of America or the BBC World Service. Other forms of digital "white noise" included trolling hash tags on Twitter and comments sections on social networking platforms in order to dilute oppositional speech with negative, contrarian, vulgar, or off-topic posts. On the more proactive side, bots were enlisted to push the popularity of Kremlin-friendly posts so that they appeared in the influential "most popular" lists of search engines, such as Yandex or Rambler (a technique sometimes called "astroturfing"). In October 2011 the Facebook community "White book" (*Belaia kniga*), after asking visitors for whom they planned to vote, saw the positive responses for Putin nearly doubled in a matter of hours because of a sudden spike in traffic from thousands of users, every one of whom cast his vote for Putin. On closer examination, it turned out that many of the "voters" featured minimalist profiles in Facebook: no profile, photos, or past posting history, just a name (in many cases, suspiciously exotic, like "Agliia Grekhovodova" and "Kharitina Zhevaakin"), confirmation that they were registered Facebook users, and their vote of support (Samsonova, Dobrokhotov, and Beniumov 2011).

The Kremlin likewise has invested considerable "administrative resources" to enlist humans to help improve its position in the online battle for public and journalistic opinion. For several years, for instance, it has invested heavily in the cultivation of Kremlin-friendly bloggers and Tweeters whose job was to embed themselves in a variety of social networking environments to promote Kremlin views (Hodge 2009, Sidorenko 2010a). According to one 2009 report,

> The ministry [of communications] said it was offering up to 5 million rubles (almost $166,000) to the company that could provide "effective mechanisms of promoting the interests of the federal bodies of the executive branch of power on specialized social networking sites." The winning bidder will also need to research the Russian-language Internet for specialized social networking sites, "draft a concept" to promote state interests through the websites, and propose "methods of monitoring" the sites in order to "boost the effectiveness" of the activities of state bodies on the sites, the documents for the tender said. (Krainova 2009)

In February 2012 the technological and economic underpinning of these efforts became clearer when someone hacked into the e-mail accounts of high-ranking officials of Nashi, the pro-Kremlin youth organization, and released thousands of exchanges between the press secretary, Kristina Potupchik, and Vasilii Iakemenko, the founder of Nashi who at the time served as head of Rosmolodezh, the Federal Agency for Youth Affairs. In addition to implicating some more broadly respected bloggers, the leaked information documented the millions of rubles that had been pumped into generating a pro-Kremlin buzz on the Internet and hacking the opposition.[8] The e-mails likewise documented a variety of other more disruptive communicative strategies, such as spamming, trolling, astroturfing, and online vote-rigging (*nakrutki*), that were clearly designed to compromise not only the "target" (*ob"ekt*), as the opposition is referred to, but to also sully the medium itself. As one of the bullet points in an e-mailed lecture by a Nashi organizer put it,

---

8. For coverage of the "Kremlingate" scandal in the Russian blogosphere, see "Perepiska nashistov" (2012).

In the network of commentaries we will increase the number of commentators, hang out to dry (*vyvialiat'*) those opponents who are conducting targeted work against us and Putin, and (we will) troll them, creating a climate in the commentaries that will force the publication to close the comment function as such. (Pyrma 2012)

One blogger drew particular attention to fact that much of this activity was being financed by the federal government (through Rosmolodezh): "The most interesting line in these budgetary expenses is the payment to a certain Arsen Mukhmatmurziev, identified as an "IT specialist, hacker" with the task of "taking opponents offline, crashing sites and web pages, and crashing accounts" (yavleev 2012).

On balance, then, the efforts outlined here suggest that, from a communicative standpoint, in 2011–2012 progovernment forces were still playing defense for the most part. Cognizant of the degree to which the medium was dominated by oppositional discourse—and discourse that was capable of attracting attention—their strategy largely amounted to *compromising* that medium, rather than offering a viable alternative, a more positive discourse of power.

The e-Government Alternative

A more proactive parallel tack taken by the government, particularly at the initiative of Medvedev, has been to promote what he has called "direct Internet democracy" (Medvedev 2010). Early signs of this came in the form of the former president's own foray into the blogosphere and his demand that other government officials likewise make themselves accessible to their constituents online. I have argued elsewhere that this has proven to be a difficult task, in part because of the antagonistic, oppositional nature of Runet and in part because of the generic traps blogging and microblogging pose to bureaucrats and elected officials affiliated with the party of power (Gorham 2012). Excessive use of either blogging or microblogging, as Medvedev found out, risks projecting an image of a political leader as one with misplaced priorities and preoccupied with frivolous niche modes of communication. Despite Medvedev's failure in this regard, he did help impress on skeptical authorities that establishing some form of positive online presence was important for one's political image.

A trend friendlier to their communicative needs evolved out of earlier "e-government" initiatives and was repackaged, in the wake of the December 2011 political turmoil, as the "Big Government" (*Bol'shoe pravitel'stvo*) project—again with Medvedev as chief advocate. In part a means of providing some relief to the sense of bureaucratic indifference that frustrated citizens (and was articulated in the statement by Kucherena quoted earlier), the "Russia without fools" website (*Rossiia bez durakov*) went online to offer citizens a mechanism for complaining about specific instances of egregious bureaucratic red tape. Promising to "change the rules of the game," the site's welcome page offers users "the real opportunity to personally find and destroy concrete idiocies [in the functioning of the state bureaucracy]."[9] Even Putin, the devout net atheist, found the need to incorporate discourse on "e-government" in his campaign literature, declaring in one policy paper,

> We need to align the "electronic government" project better to the needs and demands of citizens. Maximally and fully divulge information about the activity of organs of state and municipal power. Through electronic technology make the state mechanism comprehensible and accessible to society.
>
> Every person should clearly understand from the information on government sites what can be obtained from which agency and how, and which concrete bureaucrat needs to be asked what question. (Putin 2012)

Rather than unfettered exposure to the teeming and largely acrimonious virtual masses, the "electronic government" option allowed a medium by which government officials could provide the population with easier access to useful services and even create platforms for the solicitation of civic feedback, but on their own terms. Early examples of this could be seen in the format of Medvedev's own video blog, which had a comment section, but clearly monitored and screened messages prior to publication. It later appeared in the controversial launch of Putin's own 2012 re-election campaign website (www.putin2012.ru), which featured an interactive function, "Let's change Russia together," allowing registered users space for posting proposals on a variety of issues from housing and education to the

---

9. What it does not mention is that the site essentially clones an already existing, independently created site ("A country without idiocies") that features harder-hitting exposés (Blog Dmitriia Ternovskogo, http://ternovskiy.livejournal.com/tag/%22Страна%20без%20глупостей%22 [accessed 21 August 2012]).

political system and foreign affairs. As soon as the site went online, attentive netizens quickly posted messages suggesting that the best thing Putin could do to "change Russia" was to withdraw his name from the presidential race (e.g., "A kind request. Please leave politics. I understand power is a narcotic, but this will be a commendable move."—Andrei Antonenko ["Rossiiane pishut" 2012]). The negative comments disappeared from the site within hours, but not before they could be captured as screenshots and disseminated virally for any and all who wished to see.

Perhaps most indicative of this move from the wild world of blogging to a tamer environment of e-government is the fact that the vast majority of governors appointed in 2011 or later have opted out of maintaining a blog altogether, choosing instead to implement more controlled means of soliciting feedback from constituents online. In the period from January to May 2012 at least sixteen new governors were appointed by presidents Medvedev and Putin (Bekhbulatova and Samokhina 2012). Of these, none opted to maintain a blog with an open comment section that allowed for direct exchange between governor and constituents, but nearly all of them established alternative platforms for communicating with constitutes, most of which solicited public input while limiting the governors' exposure to public negative attacks or accusations.[10]

Collectively, the e-government initiatives resemble the more conservative interpretation of glasnost that party apparatchiks attempted to codify in the early years of perestroika—one in which the government retained full control while creating some modest mechanisms to give the public more access to information and a greater sense that their input matters. But as one critic of Putin's policy paper on democracy put it, this has done very little to change the real balance of power, the configuration of *vlast'*:

> The entire article is permeated with [the idea that] we are ready to talk.... If you want to discuss legislation, citizens, discuss them, and if you want to introduce some sort of initiatives by collecting 100 thousand signatures, collect them, but the decisions will still be made by other people. You can talk, but we will decide—that is the gist of the article, which represents Vladimir Putin's credo as far as the political structure of the country is concerned. (Cherkasov 2012)

---

10. For a detailed analysis of this trend, see Gorham (forthcoming, 2014).

Numerous examples—from bots and bloggers to trolling, astroturfing, and aggressive comment moderation—suggest three things: first, that the government is now aware of the need for a communicative presence on the Internet and has considerable resources for establishing it; second, that its presence is as much preventative as it is promotional or informative; and third, that however hard it tries, there seem to be web-savvy hacktivists who can use the technology to show that the emperor has no clothes.

Cyber Curtain?

When one looks more closely at recent state-sponsored initiatives above and beyond tactical moves in electoral politics, one finds a series of attempts to consolidate state control over the Internet through a combination of technological and economic measures. Perhaps the grandest manifestation of this effort is the creation of the Cyrillic-based first-level domain ".рф" (".rf"), a state-sponsored effort trumpeted by Medvedev soon after assuming the presidency in 2008, formally approved by the Internet Corporation for Assigned Names and Numbers (ICANN) in November 2009, and officially launched in May 2010 (Popova 2008; "O domene RF" n.d.). Justifications for the move ranged from guarantees of greater security and accessibility to a broader range of attractive URL addresses available to businesses. Underlying much of the discussion, however, was a sense of national pride that Russian Internet users would finally be able to use their native tongue to visit and mark the virtual territory of the Russian-language Internet.

Concurrently one can trace the gradual takeover of major Runet companies by Kremlin-friendly oligarchs ("Kremlin Allies'" 2010; Taratuta and Zygar' 2010; Ivanitskaia and Filippov 2008; Dorokhov and Smirnov 2013); proposals from the Ministry of Justice to register—by name—online users (Kulikov 2009); the Press Ministry's plan to monitor social networking and blogosphere "to fish out the good ideas of the network" ("E-nationalism" 2009); and a proposal for (1) a national, state-sponsored search engine—ironically dubbed "Kremlyandex" (Asmolov 2010a; "Gospoiskovik" 2010)—and (2) a state-subsidized Internet plan designed to provide affordable access to a limited number of websites and tools (Asmolov 2010c).

Collectively, these trends have led observers to surmise that, as a result of "the government's fear of the power of the new media," it is taking measures to "isolate Russian cyberspace from the global network" by creating a "national cyberzone," a "sovereign Internet" that not only makes the space "more Russian," but (more important) "more state-affiliated" as well (Sidorenko 2010b; Asmolov 2010b; Oates 2013).[11]

Legislative moves swiftly pushed through following the start of Putin's third term greatly exacerbated the impression of an impending "cyber curtain." On 8 June 2012 Putin signed new legislation authorizing Russian police to arrest citizens who "violate the order of proper conduct at public rallies," and assessing fines up to 20,000 rubles for individuals (the equivalent of the average annual salary of a Russian citizen) and up to 600,000 rubles for organizations for those deemed guilty of such violations ("Zakon o mitingakh...." 2012). The law included language forbidding web-based dissemination of information about unlawful rallies. In the closing days of the spring 2012 parliamentary session, the Russian Duma passed the "Law on the Protection of Children from Information Harmful to Their Health and Development," which in the name of protecting children from web-base pornography and the promotion of drugs and suicide, authorized the creation of a "black list" of websites containing information relating to the targeted vices. Both the details of the law and past precedent were sufficient enough to earn cries of protest from those complaining that the loose wording invited targeted blacklisting for political motivations. Critics from Navalny to the Presidential Council for the Development of Civil Society of Human Rights claimed the law amounted to censorship, would sharply impede the economic growth of Internet-related business in Russia, and would create what amounted to an "electronic curtain" around Russia (Navalny 2012; "Zaiavlenie chlenov Soveta...." 2012; Zykov 2012; Gorelik and Sindelar 2012). In January 2013 the Orthodox Church-backed "Safe Internet League" (*Liga bezopasnogo Interneta*) took the blacklist idea one

---

11. For an excellent discussion of the evolution of strategies of government control over Runet, see Deibert and Rohozinski 2010, 15–34. The digital media scholar Vlad Strukov (2009) is likewise sanguine about Runet's potential to positively shape the formation of democratic values in Russia because of the lingering and substantial digital divide between those with and without Internet access, as well as the Russian government's regulatory control over, and deep mistrust of, the Internet.

step further by announcing plans to create a "clean Internet zone" in the Kostroma oblast′ that would force Internet users to "opt out" of a restricted zone of preapproved websites (Earle 2013).

All these efforts point to a concerted strategy on the part of Putin and the ruling United Russia Party to contain, control, and contaminate the more liberal forms of glasnost and free speech emanating from web-based sources that proved so detrimental to them during the 2011–2012 electoral cycle. Putin may not have been able to mute the voice of the opposition on the Internet completely, but appeared to be wagering that, through a menu of legal and economic measures, he could compromise it enough to make it a space more feared by the networked opposition and less attractive to rank-and-file users. (In fact, in mid-2013, Russian courts had sentenced Aleksei Navalny to five years in prison for trumped up corruption charges in the Kirovles case.) But the surprisingly large response to the "snow revolution"—along with the steadily growing numbers of Internet users in Russia—cannot help but give Putin and company pause over this wager.[12] If they have learned the lessons of the first glasnost well, they will not underestimate the power of the rostrum—now virtual—to promote and bring about change more quickly and radically than proposed by the ruling party. E-government styled efforts to change the topic and tone of conversation between central authorities and citizens appear to have a greater chance than restrictive laws of limiting the Internet's ability to bring about revolutionary change in Russia, but the first year of Putin's third term suggests that more punitive approaches will be the strategy of choice. Whether these more authoritarian approaches to the language of the virtual public sphere lead to the containment or contamination of that space as a viable forum for debate, or foster its increased radicalization as an outlet for oppositional expression, remains to be seen. Putin-era policy toward "old media" has been largely successful at inoculating that space of all serious political debate, and the vast majority of Russian Internet users still spend most of their time online networking and entertaining themselves rather than fomenting revolution. But the Putin of 2013 enjoys far less popular support that the Putin of 2000, and

---

12. Polling data measuring 2012 Internet penetration and usage in Russia showed ever-faster growth at 14 percent, with the number of daily users increasing to 52.1 million Russians ("Internet v Rossii" 2013).

past experience suggests savvy net users will find creative and technical means of working around imposed legislation. Unless Putin and allies decide to go the route of China—which many now believe is untenable for economic and technical reasons, if not political ones—they will continue to fight a reactive battle against an infrastructure that is evolving far faster than any large state bureaucracy can keep up with. So while there may be some sacrificial oppositional victims in the next election season, the spate of recently dictated Internet laws will only serve to rile an already testy—and growing—population of netizen-users. Either scenario, however, ensures that the language of politics and the politics of language in Russia will remain objects of sharp symbolic contestation for the foreseeable future.

Conclusion

Linguistic innovation tends to accelerate during less stable periods of history, and the degree of success of any term, speech style, or discourse depends on the degree to which it resonates with the general population, which in turn depends on its ability to tap into underlying ideologies, economies, and technologies of language. Discussion in this book has shifted between the language of politics and the politics of language deliberately and naturally, as the two are often bundled together either in debates over national identity or the right to speak freely. Be they linguistic tussles for cultural authority or election-time battles over political control, negotiations over rights and responsibilities in language use underscore the basic role that language plays as a symbol of national identity or tool for power.

That said, how language is conceived—as identity marker or instrument—depends largely on the institutional context. Political rhetoric tends to treat language as a weapon, either for establishing and maintaining the "norms" of political behavior, as in Soviet Russian political culture, or contesting that authority through the deployment of alternative discourses. If in the perestroika era newspapers, television, and the rostrum of the First Congress of People's Deputies served as the primary technology of deployment, it was the Internet and blogosphere that served that purpose under Putin. In each of these cases, the tendency on the part of the powers that be is to dismiss oppositional speech as "empty rhetoric," contrasting it negatively to concrete deeds, or attempting to stifle it through some form of censorship. Committed as he was to his signature policy of glasnost, Gorbachev rarely exercised the formidable tools of censorship available to him as General Secretary of the Communist Party. Putin by contrast has paid only fleeting lip service to freedom of expression and swiftly reestablished state oversight of television in the early days of his presidency. He proceeded to use that outlet as a regular staging ground for projecting images of a vast, strong, and unified Russian nation led by a powerful, tough-talking, but beneficent national leader. Yet he has faced a more difficult challenge in containing oppositional speech with the rapid spread of new media technologies, the cultural history of which is closely linked to alternative notions of authority. Here, belated attempts to spam, troll, and otherwise contaminate online forums have had limited impact, though a flurry of legislative and legal efforts in the first year of his third term show every indication that containment through the manipulation of legal and economic institutions will remain at the center of his approach to oppositional speech.

Rarely, in the course of these political struggles to gain, maintain, or contest authority, have metaphors of Russian as a national treasure or living organism come into play. Only when the cultural authority of the Russian language offered the state a means of staking out its domain as "official language" within the Federation and advertising Russia's cultural allure for "compatriots" of the near and far abroad did the state invoke preservationist discourse. Otherwise, essentialist discourse has had little place in instrumental approaches to language.

Discourse on language as a marker of identity resides, instead, chiefly in cultural institutions such as the Academy and the Church. Here, too, there is no lack of struggle for authority, but rather than political authority, opposing discourses on language battle over the legitimacy of alternative forms of identity. Here, as in the political realm, these battles become more chaotic during times of radical social change. Soviet-era advocates of "speech culture" faced rather tame issues when writing about youth slang and loanwords. They limited political critiques to the popular and safe target of the convoluted language of an entrenched bureaucracy. And once the radical notions of Nikolai Marr had been discredited once and for all by Stalin, they enjoyed a near monopoly of authority with regard to language culture. When in the late 1980s institutions of censorship and state-controlled media were removed, however, the norm-based authority of the speech culture movement found itself drowned out by a cacophony of new registers—from the vulgar language of the streets to barbarisms from abroad. Just as alternative political voices filled the void created by the discrediting of political newspeak, alternative discourses in the cultural realm presented post-Soviet Russians with new alluring identities—foreign, capitalist, popular—that spread largely unabated through the early and mid-1990s. Eventually norm-based discourse on language enjoyed something of a renaissance as a growing number of Russians grew disillusioned by the unrealized promises of new capitalist or Western identities and bought into the growing drumbeat of "linguistic lawlessness" from the language guardians. Here, too, we witness a convergence of political utility and cultural moralism, a potent force that fueled the restorationist impulse of Putin's first two presidential terms. Though purists winced when he threatened to waste Chechen terrorists in the outhouse and grab tax-dodging oligarchs by the testicles, many Russians heard in Putin's salty turns the voice of a fighter for stability and order, unafraid to confront Russia's enemies and speak to them in their own language.

Events of 2011–2012, however, suggest that many Russians have grown weary of Putin's tough-talking rhetoric. Twelve years after his arrival on the political scene, Russian citizens have seen few concrete actions to buttress the talk, leading to growing skepticism and greater inclination to invoke that aspect of traditional Russian language ideology that regards colorful language with mistrust and looks instead for proof in concrete deeds ("A lot of cackle, but no eggs," as the saying goes [appendix 7.3.6]). "It turns out," as one commentator put it, "it's not enough that our president speaks well, deftly answers questions, and can cut opponents down to size.... The problem is that, with his responding blows he is defending a vacuum. There is nothing visible except for the fencer himself who in a blaze defends his place in the middle of the circle: let me stay longer, let me run the country some more, everyone step away from the tribune. For what purpose? Why? To do what?" (Baunov 2013).

The once-valued currencies of tough talk and the discourse of "stability" have seen their worth further challenged by new technologies of communication that have circumvented the stronghold of Putin-TV, to convey an alternative vision of a nation run by crooks and thieves. Indeed, it is no surprise that, while *politkonkretnost'* earned the "antiword-of-the-year" award in 2007 and exerted little impact after that (to date it shows no sign of adoption in public parlance), the honor of "word of the year" in 2011 went to *Rospil* (the title of Navalny's anticorruption project), and "phrase of the year" to "Party of Crooks and Thieves" (*Partiia zhulikov i vorov*)— two terms that have already demonstrated far greater impact, in part because of their ability to speak to broadly recognized social ills and in part thanks to the power of Internet technology in the hands of one of Russia's most followed bloggers. And yet, with the memories of the era of "lawlessness" still fresh in the minds of many, radical calls for a "Russia without Putin" still remain vulnerable to threats of apocalypse.

Politics of Language

So how, in all this web-based morass of trolling, spamming, hacking, and other forms of political mischief, does the "great and mighty" Russian language fare? As one by now could predict, new-media inspired language degradation has given rise to a drumbeat of protest among purists and language mavens in Russia, just as it has in the West. The experiences of the 1990s suggest that this is both entirely expected and largely uncalled for. Indeed, from a purely economic standpoint, as I have argued in chapter 4, institutions of Academy, state, and Church greatly benefit from such potent fuel to fire future guidebooks and conferences, sermons and lectures, laws and decrees. "Bad language" is good economics for industries that run on the preservation of norms. This is true in any culture, but particularly in Russian, where national identity is so closely linked to the mother tongue.

One could also argue that the era of new media technology brings as much potential benefit for fostering language culture as it does potential harm. Never before have language users had such easy access to tools for proper writing and speech—from spell-checkers and online dictionaries to distance-learning courses and digital corpora of the entire literary language. I have argued here that the discursive practices of the purists and monitors, while easy to dismiss as misguided prescriptivism, actually can and do have a concrete impact on general attitudes toward language, which may ultimately influence language use itself. Dominant Russian language ideologies, which tend to accentuate the literary dimension of language as a marker of national and cultural identity, set the bar particularly high when it comes to assessing norms. Even if speakers and writers do not always obey them, they learn of and acknowledge their import from an early age. As institutions of language culture gain further access to mass technologies that better spread and popularize their message, their impact has even greater potential.

Beyond these metalinguistic practices, however, one tends to see a natural swing in language attitudes that serves as a more natural regulator of proper usage. For every trendy loan that "earns the right to citizenship," dozens of others die a natural death. Many of the language innovations that inevitably arise with the advent of new ideologies, economies, or technologies run their natural course and eventually lapse, with some exceptions, into the realm of "historicism." Such was the case with the notorious "scumbag" or *padonki* language that took the Russian blogosphere by storm in the late 1990s and early 2000s: purist cries of linguistic apocalypse eventually faded as the *padonki* themselves grew tired of their creative misspellings and vulgar blog-based banter—in part because the trend had gone too mainstream (Zvereva 2012, 51–82; Zvereva and Berdicevskis, forthcoming, 2014). In a similar manner, teenage texters who clutter their online diaries and text messages with emoticons and abbreviations ultimately understand how and where that register is appropriate—until they grow up and it loses relevance altogether.[1]

Language of Politics

As for the other side of the equation that has served as the dual focus of this book, it is less clear how the rise of new media technologies will

---

1. Maksim Krongauz strikes a more cautious tone when contemplating the impact of "Olbanian" in his recent discussion of the language of the Internet, arguing that phenomena of this sort suggests that "shame [with regard to one's own illiteracy] has disappeared" (Krongauz 2013, 124).

affect the shape and form of political communication in years to come. As the two realms continue to merge, will the language of the Internet transform politics, or will politics transform the language of, and communication on, the Internet? Evidence adduced in chapter 6 provides fodder for both sides of the argument. While it may be true that the politicization of the Internet is ultimately "bad" for that environment— cluttering it with incendiary language, partisan diatribes, hacking, trolls, and spam—there is little doubt that it is largely thanks to the Internet as an alternative space for oppositional discourse and communication that Putin has had a more difficult time dictating the terms of debate. On this count, the content and reception of Putin's 2011 "Direct Line" is emblematic. Staged directly in the aftermath of the December 2011 parliamentary elections and protests, his ability to talk tough in a convincing manner was severely compromised and the coherence of the "strong, unified Russia" message disabled. Instead, linguistic practices of the street forced him to back off from the total *dramaturgia* seen in previous episodes; when he did try to talk tough, his word choice and timing seemed off, and the reaction as a result was visibly forced. With the number of users of Yandex, Russia's leading search engine, now greater than that of the state-controlled Channel One, and with the number of citations by mainstream media and news services to blog sources doubling on an annual basis, the impact of Putin-TV and its technologies of symbolic production is likely to shrink ("Auditoriia 'Iandeksa'...." 2012; "Itogi 2011" 2012). This does not mean that Runet will serve as a society-wide "kitchen" for open and frank debate, but it will have greater impact, with fewer means of outside manipulation. At the same time, oppositional forces face considerably more resistance from a party of power largely united in its drive to retain that power (in the name of "stability" and national unity) and a large portion of the electorate that has little stomach for "revolution" and the lawlessness and disarray that have come to be associated with it. Given the central role in the reform process that new media technology has played, it is here that some of the biggest battles are being waged. And while the opposition may enjoy a stronger rhetorical presence, ruling authorities, both nationally and regionally, have considerable means by which to apply economic and legal pressure to "regulate" that presence—and are hastening to do so (Gorodetskaia and Ivanov 2013).

What one can count on—in Russian as well as in other language cultures—is that tensions between innovation and purification (or between degradation and restoration, depending on one's perspective) will persist in both the politics of language and the language of politics. The specific dynamic of that tension will largely depend on ideological, economic, and technological trends that benefit one or the other side of the struggle. In the context of Russian language and society, where notions of "stability" and "norms" have traditionally overshadowed the messier discourse of democratic exchange, symbolic authority in language has tended to buttress more readily political ideologies rooted in notions of essentialism, preservation, and restoration. Regardless of the underlying ideologies, there will always be less than a one-to-one correspondence between language attitudes—how one perceives the proper place of language in culture and society—and how one actually speaks and writes. The struggle for linguistic purity, just as in the struggle for political authority, therefore, will always be tempered not only by contrary forces of degradation, innovation, resistance, and reform, but also by a fundamental gap between linguistic ideals and everyday practice. And it is in this gap that the shifting trends of continuity and change in language culture take form.

Appendix

Sayings and Proverbs about Language

1. Language as weapon (or instead of weapon), a powerful force.[1]

    1.1. Ветры горы разрушают—слово народы подымает. [226] (The winds destroy mountains, the word arouses nations.)

    1.2. Не пройми копьем—пройми языком! [231] (Pierce not with the sword, pierce with the tongue!)

    1.3. Рана от копья—на теле, рана от речей—в душе. [232] (A wound from a spear goes to the body; a wound from speeches goes to the soul.)

    1.4. Хоть слово не обух, а от него люди гибнут. [234] (While a word may not be an axe, people will perish from it.)

    1.5. Лучше говорить дельно, чем говорить много. [229] (It's better to speak sensibly than speak a lot.)

2. Language as the voice of the people (*vox populi*).

    2.1. Голос народа могучен, как океан. [18] (The voice of the people is mighty like the ocean.)

    2.2. Глас народа—глас божий. (The voice of the people is the voice of God.)

---

1. With one exception ("The voice of the people is the voice of God"), proverbs cited come from Martynova and Mitrofanova (1986), page number in brackets.

3. Kind language as a source of wealth, nourishment.
   3.1. Добрые слова дороже богатства. [46] (Kind words are dearer than wealth.)
   3.2. Добрым словом и бездомный богат. [47] (A kind word makes even the homeless rich.)
   3.3. Слово лучше доброе мягкого пирога. [227] (A kind word is better than a flaky pie.)
   3.4. Доброе слово человеку—что дождь в засуху. [227] (A kind word to a man is like rain in a drought.)

4. Power/authority linked to paucity of speech.
   4.1. Умный не тот, кто много говорит, а тот, кто много знает. [98] (Smart is not he who speaks much, but rather he who knows much.)
   4.2. Тот неглуп, кто на слова скуп. [110] (He who is sparing with words is no idiot.)
   4.3. Правда не речиста. [194] (The truth is not loquacious.)
   4.4. В запертой рот и муха не залетит. [226] (Even a fly won't fly into a closed mouth.)
   4.5. Доброе молчанье лучше пустого болтанья. [227] (Kind silence is better than empty chatter.)
   4.6. Ешь больше, а говори меньше! [227] (Eat more, speak less!)
   4.7. Коротко, да ясно, оттого и прекрасно. [228] (Short and clear—that's what make it beautiful.)
   4.8. Слово—серебро, молчание—золото. [233] (Speech is silver, but silence is golden.)

5. Weakness/lack of authority linked to verbosity.
   5.1. Где много слов, там мало правды. [226] (Where there are many words, there is little truth.)
   5.2. Говорит до вечера, а слушать нечего. [226] (He'll talk until evening, but there's nothing worth listening to.)
   5.3. Говорит красиво, да слушать тоскливо. [226] (He speaks handsomely, but it's depressing to listen.)
   5.4. Кто много болтает, тот беду на себя накликает. [229] (He who talks too much calls harm to himself.)
   5.5. Мелет день до вечера, а послушать нечего. [229] (He'll ramble on from day to night, but there's nothing worth listening to.)
   5.6. Острый язык—дарованье, длинный язык—наказанье. [231] ("A sharp tongue is a gift; a long tongue, a punishment.")
   5.7. Держи язык короче! [227] (Hold your tongue tighter!)
   5.8. Длинный язык—короткие мысли. [227] (Where tongue is long, thoughts are short.)
   5.9. Много шуму—мало толку. [230] (All noise, no substance.)

6. Varieties of morally suspect speech (flattery, gossip, stupid, hateful, or indiscrete speech).
   6.1. Льстец под словами—змей под цветами. [229] (The flatterer hides beneath words like a snake beneath flowers.)

6.2. Бабий язык—чертово помело. [226] (A woman's tongue is a witch's broom.)

6.3. Глупые речи—что пыль на ветру. [226] (Stupid speeches are like dust in the wind.)

6.4. Дурное слово, что смола: пристанет—не отлепишь. [227] (A bad word is like resin: when it sticks, you can't get it off.)

6.5. Осла узнаешь по ушам, а дурака—по словам. [231] (You can tell an ass by his ears, a fool by his words.)

6.6. За худые слова слетит и голова. [228] (For evil words the head rolls too.)

6.7. Слово—не воробей, вылетит—не поймешь. [233] (A word is not a sparrow; when if flies out, you won't catch it.)

6.8. Лишнее говорить—себе вредить. [229] (If you say too much, you hurt yourself.)

6.9. Говорить умеет, да не смеет. [227] (He knows how to speak, but doesn't dare.)

7. "Deed" is greater than or equal to "Word."

7.1. Balance between the two.

7.1.1. На великое дело—великое слово. [226] (Great words for great deeds.)

7.1.2. Если сидишь на печи, так побольше молчи. [227] (If you laze around, then keep your mouth shut.)

7.1.3. Как сказано, так и сделано. [228] (What's said is done.)

7.2. Deeds without words [+].

7.2.1. Кто мало говорит, тот больше делает. [229] (He who speaks little does more.)

7.2.2. Немного слов, да много дела. [231] (Few words, but much action.)

7.3. Words without deeds [-].

7.3.1. Иной речист, да на руку нечист. [228] (An eloquent preacher, but impure in practice.)

7.3.2. Много всего говорится, да не все в дело годится. [230] (He talks a good game, but falls short in practice.)

7.3.3. От одних слов толку мало. [231] (There's little sense to be had from words alone.)

7.3.4. От слова до дела—бабушкина верста. [231] (From word to deed is a country mile.)

7.3.5. Складно бает, да дела не знает. [232] (He talks smoothly, but doesn't know what he's doing.)

7.3.6. Много кудахтанья, а яиц нет. [230] (A lot of cackle, but no eggs.)

7.3.7. Словом и комара не убьешь. [233] (You won't even kill a mosquito with a word.)

WORKS CITED

Abdullaev, Nabi. 2006. "Making Sure Everything Looks Nice." *The Moscow Times* (27 October). http://www.themoscowtimes.com/news/article/making-sure-everything-looks-nice/201357.html (accessed 22 July 2013).

Ageev, Aleksandr. 1995. "Vostavshii 'Ъ.'" *Znamia* 4: 184–90.

Aizerman, L. S. 1990. "Uroki literatury kak dialog." *Literatura v shkole* 4: 78–86.

"Alisher Usmanov: Krupneishii igrok v svere telekommunikatsii i SMI, priverzhenets Putina." 2011. *Newsru.com* (14 December). http://www.newsru.com/background/14dec2011/usmanov.html (accessed 11 July 2012).

Alpatov, V. M. 1991. *Istoriia odnogo mifa: Marr i marrizm.* Moscow: Nauka.

———. 2000. "What Is Marxism in Linguisitics?" In *Materializing Bakhtin: The Bakhtin Circle and Social Theory,* edited by Craig Brandist and Galin Tihanov, 173–93. New York: St. Martin's Press.

Altunian, A. G. 1998. *"Politicheskie mneniia" Faddeia Bulgarina: Ideino-stilisticheskii analiz zapisok F. V. Bulgarina k Nikolaiu I.* Moscow: Izdatel'stvo URAO.

Amirov, V. M. 1997. *Rechevaia agressiia i gumanizatsiia obshcheniia v sredstvakh massovoi informatsii.* Ekaterinburg: Ural'skii gos. universitet imeni A. M. Gor'kogo, Fakul'tet zhurnalistiki.

Anderson, Benedict. 1983. *Imagined Communities: Reflections on the Origin and Spread of Nationalism.* London: Verso Editions.

Anderson, Richard D., Jr., Valery I. Chervyakov, and Pavel B. Parshin. 1995. "Words Matter: Linguistic Conditions for Democracy in Russia." *Slavic Review* 54, no. 1: 868–95.

Andreev, V. I. 1995. *Delovaia ritorika: Prakticheskii kurs delovogo obshcheniia i oratorskogo masterstva.* Moscow: Narodnoe obrazovanie.

Andrusenko, Lidiia. 2007. "Nagliadnaia agitatsiia." *Politicheskii zhurnal* 30 (29 October). http://www.politjournal.ru/index.php?action=Articles&issue=205&tek=7481&dirid=43 (accessed 19 July 2013).

Anishkin, Valerii. 1997. "Iazyk moi-vrag?" *Literaturnaia Rossiia* 7 (14 February): 3.

Annushkin, V. I. 1988. "Zachem nuzhna ritorika?" *Russkaia rech'* 5: 81–83.

Areshev, Andrei. 2008. "Virtual'naia politika, setevoi elektorat: Blogi stiraiut granitsy mezhdu nabliudateliami i igrokami." *Novaia politika* (5 February). http://www.novopol.ru/-virtualnaya-politika-setevoy-elektorat-text36121.html (accessed 22 July 2013).

Asmolov, Gregory. 2010a. "Russian Government to Develop National Search Engine." *Global Voices* (6 April). http://globalvoicesonline.org/2010/04/06/kremlyandex/ (accessed 22 July 2013).

———. 2010b. "From 'Sovereign Democracy' to 'Sovereign Internet'?" *Global Voices* (10 June). http://globalvoicesonline.org/2010/06/13/russia-from-sovereign-democracy-to-sovereign-internet/ (accessed 22 July 2013).

———. 2010c. "Flaws and Pitfalls of the Subsidized 'Social' Internet Plan." *Global Voices* (21 June). http://globalvoicesonline.org/2010/06/21/russia-flaws-and-pitfalls-of-the-subsidized-"social"-internet-plan/ (accessed 22 July 2013).

"Auditoriia 'Iandeksa' privysila chislo zritelei Pervogo kanala." 2012. *Lenta.ru* (25 May). http://lenta.ru/news/2012/05/25/overtake/ (accessed 22 July 2013).

Austin, J. L. 1962. *How to Do Things with Words: The William James Lectures Delivered at Harvard University in 1955.* Edited by J. O. Urmson. Oxford: Clarendon.

Azimov, P. A., Iu. D. Desheriev, and F. P. Filin, eds. 1972. *Problemy dvuiazychiia i mnogoiazychiia.* Moscow: Nauka.

Babich, Dmitry. 2006. "The Goodness Inside the Kremlin." *Russian Profile* (25 October), as reprinted in *Johnson's Russia List,* no. 239 (2006).

Baker, Keith Michael. 1990. *Inventing the French Revolution: Essays on French Political Culture in the Eighteenth Century.* Cambridge: Cambridge University Press.

Bakhtin, M.M. 1981. "The Epic and the Novel: Towards a Methodology for the Study in the Novel." In *The Dialogic Imagination,* edited by Michael Holquist, 3–40. Austin: University of Texas Press.

———. 1986. "The Problem of Speech Genres." In *Speech Genres and Other Late Essays,* edited by Caryl Emerson and Michael Holquist, translated by Vern W. McGee, 60–102. Austin: University of Texas Press.

Baldaev, D. S., V. K. Belko, and I. M. Isupov, eds. 1992. *Slovar' tiuremno-lagerno-blatnogo zhargona (Rechevoi i graficheskii portret sovetskoi tiur'my).* Moscow: Kraia Moskvy.

Balmforth, Tom. 2011. "Russian Protesters Mobilize via Social Networks, as Key Opposition Leaders Jailed." Radio Free Europe/Radio Liberty (8 December). http://www.rferl.org/content/russian_protesters_mobilize_online_as_leaders_jailed/24414881.html (accessed 22 July 2013).

Baraulina, Anna. 2006. "Kul't distantsionnogo upravleniia." *Russkii Newsweek* 6 (13–19 February): 24–27.

Barkhudarov, S. G. 1951. "Itogi perspektivy perestroika iazykovedcheskoi raboty v svete stalinskogo ucheniia o iazyke." *Russkii iazyk v shkole* 5: 1–11.

Baron, Dennis E. 1982. *Grammar and Good Taste: Reforming the American Language*. New Haven: Yale University Press.

Baudrillard, Jean. 1983. *Simulations*. New York: Semiotext(e).

———. 1994. *Simulacra and Simulation*. Ann Arbor: University of Michigan Press.

Baunov, Aleksandr. 2011. "Partiia zhulikov i vorov: Filologicheskii analiz." *Slon* (24 November). http://slon.ru/world/zhuliki_i_vory-714211.xhtml (accessed 22 July 2013).

———. 2013. "Pochemu Putina bol'she ne slushaiut." *Slon* (25 April). http://slon.ru/russia/putin_ritor-733404.xhtml (accessed 19 July 2013).

Bekhbulatova, Taisiia, and Sof'ia Samokhina. 2012. "Gubernatory ispolnili svoe naznachenie." *Kommersant* (31 May). http://www.kommersant.ru/doc/1947363 (accessed 22 July 2013).

Beloded, I. K. 1971. "Problemy izucheniia iazyka V. I. Lenina." *Russkaia rech'* 2: 8–15.

Bennett, Brian P. 2011. *Religion and Language in Post-Soviet Russia*. New York: Routledge.

Bernaskoni, Elena. 2001. "Iazyk, kak zhenshchina: Ego nado liubit' i zashchishchat'." *Ekho Planety* 8 (16 February): 26.

Bilaniuk, Laada. 2005. *Contested Tongues: Language Politics and Cultural Correction in Ukraine*. Ithaca: Cornell University Press.

Birch, David. 2002. "In Russia, a New Battle of Morals." *Baltimore Sun,* 9 December. http://articles.baltimoresun.com/2002-12-09/news/0212090265_1_russian-literature-russian-culture-putin (accessed 19 July 2013).

Blokhina, N. G. 1993. "Problemy formirovaniia iazykovoi lichnosti uchitelia." *Russkii iazyk v shkole* 6: 94–95.

Bogomolov, Iurii. 2000. "Vse-svoi—skazal president." *Izvestiia,* 2 November.

Bogomolov, N., ed. 1996. *Anti-mir russkoi kul'tury: Iazyk. Fol'klor. Literatura*. Moscow: Ladomir.

Borenstein, Eliot. 2008. *Overkill: Sex and Violence in Contemporary Russian Popular Culture*. Ithaca: Cornell University Press.

Bourdieu, Pierre. 1984. *Distinction: A Social Critique of the Judgment of Taste*. Translated by Richard Nice. Cambridge: Harvard University Press.

———. 1991. *Language and Symbolic Power*. Edited by John B. Thompson and translated by Gino Raymond and Matthew Adamson. Cambridge: Harvard University Press.

———. 1991. "The Production and Reproduction of Legitimate Language." In Bourdieu, *Language and Symbolic Power,* 43–65.

Boym, Svetlana. 1994. *Common Places: Mythologies of Everyday Life in Russia*. Cambridge: Harvard University Press.

Bruchis, Michael. 1984. "The Language Policy of the CPSU and the Linguistic Situation in Soviet Moldavia." *Soviet Studies* 36, no. 1: 108–26.

Brusser, Anna, and Mariia Ossovskaia. 2005. *104 uprazhneniia po diktsii i orfoepii dlia samostoiatel'noi raboty*. Moscow: Reglant.

Bui, Vasilii. 1995. *Russkaia zavetnaia idiomatika (Veselyi slovar' krylatykh vyrazhenii).* Moscow: Pomovskii i partnery.

———. 2005. *Russkaia zavetnaia idiomatika: Veselyi slovar' narodnykh vyrazhenii.* 2nd ed., corrected and expanded. Moscow: Al'ta-Print.

Bukchina, B. Z. 1967. "G 6-18-43 (Spravochnoe biuro Instituta russkogo iazyka AN SSSR)." *Russkaia rech'* 1: 99–102.

Burke, Peter. 1987. "Introduction." In *The Social History of Language,* edited by Peter Burke and Roy Porter, 1–20. Cambridge: Cambridge University Press.

Cameron, Deborah. 1990. "Demythologizing Sociolinguistics: Why Language Does Not Reflect Society." In *Ideologies of Language,* edited by John E. Joseph and Talbot J. Taylor, 79–93. London: Routledge.

———. 1995. *Verbal Hygiene: The Politics of Language.* London: Routledge.

Cassiday, Julie A. 2000. *The Enemy on Trial: Early Soviet Courts on Stage and Screen.* DeKalb: Northern Illinois University Press.

Cassiday, Julie A., and Emily D. Johnson. 2013. "A Personality Cult for the Postmodern Age: Reading Vladimir Putin's Public Persona." In Goscilo, *Putin as Celebrity and Cultural Icon,* 37–64.

"Chelovek iz televizora." 2007. *Radio Ekho Moskvy* (20 October). http://echo.msk.ru/programs/persontv/55728/index.phtml (accessed 22 July 2013).

Chel'tsova, L. K. 1991. "Kak pisat': Bog ili bog?" *Russkaia rech'* 4: 64–69.

Cherkasov, Gleb. 2012. "'Vy mozhete pogovorit', no reshaem my—V etom sut' stat'i Putina.'" *Kommersant" FM* (6 February). http://www.kommersant.ru/doc/1866955 (accessed 19 July 2013).

Chernyshev, V. I. 1911. *Pravil'nost' i chistota russkoi rechi: Opyt russkoi stilisticheskoi grammatiki.* St. Petersburg: Tipografiia Morskogo ministerstva.

"Chislo Internet-pol'zovatelei v Rossii vyroslo do 70 millionov chelovek, sostaviv 49% naseleniia." 2011. *Gazeta.ru* (26 January). http://www.gazeta.ru/news/lenta/2011/12/26/n_2148486.shtml (accessed 22 July 2013).

Christians, Dagmar. 1983. *Die Sprachrubrik der "Literaturnaja Gazeta" von 1964 bis 1978: Dokumentation und Auswertung.* Munich: Otto Sagner.

Chudinov, A. P. 2001. *Rossiia v metaforicheskom zerkale: Kognitivnoe issledovanie politicheskoi metafory (1991–2000).* Ekaterinburg: Uralskii gosudarstvennyi pedagogicheskii universitet.

Colley, Carroll. 2012. "Kremlin's Planned Internet Ownership Limits Raise State Control Fears." *Financial Times,* 28 June. http://blogs.ft.com/beyond-brics/2012/06/27/guest-post-kremlins-planned-internet-ownership-limits-raise-state-control-fears/ (accessed 19 July 2013).

Crowley, Tony. 1996. *Language in History: Theories and Texts.* London: Routledge.

Dal', Vladimir. [1882] 1980. *Tolkovyi slovar' zhivogo velikorusskogo iazyka.* Moscow: Russkii iazyk.

Davydov, G. 1998. "Russkoi istorii nuzhen Moisei." *Nezavisimaia gazeta,* 16 September.

Deibert, Ronald, and Rafal Rohozinski. 2010. "Control and Subversion in Russian Cyberspace." In *Access Controlled: The Shaping of Power, Rights, and Rule in Cyberspace,* edited by Ronald J. Deibert, John G. Palfrey, Rafal Rohozinski, and Jonathan Zittrain, 15–34. Cambridge: MIT Press.

Denisova, M. A. 1993. "'Narod i iazyk odin bez drugogo predstavlen byt' ne mozhet....'" *Russkii iazyk v shkole* 5: 68–89.

———. 1997. "Russkoe slovo i russkii mir." *Russkii iazyk v skole* 2: 87–93.

XIX Vsesoiuznaia konferentsiia Kommunisticheskoi Partii Sovetskogo Soiuza 28 iiuniia–1 iiuliia 1988 goda: Stenograficheskii otchet. 1988. 2 vols. Moscow: Izdatel'stvo politicheskoi literatury.

Dmitrienko, Dmitrii. 2012. "Naval'nyi za nedeliu nashel 10,000 potentsial'nykh nabliudatelei." *Vedomosti* (31 January). http://www.vedomosti.ru/politics/news/1490165/navalnyj_za_nedelyu_nashel_10_000_potencialnyh_nablyudatelej (accessed 22 February 2013).

Dobromyslov, V. A. 1951. "God raboty na osnove trudov I. V. Stalina po iazykoznaniiu." *Russkii iazyk v shkole* 4: 1–10.

Dobromyslov, V. A., and N. V. Solov'ev. 1951. "Osnovnye zadachi prepodavaniia russkogo iazyka v shkole v svete ucheniia I. V. Stalina o iazyke." *Russkii iazyk v shkole* 1: 15–25.

Dorokhov, Roman and Sergei Smirnov. 2013. "48% 'V kontakte' kupil fond Shcherbovich." *Vedomosti* (17 April). http://www.vedomosti.ru/companies/news/11258121/ucp_scherbovicha_pokupaet_48_v_kontakte (accessed 18 July 2013).

Dudnikov, A. V. 1988. "Puti perestroiki prepodavaniia rodnogo russkogo iazyka v srednei shkole." *Russkii iazyk v shkole* 4: 41–44.

Dziubenko, O. G. 1988. "Obuchenie diskussionnoi rechi." *Russkii iazyk v shkole* 6: 30–35.

Dulichenko, Aleksandr D. 1999. *Etnosotsiolingvistika "Perestroiki" v SSSR: Antologiia zapechatlennogo vremeni.* Munich: Otto Sagner.

Earle, Jonathan. 2013. "Smut-free Web Evokes Censorship Fears," *Moscow Times* (5 February). http://www.themoscowtimes.com/news/article/smut-free-web-evokes-censorship-fears/475033.html (accessed 22 July 2013).

"Edinoros ne smog zasudit—Naval'nogo za 'partiiu zhulikov i vorov.'" 2011. *Lenta.ru* (11 October). http://lenta.ru/news/2011/10/11/navalny/ (accessed 22 July 2013).

"Edinoros opublikoval rolik o 'partii zhulikov i vorov.'" 2011. *Lenta.ru* (2 December). http://lenta.ru/news/2011/12/02/bob/ (accessed 22 July 2013).

Elistratov, V. S. 2000. "Argo i kul' ura." In *Slovar' russkogo argo (materialy 1980–1990-kh gg.),* edited by V. S. Elistratov, 574–683. Moscow: Russkie slovari.

———. 2001. "Natsional'nyi iazyk i natsional'naia ideia." *Gramota.ru* (2 February). http://www.gramota.ru/biblio/magazines/gramota/28_54 (accessed 22 July 2013).

Emerson, Caryl. 1992. "The Shape of Russian Cultural Criticism in the Post-communist Period." *Canadian Slavonic Papers/Revue canadienne des slavistes* 34, no. 4: 353–71.

Emirova, A. M. 1990. "Frazeologiia perestroiki: Tematika i semantika." *Russkii iazyk v shkole* 3: 77–81.

"E-nationalism." 2009. *Vedomosti,* 29 November.

Enikeeva, Dilara. 1996. "Dusha moia maslenitsa." *Moskovskaia Pravda,* 24 February.

Epshtein, Mikhail. 2008. "Glamurnyi god pod znamenem politkonkretnosti." *NG Ex Libris* (17 January). http://www.ng.ru/ng_exlibris/2008-01-17/4_slovo.html (accessed 22 July 2013).

Erofeev, Viktor. 2003. "Dirty Words." *The New Yorker,* 15 September, 42–48.

———. 2004. "Tsarstvo-mata," *Moskovskie novosti* 27 (23 July): 16.

"Evangel'skii tekst i frazeologiia russkogo iazyka." 1995. *Russkii iazyk v shkole* 3: 49–52.

Ewing, E. Thomas. 1994. "How Soviet Teachers Taught: Classroom Practices and Stalinist Pedagogy, 1931 to 1939." *East/West Education* 15, no. 2: 117–52.

Fairclough, Norman. 2003. "'Political Correctness': The Politics of Culture and Language." *Discourse and Society* 14, no. 1: 17–28.

Filin, F. P. 1966. "Neskol'ko slov o iazykovoi norme i kul'ture rechi." *Voprosy rechevoi kul'tury* 7: 15–22.

———. 1968. "K probleme sotsial'noi obuslovlennosti iazyka." In *Iayzk i obshchestvo,* edited by F. P. Filin, 3–22. Moscow: Nauka.

Filippov, Aleksei. 1999. "Bodalsia kanal s kanalom." *Izvestiia* 184 (1 October). http://dlib.eastview.com.lp.hscl.ufl.edu/browse/doc/3177743 (accessed 19 July 2013).

Franklin, Simon. 2002. *Writing, Society, and Culture in Early Rus'.* Cambridge: Cambridge University Press.

Foucault, Michel. 1972. *The Archaeology of Knowledge and the Discourse on Language.* New York: Pantheon Books.

Gal, Susan, and Kathryn A. Woolard. 1995. "Constructing Languages and Publics: Authority and Representation." *Pragmatics* 5: 129–38.

Ganina, Maia. 2001. "Chtoby ne sgoret' na vode.... (O russkom iazyke i o russkoi zhizni)." *Nash sovremennik* 9: 242–51.

Gasparov, Boris. 2004. "Identity in Language?" In *National Identity in Russian Culture,* edited by Simon Franklin and Emma Widdis, 132–48. Cambridge: Cambridge University Press.

Gavrilov, K., E. Kozievskaia, and E. Iatsenko. 2008. "Russkii iazyk v novykh nezavisimykh gosudarstvakh: Tekushchee sostoianie i perspektivy." *Ekonomicheskoe obozrenie* 1: 9–14.

Gellner, Ernest. 1983. *Nations and Nationalism.* Ithaca: Cornell University Press.

"Glasnost' v rabote sovetov." 1980. *Izvestiia,* 15 February.

Gogol', N. V. [1842] 1951. *Mertvye dushi.* In *Polnoe sobranie sochinenii,* vol. 6. Moscow: Izdatel'stvo akademii nauk SSSR.

"Golosui za partiiu zhulikov i vorov!!!" 2011. YouTube. http://www.youtube.com/watch?v = FAv54E-zrC4&lr = 1 (accessed 8 February 2011).

Golovin, B. N. 1956. *O kul'ture russkoi rechi: Nauchno-populiarnyi ocherk.* Vologda: Pedogogicheskii institute im. Molotova.

Gorbachev, Mikhail. 1987. *Izbrannye rechi i stat'i.* 6 vols. Moscow: Izd. politicheskoi literatury.

———. 1988. *Perestroika i novoe myshlenie dlia nashei strany i dlia vsego mira.* Moscow: Izd. politicheskoi literatury.

———. 1996. *Memoirs.* New York: Doubleday.

Gorbachev, Michael, and Zdenek Mlynar. 2002. *Conversations with Gorbachev: On Perestroika, the Prague Spring, and the Crossroads of Socialism.* Translated by George Shriver. New York: Columbia University Press.

Gorelik, Kristina, and Daisy Sindelar. 2012. "Russian NGOs Say New Bill Will Hurt Cancer Care, Environment, Businesses." Radio Free Europe/Radio Liberty (13 July). http://www.rferl.org/content/russia-ngos-bill-foreign-agents-foreign-funding-duma/24644355.html (accessed 13 July 2012).

Gorham, Michael S. 1996. "From Charisma to Cant: Models of Public Speaking in Early Soviet Russia." *Canadian Slavonic Papers/Revue canadienne des slavistes* 38 (September–December): 331–55.

———. 2000. "Mastering the Perverse: State-Building and Language 'Purification' in Early Soviet Russia." *Slavic Review* 59: 133–53.

———. 2003. *Speaking in Soviet Tongues: Language Culture and the Politics of Voice in Revolutionary Russia.* DeKalb: University of Northern Illinois Press.

———. 2006. "Vladimir Putin and the Rise of the New Russian Vulgate." *Groniek: Historisch Tijdschrift* 39, no. 172: 297–307.

———. 2011. "Virtual Rusophonia: Language Policy as 'Soft Power' in the New Media Age." *Digital Icons: Studies in Russian, Eurasian, and Central European New Media* 5: 23–48. http://www.digitalicons.org/issue05/michael-gorham/ (accessed 28 July 2012).

———. 2012. "Medvedev's New Media Gambit: The Language of Power in 140 Characters or Less." In *Power and Legitimacy: Challenges from Russia,* edited by Per-Arne Bodin, Stefan Hedlund, and Elena Namli, 199–219. London: Routledge.

———. 2013. "Putin's Language." In Goscilo, *Putin as Celebrity and Cultural Icon,* 82–103.

———. Forthcoming, 2014. "Politicians Online: The Prospects and Perils of 'Direct Internet Democracy.'" In Gorham, Lunde, and Paulsen, *Digital Russia.*

Gorham, Michael S., Ingunn Lunde, and Martin Paulsen. eds. Forthcoming, 2014. *Digital Russia: The Language, Culture, and Politics of New Media Communication.* New York: Routledge.

Gorny, Evgenii. 2007. "Russkii LiveJournal: Vlianie kul'turnoi identichnosti na razvitie virtual'nogo soobshchestva." In Konradova, Teubener, and Schmidt, *Control + Shift,* 109–30. http://www.ruhr-uni-bochum.de/russ-cyb/library/texts/ru/control_shift/Schmidt_Teubener.pdf (accessed 10 February 2012).

Gorodetskaia, Natal'ia, and Maksim Ivanov. 2013. "Obshchestvenniki sistemiziruiut internet." *Kommersant"* (15 July). http://kommersant.ru/doc/2234001 (accessed 19 July 2013).

Goscilo, Helena, ed. 2013. *Putin as Celebrity and Cultural Icon.* New York: Routledge.

———. "Russia's Ultimate Celebrity: VVP as VIP Objet d'Art." In Goscilo, *Putin as Celebrity and Cultural Icon,* 6–36.

"Gosduma priniala zakonoproekt o razoblachenii 'inostrannykh agentov' sredi NKO." 2012. *Pravo.ru* (6 July). http://pravo.ru/news/view/74727/ (accessed 10 July 2012).

"Gospoiskovik: Chinovniki 'slivaiut' v Internet podrobnosti i vedut podkovernuiu bor'bu." 2010. *CNews.ru* (15 July). http://www.internet.cnews.ru/news/top/index.shtml?2010/07/15/401020 (accessed 4 November 2010).

Goux, Jean-Joseph. 1990. *Symbolic Economies: After Marx and Freud.* Translated by Jennifer Curtis Gage. Ithaca: Cornell University Press.

———. 1999. "Cash, Check, or Charge?" In Woodmansee and Osteen, *New Economic Criticism,* 115–27.

"'Govorit Moskva….'" 1970. *Russkaia rech'* 4: 49–52.

Grachev, M. A. 2001. "V pogone za effektom (Blatnye slova na gazetnoi polose)." *Russkaia rech'* 5: 67–72.

Graham, Seth. 2000. "*Chernukha* and Russian Film." *Studies in Slavic Culture* 1: 9–27.

Granovskaia, L. M. 1998. "Bibleiskie frazeologizmy: Opyt slovaria." *Russkaia rech'*: 1–5.

Graudina, L. K., O. A. Dmitrieva, N. V. Novikova, and E. N. Shiriaev, eds. 1995. *My sokhranim tebia, russkaia rech'!* Moscow: Nauka.

Graudina, L. K., and E. N. Shiriaev, eds. 1994. *Kul'tura parlamentskoi rechi.* Moscow: Nauka.

————. 2000. *Kul'tura russkoi rechi: Uchebnik dlia vuzov.* Moscow: NORMA.

Grigor'ev, V. P. 1963. "Kul'tura iazyka i iazykovaia politika (Vmesto retsenzii na knigu K. I. Chukovskogo)." *Voprosy kul'tury rechi* 4: 5–20.

Grigor'eva, Ekaterina. 2007. "Vladimir Putin: 'Chtoby stat' prezidentom, nado uchastvovat' v vyborakh i pobedit.'" *Izvestiia.ru* (18 October). http://www.izvestia.ru/russia/article3109471 (accessed 5 August 2013).

Grillo, R. D. 1989. *Dominant Languages: Language and Hierarchy in Britain and France.* Cambridge: Cambridge University Press.

Grishina, N. S. 2006. "Spravochno-informatsionnye sluzhby russkogo iazyka: Traditsii i sovremennost'." *Russkaia rech'* 6: 47–50.

Gritsenko, A. P. 2007. "Privetstvennoe slovo Predsedatelia VR ARK A. P. Gritsenko na otkrytii Mezhdunarodnoi nauchno-prakticheskoi konferentsii 'Russkii iazyk v polikul'turnom mire.'" In Gritsenko, *Russkii iazyk v polikul'turnom mire,* 3–8.

Gritsenko, A. P., ed. 2007. *Russkii iazyk v polikul'turnom mire: Materialy mezhdunarodnoi nauchno-prakticheskoi konferentsii.* Simferopol': Sonat.

Guboglo, M. N. 1998. *Iazyki etnicheskoi mobilizatsii.* Moscow: Shkola "Iazyki russkoi kul'tury."

Guseinov, Gasan. 2004. *D.S.P.: Sovetskie ideologemy v russkom diskurse 1990-kh.* Moscow: Tri kvadrata.

————. 2005. *Karta nashei rodiny: Ideologema mezhdu slovom i telom.* Moscow: OGI.

————. 2012. *Nulevye na konchike iazyka: Kratkii putevoditel' po russkomu diskursu.* Moscow: Delo.

Gustafson, Thomas. 1992. *Representative Words: Politics, Literature, and the American Language, 1776–1865.* Cambridge: Cambridge University Press.

Habermas, Jürgen. [1964] 1974. "The Public Sphere: An Encyclopedia Article." *New German Critique* 3: 49–55.

Hall, Stuart. 1990. "Cultural Identity and Disapora." In *Identity: Community, Culture, Difference,* edited by J. Rutherford, 222–37. London: Lawrence and Wishart.

————. 1996. "Who Needs 'Identity'?" In *Questions of Cultural Identity,* edited by Stuart Hall and Paul Du Gay, 1–17. London: Sage.

Hardt, Michael, and Kathi Weeks, eds. 2000. *The Jameson Reader.* Oxford, UK: Blackwell.

Hata, Shojun, Koji Abe, and Yosuke Takagi. 2003. *Putin: Stairway to Power.* Films for the Humanities and Sciences. New York, NY: Film Media Group.

Hodge, Nathan. 2009. "Kremlin Launches 'School of Bloggers'." *Wired* (27 May). http://www.wired.com/dangerroom/2009/05/kremlin-launches-school-of-bloggers/ (accessed 18 July 2013).

Hughes, Geoffrey. 2010. *Political Correctness: A History of Semantics and Culture.* West Sussex, UK: Wiley-Blackwell.

Hunt, Lynn. 1984. *Politics, Culture, and Class in the French Revolution.* Berkeley: University of California Press.

"Ia idu nabliudatelem na vybory." 2012. YouTube. http://www.youtube.com/watch? v = HGwOmBsAAwQ (accessed 15 February 2012).

Iakovlev, Aleksandr. 2001. *Omut pamiati: Ot Stolypina do Putina.* Moscow: Vagrius.

Iatsenko, E. V., E. V. Kozievskaia, and K. A. Gavrilov, eds. 2008. *Russkii iazyk v novykh nezavisimykh gosudarstvakh.* http://www.fundeh.org/publications/books/2/ (accessed 6 June 2010).

Iatsiuk, T. A. 1991. "'Terminotvorchestvo' totalitarnogo pravosudiia." *Russkaia rech'* 3: 52–57.

"Iazyk gazety." 1969. *Russkaia rech'* 3: 48–66, and 4: 66–82.

Iazyk moi—vrag moi: O grekhe prazdnosloviia. 2000. Moscow: Blago.

Iazyk moi—vrag moi: O grekhe slovom. 1998. Moscow: Izdatel'stvo "Otchii dom."

Iazykovod. n.d. Tsentr tvorcheskogo razvitiia russkogo iazyka. http://www.russkoes lovo.org/yazykovod (accessed 4 November 2008).

Il'inskaia, I. S., ed. 1969. *Kniga o russkom iazyke.* Moscow: Izdatel'stvo "Znanie."

International Forum: The 2005 Federation Law on the Russian Language. 2006. *Russian Language Journal* 56: 1–100.

"Internet v Rossii: dinamika proniknoveniia. Vesna 2013." 2013. FOM Internet (11 June). http://runet.fom.ru/posts/10950 (accessed 22 July 2013).

"Interv'iu ital'ianskim informatsionnomu agentstvu ANSA, gazete *Kor'ere della sera* I telekomanii RAI." 2003. *Kremlin.ru,* 3 November. http://archive.kremlin.ru/ appears/2003/11/03/2200_type63379_54926.shtml (accessed 12 May 2011).

"Interv'iu Prezidenta Rossii telekanalu RTR v sviazi s tragediei na atomnoi podvod-noi lodke 'Kursk.'" 2000. *Kremlin.ru,* 23 August. http://archive.kremlin.ru/text/ appears/2000/08/28834 (accessed 24 April 2013).

Ioann, Mitropolit Sankt-Peterburgskii i Ladozhskii. 1995. "Vremeni ostaetsia vse men'she i men'she." *Sovetskaia Rossiia,* 4 December.

"Istochnik dukhovnogo obogashcheniia." 1986. *Russkaia rech'* 5: 3–10.

"Itogi 2011: Vlast' ot bloga." 2012. *Public.ru.* http://www.public.ru/blogsmi2011 (accessed 24 August 2012).

Iugov, A. 1959. "Epokha i iazykovoi 'piatachok.'" *Literaturnaia gazeta,* 15–17 January.

Ivanitskaia, Nadezhda, and Ivan Filippov. 2008. "Suverennyi Internet: Gosudarstvo ne khochet davat' inostrannym investoram svobodu vladeniia Internet-provaiderami, a takzhe tipografiiami i pechatnymi SMI." *Vedomosti,* 5 March.

Ivanova, S. F. 1991a. "Ritorika zavoevyvaet mesto v shkole." *Russkii iazyk v shkole* 2: 8–13.

———. 1991b. "Esli bez ritoriki...." *Narodnoe obrazovanie* 6: 50–52.

Ivanova, V. F. 1998. "Vesti iz Orfograficheskoi komissii RAN." *Russkaia rech'* 6: 48–51.

"Iz shestodneva Ioanna Ekzarkha Bolgarskogo." 1998. *Russkaia rech',* vols. 1–6.

"Iz ust reformatora: Do sikh por begut murashki po spine, kogda ia slyshu gimn SSSR...." 1996. *Sovetskaia Rossiia,* 14 May.

Jameson, Fredric. [1984] 1991. *Postmodernism, or, The Cultural Logic of Late Capitalism.* Durham: Duke University Press.

Joseph, John E. 2006. "'The Grammatical Being Called a Nation': History and the Construction of Political and Linguistic Nationalism." In *Language and History: Integrationist Perspectives,* edited by Nigel Love, 120–41. London: Routledge.

Kalashnikov, V. 1986. "Sila glasnosti." *Kommunist* 13: 46–56.

Kalashnikova, Marina. 2000. "Polnomochnyi predstavitel' Prezidenta v Privolzhskom Federal'nom Okruge Sergei Kirienko schitaet, chto institut polpredov— promezhutochnyi." *Nezavisimaia gazeta,* 25 October.

Kantor, Iulii. 2000. "Naselenie—288 millionov." *Izvestiia,* 27 October.

Karta pomoshchi. n.d. http://russian-fires.ru/ (accessed 10 February 2012).

"K chitateliu." 1968. *Russkaia rech'* 1: 3–4.

Kara-Murza, E. S. 2001. "Chto v imeni tebe moem." In "'Divnyi novyi mir' rossiiskoi reklamy: Sotsiokul'turnye, stilisticheskie i kul'turno-rechevye aspekty, part 7." *grammota.ru.* http://www.gramota.ru/biblio/magazines/gramota/advertizing/28_47 (accessed 2 July 2012).

Karaulov, Iu. N. 1987. *Russkii iazyk i iazykovaia lichnost'.* Moscow: Nauka.

Kazumova, Emiliia and Natal'ia Fil'kina. 2007. "Eto priamo Putin kakoi-to!" *Pressmon.com* (22 October). http://www.pressmon.com/cgi-bin/press_view.cgi?id=2115342 (accessed 22 July 2013).

Khan-Pira, Er. 1990. "Stalinizm i stalinshchina." *Russkaia rech'* 2: 142–45.

Kharchenko, V. K. 1997. "Molodezhi o skvernoslovii." *Russkii iazyk v shkole* 1: 97–101.

Kharitonov, Valerii. 1994. "Antei, sgoniaemyi s zemli (Besedy o russkom). *Moskva* 2: 116–19.

Kitaev-Smyk, L. A. 2005. "Seksual'no-verbal'nye zashchita i agressiia (Maternaia rech' i maternaia rugan')." In *Rechevaia agressiia v sovremennoi kul'ture: Sbornik nauchnykh trudov,* edited by M. V. Zagidullina, 17–21. Cheliabinsk: Cheliabinskii gosudarstvennyi universitet.

Kobzev, Artem. 2012. "Protiv zhulikov i vorov." *Moskovskie novosti,* 13 December.

Kolesov, V. V. 2001. *Kak nashe slovo otozvettsa.* St. Petersburg: Ivan Fedorov.

———. 2004a. *Iazyk i mental'nost'.* St Petersburg: Peterburgskoe vostokovedenie.

———. 2004b. *Slovo i delo: Iz istorii russkikh slov.* St. Petersburg: St. Petersburg University Press.

Kolymagin, Boris. 1998. "Iazyk tserkvi." *Literaturnaia gazeta,* 30 November.

Koniaev, N. 2007. "Polittekhnologicheskie itogi: God russkogo iazyka." December. http://www.voskres.ru/idea/konjaev2.htm (accessed 23 April 2008).

Konradova, Natal'ia, Katy Teubener, and Henrike Schmidt, eds. 2007. *Control + Shift: Publichnoe i lichnoe v russkom Internete.* http://www.ruhr-uni-bochum.de/russ-cyb/ library/texts/ru/control_shift/Schmidt_Teubener.pdf (accessed 10 February 2012).

"Konstitutsiia Soiuza Sovetskikh Sotsialisticheskikh Respublik." 1977. *Istoricheskii fakul'tet MGU* (7 October). http://www.hist.msu.ru/ER/Etext/cnst1977.htm (accessed 7 November 2011).

"Kontseptsiia vneshnei politiki 2010 Rossiiskoi Federatsii." 2008. *Kremlin.ru* (12 July). http://archive.kremlin.ru/text/docs/2008/07/204108.shtml (accessed 7 June 2010).

Korchenkova, Natal'ia and Sof'ia Samokhina. 2013. "Primaia liniia sobrala ne vsekh." *Kommersant"* (30 April). http://kommersant.ru/doc/2182375 (accessed 18 July 2013).

Korolev, Anatolii. 2001. "Oskrblenie sakral'nogo: Matershchina—magiia novogo vremeni." *Literaturnaia gazeta,* 11 April, p. 12.

Koroleva, Marina. 2003. *Govorim po-russki s Marinoi Korolevoi.* Moscow: Slovo.

Koselleck, Reinhart. 2002. *The Practice of Conceptual History: Timing History, Spacing Concepts.* Translated by Todd Samuel Presner et al. Stanford: Stanford University Press.

Kostomarov, V. G. 1959. "Otkuda slovo 'stiliaga'?" *Voprosy kul'tury rechi* 2: 168–75.

———. 1961. "Zheleznyi zanaves." *Voprosy kul'tury rechi* 3: 194–201.

———. 1966. "Aktual'nye voprosy kul'tury rechi." *Voprosy kul'tury rechi* 7: 11–14.

———. 1994. *Iazykovoi vkus epokhi: Iz nabliudenii nad rechevoi praktikoi mass-media.* Moscow: Pedagogika Press.

———. 1999. "Bez russkogo iazyka u nas net budushchego." *Russkaia rech'* 4: 3–10.

Kostomarov, V. G., and L. I. Skvortsov, eds. 1970. *Aktual'nye problemy kul'tury rechi.* Moscow: Nauka.

Kotriakhov, N. V., and L. E. Holmes. 1993. *Teoriia i praktika trudovoi shkoly v Rossii (1917–1932 gg).* Kirov: Kirovskii gosudarstvennyi pedagogicheskii institute im. V. I. Lenina.

Kozenko, Andrei, and Lolita Gruzdeva. 2012. "K Vladimiru Putinu obratilis' iazykom plakata." *Kommersant''* (1 February). http://www.kommersant.ru/doc/1863345 (accessed 6 February 2012).

Kozhemiako, Viktor. 1995. "Chto predlagaet chitateliam Aleksandr Prokhanov *Zavtra.*" *Sovetskaia Rossiia,* 4 December.

Kozhin, A. N. 1969. "Voennoe slovo v rechi V. I. Lenina." *Russkaia rech'* 4: 3–6.

———. 1973. "Slovo Ia. M. Sverdlova-propagandista." *Russkaia rech'* 1: 84–86.

Kramer, Andrew E. 2011. "Russian Site Smokes Out Corruption." *New York Times,* 27 March. http://www.nytimes.com/2011/03/28/business/global/28investor.html? pagewanted = all (accessed 20 February 2012).

Kratkii politicheskii slovar'. 1989. Moscow: Izd. Politicheskoi literatury.

"Kremlin Allies' Expanding Control of Runet Provokes Only Limited Opposition." 2010. *U.S. Office of the Director of National Intelligence: Open Source Center* (28 February). http://www.fas.org/irp/dni/osc/runet.pdf (accessed 3 May 2010).

Krongauz, Maksim. 2003. "Slovo pod lupoi." *Otechestvennye zapiski* 4. http://www. strana-oz.ru/2003/4/slovo-pod-lupoy (accessed 13 August 2012).

———. 2005. "Zametki rasserzhennogo obyvatelia." *Otechestvennye zapiski* 2. http:// www.strana-oz.ru/2005/2/zametki-rasserzhennogo-obyvatelya (accessed 25 July 2012).

———. 2007. "'Lingvist ne mozhet byt' diktatorom....'" *Russkii zhurnal,* 10 December. www.russ.ru//culture/besedy/lingvist_ne_mozhet_byt_diktatorom (accessed 10 December 2007).

———. 2008. *Russkii iazyk na grani nervnogo sryva.* Moscow: Znak "Iazyki slavianskikh kul'tur."

———. 2013. *Samouchitel' Olbanskogo.* Moscow: AST.

Kulikov, Vladislav. 2009. "Imennoi fond Interneta." *Rossiiskaia gazeta,* 29 September.

Laruelle, Marlene. 2006. "'Russkaia diaspora' i 'rossiiskie sootechestvenniki'." In *Demokratiia vertikali,* edited by A. Verkhovskii, 185–212 (Moscow: Tsentr 'Sova').

Lastochkin. Viktor. 2010. "Putin skazal vsiu pravdu ob Internete: 50%—eto pornografiia." *UralDaily.ru* (25 January). http://uraldaily.ru/politika/381.html (accessed 18 May 2010).

Latukhina, Kira. 2011. "Vsegda govorit' pravdu: Vladimir Putin otvetil kritikam 'Edinoi Rossii'—Rezul'tat u partii khoroshii." *Rossiiskaia gazeta,* 7 December. http://www.rg.ru/2011/12/07/putin.html (accessed 22 February 2012).

Lenin, V. I. 1902. "Chto delat'?: Nabolevshie voprosy nashego dvizheniia." *Biblioteka gazety "Revoliutsii."* http://www.revolucia.ru/chto_del2.htm (accessed 7 November 2011).

Lévy, Pierre. 2001. *Cyberculture.* Translated by Robert Bononno. Electronic Mediations 4. Minneapolis: University of Minnesota Press.

Likhachev, D. S. [1935] 1992. "Cherty pervobytnogo primitivizma vorovskoi rechi." In Baldaev, Belko, and Isupov, *Slovar' tiuremno-lagerno-blatnogo zhargona,* 354–98.

Lincoln, W. Bruce. 1982. *In the Vanguard of Reform: Russia's Enlightened Bureaucrats, 1825–1861.* DeKalb: Northern Illinois University Press.

Liuboshits, S. M. 1991. "Shtampy: Moda ili neobkhodimost'?" *Russkaia rech'* 2: 66–70.

Liustrova, Z. N., and L. I. Skvortsov. 1972. *Mir rodnoi rechi: Besedy o russkom iazyke i kul'ture rechi.* Moscow: Izdatel'stvo Znanie.

Liustrova, Z. N., L. I. Skvortsov, and V. Ia. Deriagin. 1987. *O kul'ture russkoi rechi.* Moscow: Znanie.

Lotman, Iu., and B. Uspenskii. 1975. "Spory o iazyke v nachale XIX v. kak fakt russkoi kul'tury ('Proisshestvie v tsarstve tenei, ili sud'bina rossiiskogo iazyka'—Neizvestnoe sochinenie Semena Bobrova)." In *Trudy po russkoi i slavianskoi filologii, XXIV: literaturovedenie,* edited by B. F. Egorov and B. Gasparov, 168–254. Uchenye zapiski tartuskogo gosudarstvennogo universiteta 358. Tartu: Tartuskii gosudarstvennyi universitet.

Lynch, Kevin. 1960. *The Image of the City.* Cambridge: MIT Press.

Makarov, Iurii. 1996. "Otvet'te mne oral'no, pristebyvaia gubami (Otkrytoe pis'mo diktoru radio rossii T. Vizbor)." *Molodaia gvardiia* 5: 239–57.

Mal'tsev, Vladislav. 2012. "Sakramental'noe prestuplenie Pussy Riot." *Nezavisimaia gazeta—NG Religiia,* 13 July. http://www.ng.ru/regions/2012-07-13/1_riot.html (accessed 18 July 2012).

"Mama umiraet!" 2012. *Onlain-priemnaia Gubernatora Vologodskoi oblasti Olega Kuvshinnikova* (26 April). http://www.vopros.vologda-oblast.ru/requests/4800.html (accessed 20 July 2012).

Marr, N. Ia. 1927. *Iafeticheskaia teoriia: Programma obshchego kursa ucheniia ob iazyke.* Baku: AzGIZ.

———. 1930. "K reforme pis'ma i grammatiki." *Russkii iazyk v sovetskoi shkole* 4: 44–48.

———. [1931] 1977. "Iazyk i myshlenie." In *Iazyk i myshlenie.* Russian Titles for the Specialist 107. Letchworth, UK: Prideaux Press.

Martynova, A. N., and V. V. Mitrofanova, eds. 1986. *Poslovitsy. Pogovorki. Zagadki.* Moscow: Sovremennik.

Martyshchuk, Dar'ia. 2011. "'Edinaia Rossiia' gotovitsia podat' v sud na Alekseia Naval'nogo." *Kommersant",* 16 February. http://www.kommersant.ru/doc/1586410 (accessed 5 August 2013).

McLuhan, Marshall. [1964] 2003. *Understanding Media: The Extensions of Man.* Critical ed. Edited by W. Terrence Gordon. Corte Madera, CA: Gingko Press.

Medvedev, Dmitrii. 2010. "Griadet epokha vozvrashcheniia neposredstvennoi demokratii." *Videoblog Dmitriia Medvedeva* (31 May). http://blog-medvedev.livejournal.com/49512.html (accessed 7 March 2013).

Medvedev, S. 1995. "SSSR: Dekonstruktsiia teksta (K 77-letiiu sovetskogo diskursa)." In *Inoe: Khrestomatiia novogo rossiiskogo samosoznaniia.* http://old.russ.ru:8083/antolog/inoe/medved.htm (accessed 25 July 2012).

Medvedeva, Irin, and Tat'iana Shishova. 1997. "Strakhi vzroslye i detskie." *Oktiabr'* 9: 133–45.

Mickiewicz, Ellen. 1991. "Ethnicity and Soviet Television News." The Carter Center. http://www.cartercenter.org/documents/1221.pdf (accessed 17 August 2012).

Miroshnichenko, Nadezhda. 1996. "Ochishchenie natsional'nogo soznaniia." *Literaturnaia Rossiia* 26.

Mishatina, N. L. 1996. "Obraz Rossii na rechevedcheskikh urokakh v piatom klasse." *Russkii iazyk v shkole* 2: 41–45.

Miller, James. 2000. "Is Bad Writing Necessary?: George Orwell, Theodor Adorno, and the Politics of Literature." *Lingua Franca* 9, no. 9. http://linguafranca.mirror.theinfo.org/9912/writing.html (accessed 28 March 2008).

"Mochit' v peshchere." 2006. *Kommersant''* 22 (8 February). www.kommersant.ru/doc/html?docId-647638 (accessed 16 April 2006).

"Moia prekrasnaia niania." n.d. *vilavi.ru.* http://www.vilavi.ru/sud/310508/310508.shtml (accessed 19 July 2011).

Mokienko, V. M. 1994. "Substandartnaia frazeologiia russkogo iazyka i nekotorye problemy ee lingvisticheskogo izucheniia." In *Dinamika russkogo slova: Mezhvuzovskii sbornik statei k 60-letiiu Prof. V. V. Kolesova,* edited by V. M. Mokienko, 154–73. St. Petersburg: St. Petersburg University Press.

Mokienko, V. M., and T. G. Nikinitan. 1998. *Tolkovyi slovar' iazyka Sovdepiia.* St. Petersburg: Folio-Press.

Morozov, Sergei. 1997. "'…Nash dar bessmertnyi-rech'.'" *Narodnoe obrazovanie* 9: 197–200.

Moslakova, Vera. 2012. "Effektivnye uvol'neniia." *Novye izvestiia,* 8 June. http://www.newizv.ru/economics/2012-06-08/164723-effektivnye-uvolnenija.html (accessed 11 July 2012).

Naidich, Larisa. 1995. *Sled na peske: Ocherki o russkom iazykovom uzuse.* St. Petersburg: St. Petersburg University Press.

Navalny, Aleksei. 2011a. "Spoem?" 28 September. *Naval'nyi.* http://navalny.livejournal.com/625374.html (accessed 22 February 2012).

———. 2011b. "Tvoia pesenka speta." *Naval'nyi.* http://navalny.livejournal.com/664805.html (accessed 8 February 2012).

———. 2012. "'Chernye spiski runeta.'" *Navalny* (10 July). http://navalny.livejournal.com/719705.html (accessed 12 July 2012).

"Navstrechu XXIV s''ezdu partii." 1971. *Russkaia rech'* 2: 3–7.

Neidhart, Christoph. 2003. *Russia's Carnival: The Smells, Sights, and Sounds of Transition.* New York: Rowman & Littlefield.

"New Putin's Dialogue with Russians Has Every Chance to Set New Record." 2007. *Itar-Tass* (14 October), as reported on *Johnson's Russia List,* no. 215 (2007).

"Novye slova." 1968. *Russkaia rech'* 5: 107–9.

Novyi slovar' russkogo iazyka. n.d. *Rubrikon.* www.rubrikon.com (accessed 17 July 2013).

Oates, Sarah. 2013. *The Political Limits of the Internet in the Post-Soviet Sphere.* Oxford: Oxford University Press.

Obnorskii, S. P. [1944] 1960. "Pravil'nosti i nepravil'nosti sovremennogo russkogo literaturnogo iazyka." In Obnorskii, *Izbrannye raboty po russkomu iazyku,* 253–72.

———. [1949] 1960. "Kul'tura russkogo iazyka." In Obnorskii, *Izbrannye raboty po russkomu iazyku,* 272–93.

———, ed. 1960. *Izbrannye raboty po russkomu iazyku.* Moscow: Gosudarstvennoe uchebno-pedagogicheskoe izdatel'stvo Ministerstva Prosveshcheniia RSFSR.

"O domene RF." n.d. *RF—Domen Rossii!* http://za-rf.ru/node/5 (accessed 16 July 2010).

"O federal'noi tselevoi programme 'Russkii iazyk.'" 1997. *Russkaia rech'* 1: 36.

"O federal'noi tselevoi programme 'Russkii iazyk.'" 2002. *Informatsionno-analiticheskie materialy Gosudarstvennoi Dumy.* http://iam.duma.gov.ru/node/2/4422/14451 (accessed 7 August 2012).

Ofitova, Svetlana. 2000. "Putin mozhet delat' vse, chto zakhochet." *Segodnia* 44 (28 February). http://dlib.eastview.com.lp.hscl.ufl.edu/browse/doc/1986062 (accessed 5 August 2013).

"O Fonde." n.d. *Fond Russkii Mir.* http://www.russkiymir.ru/russkiymir/ru/fund/about (accessed 19 February 2010).

Ol'bik, Aleksandr. 2002. *Prezident.* Donetsk: Stalker.

"Oppozitsionery povesili naprotiv Kremlia antiputinskii banner." 2012. *Ridus* (1 February). http://www.ridus.ru/news/20176/ (accessed 20 February 2012).

Orwell, George. [1946] 1981. "Politics and the English Language." In *A Collection of Essays,* 156–70. San Diego: Harcourt Brace Jovanovich.

Osteen, Mark, and Martha Woodmansee. 1999. "Taking Account of the New Economic Criticism: An Historical Introduction." In Woodmansee and Osteen, *New Economic Criticism,* 3–50.

Ozhegov, S. I. 1955a. [preface]. *Voprosy kul'tury rechi* 1: 1–4.

———. 1955b. "Ocherednye voprosy kul'tury rechi." *Voprosy kul'tury rechi* 1: 5–33.

Parnakh, Aleksandr. 1997. "Govoriat, kak pishut." *Znamia* 10: 236.

Parthé, Kathleen. 1997. "Russia's 'Unreal Estate': Cognitive Mapping and National Identity." Washington, DC: Woodrow Wilson Center, Kennan Institute for Advanced Russian Studies.

Paulsen, Martin. 2009. "Hegemonic Language and Literature: Russian Metadiscourse on Language in the 1990s." PhD diss., University of Bergen, Norway.

Pavlov, Ivan. 2012. "'Edinoi Rossii' gotoviat reorganizatsiiu." *Novaia politika* (9 February). http://www.novopol.ru/—edinoy-rossii-gotovyat-reorganizatsiyu-text117406.html (accessed 13 February 2012).

"Perekoshennye khari." 2000. *Delovye liudi* 115 (1 October).

"Perepiska nashistov." 2012. *Besttoday.ru.* http://besttoday.ru/subjects/952_2.html (accessed 19 April 2013).

Pervyi s"ezd narodnykh deputatov SSSR, 25 maia–9 iiunia 1989 g.: Stenograficheskii otchet. 1989. 2 vols. Moscow: Izd. Verkhovnogo soveta SSSR.

"Peskov oprovergaet tsenzuru na saite 'Putin-2012.'" 2012. *Novyi region 2* (12 January). http://www.nr2.ru/election/367151.html (accessed 26 February 2012).

Pesmen, Dale. 2000. *Russia and Soul: An Exploration.* Ithaca: Cornell University Press.

Petrova, E. N. 1949. "Nikolai Iakovlevich Marr i ego znachenie dlia sovetskoi shkoly." *Russkii iazyk v shkole* 5: 26–32.

Petukhov, A. S. 1992. "Iazyk perestroiki ili perestroika iazyka?: Deeprichastie v usloviiakh glasnosti." *Russkaia rech'* 2: 57–63.

"Phone-in with Putin: No Drinking, No Smoking, No Chewing during the Broadcast." 2006. *Regnum.ru* (25 October). http://www.regnum.ru/english/727989.html (accessed 26 July 2012).

Piniashev, N. F. 1987. "Vospitanie grazhdanstvennosti na urokakh russkogo iazyka v VII–VIII klassakh." *Russkii iazyk v shkole* 3: 46–47.

Pinsker, Dmitrii. 2000. "Poligon." *Itogi* 46 (14 November): 25–28.

Plato. 1994. *Gorgias.* Translated by Robin Waterfield. Oxford: Oxford University Press.

Plutser-Sarno, Aleksei. 2000. "Russkii vorovskoi slovar' kak kul'turnyi fenomen." *Logos* 2: 209–17.

———. 2001. "Maternyi slovar' kak fenomen russkoi kul'tury: Russkaia nepristoinaia leksika v slovariakh XIX–XX vv." In *Bol'shoi slovar' mata,* vol. 1, edited by A. Plutser-Sarno, 49–74. St. Petersburg: Limbus Press.

"Pochta *Russkoi rechi.*" 1967. *Russkaia rech'* 4: 78–86, and 5: 111–17.

"Pochta *Russkoi rechi.*" 1968. *Russkaia rech'* 4: 110–24.

"Pochta *Russkoi rechi.*" 1969. *Russkaia rech'* 1: 120–25.

Popova, Mariia. 2008. "Kirillicheskii zanaves." *Kommersant"-Biznes* (25 September). http://www.kommersant.ru/doc.aspx?DocsID = 1027838 (accessed 16 July 2010).

Popova, Z. D., and I. A. Sternin, eds. 2002. *Iazyk i natsional'noe soznanie: Nauchnoe izdanie.* 3rd ed. Voronezh: Istoki.

"Por'vu za Putina!" 2011. YouTube (uploaded by *Armiia Putina* on 13 July). http://www.youtube.com/watch?v = 1Easr8WTwxs (accessed 22 February 2012).

Postman, Neil. 1992. *Technopoly: The Surrender of Culture to Technology.* New York: Alfred A. Knopf.

Potapov, N. 1991. "Mat v pereplete." *Pravda,* 21 November. Reprinted in *Etnosotsiolingvistika "Perestroiki" v SSSR: Antologiia zapechatlennogo vremeni,* edited by Aleksandr D. Dulichenko, 240. Munich: Otto Sagner, 1999.

"Press-konferentsiia Prezidenta." 2001. *Prezident Rossii* (18 July). http://archive.kremlin.ru/appears/2001/07/18/0000_type63380type82634_28591.shtml (accessed 27 April 2013).

"Press-konferentsiia Prezidenta Rossii." 2002. *Prezident Rossii* (24 June). http://archive.kremlin.ru/text/appears/2002/06/29002.shtml (accessed 27 April 2013).

"Prezentatsionnyi rolik Fonda 'Russkii Mir.'" n.d. *Fond Russkii Mir.* http://www.russkiymir.ru/russkiymir/ru/video/presentation.html (accessed 2 April 2010).

Priadko, P. 2001. "Doreformennaia orfografiia i sovremennaia reklama." *Russkii iazyk* (9 February). http://www.gramota.ru/biblio/magazines/gramota/28_57 (accessed 9 August 2012).

"Priamaia liniia s Prezidentom Rossii Vladimirom Putinym." 2006. http://www.president-line.ru/ (accessed 26 July 2012).

"Protiv idealizma v iazykoznanii." 1949. *Russkii iazyk v shkole* 1: 70–73.

"Protiv PZhiV." 2012. "Konkurs spoem." YouTube. http://www.youtube.com/playlist?list = 076597D3249D81B8 (accessed 22 February 2012).

Putin, Vladimir. 2000. *First Person: An Astonishingly Frank Self-Portrait by Russia's President.* New York: Public Affairs.

————. 2001a. "Interv'iu nemetskomu zhurnalu *Fokus.*" *Prezident Rossii: Ofitsial'nyi sait* (19 September). http://archive.kremlin.ru/text/appears/2001/09/28637.shtml (accessed 1 May 2012).

————. 2001b. "Vystuplenie Prezidenta Rossiiskoi Federatsii V. V. Putina na Kongresse sootechestvennikov, prozhivaiushchikh za rubezhom." (11 October). http://www.mosds.ru/Meria/meria_merop_KongPut.shtml (accessed 14 June 2010).

————. 2006. "Vystuplenie na gosudarstvennom prieme, posviashchennom Dniu narodnogo edinstva." *Kremlin.ru* (4 November). http://archive.kremlin.ru/appears/2006/11/04/1601_type82634type122346_113418.shtml (accessed 5 November 2010).

————. 2007. "Poslanie Federal'nomu Sobraniiu Rossiiskoi Federatsii." *Kremlin.ru* (26 April). http://archive.kremlin.ru/appears/2007/04/26/1156_type63372type63374type82634_125339.shtml (accessed 24 September 2010).

————. 2012. "Demokatiia i kachestvo gosudarstva." *Kommersant''* (6 February). http://www.kommersant.ru/doc/1866753 (accessed 6 February 2012).

Putinki: Kratkii sbornik izrechenii prezidenta. 2004. Moscow: Ekho buk.

Pyrma, Roman. 2012. Personal e-mail to Artem Lazarev, 20 January, re-posted at kremlingate (24 February 2012). http://lj.rossia.org/users/kremlingate/ (accessed 19 April 2013).

Radzikhovskii, Leonid. 1999. "Shchedraia na razrushenie dusha." *Segodnia* 254 (10 November). http://dlib.eastview.com.lp.hscl.ufl.edu/browse/doc/2072495 (accessed 5 August 2013).

————. 2008. "Led taet, no klimat ne meniaetsia." *Rossiiskaia gazeta,* 3 March.

Ramenskii, Evgenii. 1998. "Nash novoiaz—iavilsia anglofenei: O iazyke i natsional'nom chuvstve." *Literaturnaia gazeta,* 24 June.

Reshetov, Ivan. 1999. "Kolokola pechal'noi vesti." *Sovetskaia Rossiia,* 9 February.

Reznichenko, I. L. 1997. "Novye knigi po kul'ture rechi." *Russkii iazyk v shkole* 2: 108–12.

Ries, Nancy. 1997. *Russian Talk: Culture and Conversation during Perestroika.* Ithaca: Cornell University Press.

Rodchenko, O. D., and L. A. Koreneva. 1990. "Diskussiia kak forma obshcheniia na uroke russkogo iazyka." *Russkii iazyk v shkole* 4: 7–16.

Rodnianskaia, Irina. 1997. "Iazyk pravoslavnogo bogosluzheniia kak prepiatstvie k raskul'turivaniiu sovremennoi Rossii." *Literaturnaia ucheba* 5–6: 86–93.

Rogozin, Dmitrii. 2011. "Slava Rossii: Dmitrii Rogozin protiv zhulikov, vorov i predatelei." *Rodina.ru.* http://rodina.ru/kronews.php?id = 340 (accessed 16 February 2012).

Rollins, Patrick J., ed. 1993. *First Congress of People's Deputies of the USSR, 25 May–9 June 1989: The Stenographic Record.* Vols. 1–2. Gulf Breeze, FL: Academic International Press.

Romashkova, Natal'ia. 2013. "Vladimir Zhirinovskii predlagaet ochistet' russkii iazyk ot amerikanizmov." *Novosti@mail.ru* (22 January). http://news.mail.ru/politics/11692099/ (accessed 5 April 2013).

Rosenberg, Scott. 2009. *Say Everything: How Blogging Began, What It's Becoming, and Why It Matters.* New York: Three Rivers Press.

"Rossiia bez Putina?: Apokalipsis zavtra!" 2012. YouTube (uploaded on 3 February by genrihlkov1223). http://www.youtube.com/watch?v = -9-5NBaAEsI (accessed 22 February 2012).

"Rossiiane pishut predlozheniia na predvybornyi sait Putina, samoe populiarnoe—ukhodite." 2012. *Gazeta.ru* (12 January). http://www.gazeta.ru/news/blogs/2012/01/12/n_2163149.shtml (accessed 21 August 2012).

Rudniakov, A. N. 2007. "Russkii iazyk v polikul'turnom mire." In Gritsenko, *Russkii iazyk v polikul'turnom mire,* 15–16.

Rudnitskii, Valerii, Vladimir Parfenov, Anatolii Larchenkov, and Vladimir Khristoforov. 1996. "Nuzhen zakon o zashchite chistoty russkogo iazyka." *Literaturnaia Rossiia* 13 (29 March): 11.

"Russian Bank Used by Anti-govt. Blogger Investigated." 2012. *Reuters* (15 February). http://www.reuters.com/article/2012/02/15/russia-blogger-idUSL5E8DF6KI20120215 (accessed 20 February 2012).

"Russian TV Highlights, 23–29 October 2006." 2006. *BBC Monitoring* (30 October), as reprinted in *Johnson's Russia List,* no. 244 (2006).

"Russian Twitter Political Protests 'Swamped by Spam.'" 2011. *BBC News: Technology* (9 December). http://www.bbc.co.uk/news/technology-16108876 (accessed 13 July 2012).

"Russkii kak inostrannyi." 2006. *Kommersant"* (17 August): 7.

Ryazanova-Clarke, Lara. 2006. "'The Crystallization of Structures': Linguistic Culture in Putin's Russia." In *Landslide of the Norm: Language Culture in Post-Soviet Russia,* edited by Ingunn Lunde and Tine Roesen, 31–63. Bergen, Norway: Slavica Bergensia.

———. 2008. "Putin's Nation: Discursive Construction of National Identity in *Direct Line with the President.*" In *Instrumentarii rusistiki: Korpusnye podkhody,* Slavica Helsingiensia 34, edited by A. Mustaioki, M. V. Kopotev, L. A. Biriulina, and E. Iu. Protasova, 311–31. Helsinki: Slavica Helsingiensia.

Ryl'nikova, I. L. 1990. "Iz istorii russkoi shkol'noi ritoriki." *Russkii iazyk v shkole* 4: 23–27.

Sakharov, Andrei. 1992. *Moscow and Beyond: 1986 to 1989.* New York: Vintage.

Saliaev, V. A. 1995. "O sotsial'nykh dialektakh russkogo iazyka." *Russkii iazyk v shkole* 3: 78–84.

———. 1996. "Ob osnovnykh etapakh evoliutsii argoticheskogo slova." *Russkii iazyk v shkole* 5: 90–93.

Samsonova, Tonia, Roman Dobrokhotov, and Konstantin Beniumov. 2011. "Vybory nachalis'?: V 'Feisbuke' rastet aktivnost' politicheskikh botov." *Slon.ru* (12 October). http://www.slon.ru/russia/kremlevskie_trolli-688096.xhtml (accessed 24 February 2012).

Sarnov, Benedikt. 2005. *Nash sovetskii novoiaz: Malen'kaia entsiklopediia real'nogo sotsializma.* Moscow: Eksmo.

Saussure, Ferdinand de. 1993. *Third Course of Lectures in General Linguistics (1910–1911): From the Notebooks of Emile Constantin.* Language and Communication Library 12. Translated and edited by E. Komatsu and R. Harris. Oxford: Pergamon.

Schmidt, Henrike, and Katy Teubener. 2006. "'Our RuNet'?: Cultural Identity and Media Usage." In Konradova, Teubener, and Schmidt, *Control + Shift,* 14–21. http://www.ruhr-uni-bochum.de/russ-cyb/library/texts/en/control_shift/Schmidt_Teubener_Identity.pdf (accessed 24 August 2012).

————. 2007. "Rossiiskii Internet kak (al'ternativnaia) publichnaia sfera?" In Konradova, Teubener, and Schmidt, *Control + Shift,* 75–107. http://www.ruhr-uni-bochum.de/russ-cyb/library/texts/ru/control_shift/Schmidt_Teubener.pdf (accessed 10 February 2012).

Sedakov, Pavel. 2013. "Lesnoe pravo: Kak delo 'Kirovlesa' dovelo Alekseia Naval'nogo do suda." *Forbes,* 17 April. http://www.forbes.ru/sobytiya/obshchestvo/237700-lesnoe-pravo-kak-delo-kirovlesa-dovelo-alekseya-navalnogo-do-suda (accessed 19 April 2013).

Seifrid, Thomas. 2005. *The Word Made Self: Russian Writings on Language, 1860–1930.* Ithaca: Cornell University Press.

Seriot, Patrick. 1985. *Analyse du discours politique soviétique.* Cultures et sociétés de l'Est 2. Paris: Institut d'études Slaves.

Severskaia, Ol'ga. 2004. *Govorim po-russki s Ol'goi Severskoi.* Moscow: Slovo.

Sewell, William H., Jr. 1999. "The Concept(s) of Culture." In *Beyond the Cultural Turn: New Directions in the Study of Society and Culture,* edited by Victoria E. Bonnell and Lynn Hunt, 35–61. Berkeley: University of California Press.

Shanskii, N. M. 1980. "Novye slova sovetskoi epokhi." *Russkaia rech'* 5: 3–9.

Shaposhnikov, V. N. 1998. *Russkaia rech' 1990-kh: Sovremennaia Rossiia v iazykovom otobrazhenii.* Moscow: MALP.

Shapovalov, Vladimir. 1991. "Kto nas uchit russkomu iazyku." *Molodaia gvardiia* 2: 272–81.

Shchedrovitskii, Petr. 2000a. "Russkii mir: Vozmozhnye tseli samoopredeleniia." *Nezavisimaia gazeta,* 11 February.

————. 2000b. "Gosudarstvo v epokhu gumanitarnykh tekhnologii." *Russkii zhurnal,* 21 July. http://old.russ.ru/politics/meta/20000721_sch.html (accessed 9 June 2010).

Shcherba, L. V. [1931] 1974. "O troiakom aspekte iazykovykh iavlenii i ob eksperimente v iazykoznanii." In L. V. Shcherba, *Iazykovaia sistema i rechevaia deiatel'nost',* 24–39. Leningrad: Izd. Nauka, Leningradskoe otdelenie.

————. [1939] 1957. "Sovremennyi russkii literaturnyi iazyk." In L. V. Shcherba, *Izbrannye raboty po russkomu iazyku,* 113–29. Moscow: Gosudarstvennoe uchebno-pedagogichskoe izdatel'stvo Ministerstva prosveshcheniia RSFSR.

Shchuplov, Aleksandr. 2002. "Kanaet vor, nasadkoi laviruia....Nadolgo l' nynche zadremala dusha v ob'iatiiakh kriminala?" *Nezavisimaia gazeta* 169 (16 August).

Shmelev, Aleksei Dmitrievich. 1996. "Leksicheskii sostav russkogo iazyka kak otrazhenie 'russkoi dushi.'" *Russkii iazyk v shkole* 4: 83–90.

————. 1998. "'Shirokaia' russkaia dusha." *Russkaia rech'* 1: 48–55.

————. 2005. "Lozhnaia trevoga i podlinnaia beda." *Otechestvennye zapiski* 2. http://magazines.russ.ru/oz/2005/2/2005_2_2-pr.html (accessed 13 February 2006).

Shvartskopf, B. S. 1970. "Ocherk razvitiia teoreticheskikh vzgliadov na normu v sovetskom iazykoznanii." In *Aktual'nye problemy kul'tury rechi,* edited by V. G. Kostomarov and L. I. Skvortsov, 369–404. Moscow: Izdatel'stvo "Nauka."

Shvedova, N. Iu., et al. 2001. *Slovar' i kul'tura russkoi rechi: K 100-letiiu so dnia rozhde-niia S. I. Ozhegova.* Moscow: Indrik.

Shvetsova, Elena. 1996. "Kak nashe slovo otzovetsia...." *Novyi mir* 5: 230–35.

Sidorenko, Alexey. 2010a. "Networks of Paid Bloggers Exposed." *Global Voices* (10 June). http://globalvoicesonline.org/2010/06/10/russia-networks-of-paid-bloggers-exposed/ (accessed 24 February 2012).

———. 2010b. "Russia: New Initiatives Indicate Government's Fear of the New Media." *Global Voices* (28 June). http://globalvoicesonline.org/2010/06/28/russia-new-initiatives-indicate-governments-fear-of-the-new-media/ (accessed 13 July 2010).

———. 2011. "Election Day DDoS-alypse." *Global Voices* (5 December). http://www.globalvoicesonline.org/2011/12/05/russia-election-day-ddos-alypse/ (accessed 22 February 2012).

"Sila glasnosti." 1984. *Izvestiia,* 25 May.

Skatov, Nikolai. 1996. "'...i slovo bylo Bog.'" *Nash sovremennik* 9: 153–60.

"Skoraia Lingvisticheskaia." 1974. *Russkaia rech'* 3: 80–83.

Skvortsov, L. I. 1964. "Ob otsenkakh iazyka molodezhi (zhargon i iazykovaia politika)." *Voprosy kul'tury rechi* 5: 45–70.

———. 1969. "Osnovy normalizatsii russkogo iazyka." *Russkaia rech'* 4: 42–51.

———. 1980. *Teoreticheskie osnovy kul'tury rechi.* Moscow: Izdatel'stvo Nauka.

———. 1988. "Kul'tura iazyka i ekologiia iazyka." *Russkaia rech'* 5: 3–9.

———. 1994a. "Iazyk, obshchenie i kul'tura (Ekologiia i iazyk)." *Russkii iazyk v shkole* 1: 81–86.

———. 1994b. "Iazyk, kul'tura i nravstvennost'." *Russkii iazyk v shkole* 2: 100–106.

———. 1994c. "Chto ugrozhaet literaturnomu iazyku? (Razmyshleniia o sostoianii sovremennoi rechi)." *Russkii iazyk v shkole* 5: 99–105.

Slepak, Vladimir. 2012. "Davai vpered, Vladimir Putin!" YouTube (uploaded on 11 January). http://www.youtube.com/watch?v = RNFaHppNrXc (accessed 25 Februrary 2012).

"Sluzhba iazyka." 1965. *Voprosy kul'tury rechi* 6: 196–217.

Solzhenitsyn, A. I. 1990. *Russkii slovar' iazykovogo rasshireniia.* Moscow: Nauka.

"Soveshchanie, posviashchennoe tvorcheskomu naslediiu Akademika N. Ia. Marra." 1945. *Russkii iazyk v shkole* 3: 67–73.

"Sovet po russkomu iazyku pri Prezidente Rossiiskoi Federatsii." 1996. *Russkaia rech'* 4: 52.

Stalin, I. 1950. *Marksizm i voprosy iazykoznaniia.* Moscow: 3-ia tipografiia "Krasnyi proletarii" Glavpoligrafizdata pri Sovete Ministrov SSSR.

Stanovaya, Tatiana. 2013. "Vladimir Putin's 'Indirect Line'." *Institute of Modern Russia* (2 May). http://www.imrussia.org/en/politics/451-vladimir-putins-qindirect-lineq?utm_source=Institute+of+Modern+Russia+newsletter&utm_campaign=136cfb8acf-Newsletter+05%2F03%2F2013_English&utm_medium=email&utm_term=0_279627583b-136cfb8acf-321631577 (accessed 18 July 2013).

Starkova, N. V. 1992. "Imidzh." *Russkaia rech'* 5: 61–62.

Starkovskii, A.M. 1986. "O propagande russkogo iazyka v shkole." *Russkii iazyk v shkole* 2: 34–35.

"Statisticheskie dannye ob obrashcheniiakh grazhdan v khode 'Priamoi linii s Prezidentom Rossii.'" 2006. *Prezident Rossii*. www.kremlin.ru/events/articles/2006/10/112759/113198.html (accessed 8 November 2006).

"Stenogramma priamogo tele- i radioefira ('Priamaia linia s Prezidentom Rossii')." 2001. *Prezident Rossii* (24 December). http://archive.kremlin.ru/text/appears/2001/12/28759.shtml (accessed 26 July 2012).

"Stenogramma priamogo tele- i radioefira ('Priamaia linia s Prezidentom Rossii')." 2002. *Prezident Rossii* (19 December). http://archive.kremlin.ru/text/appears/2002/12/29647.shtml (accessed 26 July 2012).

"Stenogramma priamogo tele- i radioefira ('Priamaia linia s Prezidentom Rossii')." 2003. *Prezident Rossii* (18 December). http://www.archive.kremlin.ru/text/appears/2003/12/57398.shtml (accessed 26 July 2012).

"Stenogramma priamogo tele- i radioefira ('Priamaia linia s Prezidentom Rossii')." 2005. *Prezident Rossii* (27 September). http://www.archive.kremlin.ru/text/appears/2005/09/94308.shtml (accessed 26 July 2012).

"Stenogramma priamogo tele- i radioefira ('Priamaia linia s Prezidentom Rossii')." 2006. *Prezident Rossii* (25 October). http://archive.kremlin.ru/text/appears/2006/10/112959.shtml (accessed 26 July 2012).

"Stenogramma priamogo tele- i radioefira ('Priamaia linia s Prezidentom Rossii')." 2007. *Prezident Rossii* (18 October). http://archive.kremlin.ru/appears/2007/10/18/1259_type82634type146434_148629.shtml (accessed 26 July 2012).

"Stenogramma 'Priamoi linii s Prezidentom Rossii.'" 2002. Moscow, Kremlin (19 December).

"Stenogramma programmy 'Razgovor s Vladimirom Putinym: Prodolzhenie.'" 2011. *Pravitel'stvo Rossiiskoi Federatsii* (15 December). http://premier.gov.ru/events/news/17409/index.html (accessed 6 July 2012).

Stepanov, Anatolii. 1997. "V poiskakh smysla." *Sovetskaia Rossiia*, 4 January.

Stepanov, A., and A. Tolmachev. 1966. *Sputnik oratora*. Moscow: Izdatel'stvo Sovetskaia Rossiia.

Stepanov, Iu. 2004. *Konstanty: Slovar' russkoi kul'tury*. 3rd ed. Moscow: Akademicheskii Proekt.

Strukov, Vlad. 2009. "Russia's Internet Media Policies: Open Space and Ideological Closure." In *The Post-Soviet Russian Media: Conflicting Signals,* edited by Birgit Beumers, Stephen Hutchings, and Natalia Rulyova, 209–22. London: Routledge.

Suhr, Stephanie, and Sally Johnson. 2003. "Re-visiting 'PC': Introduction to Special Issue on 'Political Correctness.'" *Discourse and Society* 14, no. 1: 5–16.

"Sukhoi ostatok." 2011a. "Pil, RosPil, osvoenie. Gosudarstvo, criminal, biznes. Kakim budet final?" *FinamFM* (2 February). http://finam.fm/archive-view/3626/ (accessed 22 February 2012).

"Sukhoi ostatok." 2011b. "'Edinaia Rossiia'—Partiia vorov i korruptsionerov ili chestnykh printsipial'nykh patriotov?" *FinamFM* (23 February). http://finam.fm/archive-view/3719/ (accessed 22 February 2012).

Surkov, Vladislav. 2006. "Natsionalizatsiia Budushchego." *Ekspert* 43 (20 November): 102–8.

Taratuta, Iuliia, and Mikhail Zygar'. 2010. "Vy u nas eshche popishite." *Russkii News-week* 18–19 (26 April–9 May). http://www.runewsweek.ru/country/34013/ (accessed 5 May 2010).

Tekuchev, V. 1937. "Na soveshchanii uchitelei-otlichnikov (Moskva)." *Russkii iazyk v shkole* 1: 120–23.

Theen, Rolf H. W., ed. 1991. *The U.S.S.R. First Congress of People's Deputies: Complete Documents and Records, May 25, 1989-June 10, 1989.* Vols. 1–4. New York: Paragon House.

Thompson, John B. 1991. "Editor's Introduction." In Bourdieu, *Language and Symbolic Power,* 1–31.

Tirmast, Mariia-Luiza. 2004. "'Neobkhodimo opuskat' Edinuiu Rossiiu gde tol'ko mozhno: Oppozitsiia gotovitsia k ulichnoi bor'be s rezhimom." *Kommersant" daily* 188 (8 October): 3.

Trudoliubov, Maksim. 2012. "Chto-to pokhozhee na obshchestvo." *Vedomosti* (3 February). http://friday.vedomosti.ru/article/2012/02/03/18234 (accessed 6 February 2012).

Tumber, Howard. 2001. "Democracy in the Information Age: The Role of the Fourth Estate in Cyberspace." In *Culture and Politics in the Information Age: A New Politics?,* edited by Frank Webster, 17–31. London: Routledge.

Turgenev, Ivan. [1882] 1988. "Russkii iazyk." Quoted in *Russkie poslovitsy, pogovorki i krylatye vyrazheniia: Lingvostranovedcheskii slovar',* edited by E. M. Vereshchagin and V. G. Kostomarov, 174. Moscow: Russkii iazyk.

Ulukhanov, I. S. 1974. "*Russkaia rech'* na golubom ekrane." *Russkaia rech'* 12: 60–66.

Ushakov, D. N., ed. 1935. *Tolkovyi slovar' russkogo iazyka.* Moscow: OGIZ.

Uspenskii, B. A. 1994. *Kratkii ocherk istorii russkogo literaturnogo iazyka (XI–XIX vv.).* Moscow: Gnosis.

———. 1996. "Mifologicheskii aspect russkoi ekspressivnoi frazeologii." In Bogomolov, *Anti-mir russkoi kul'tury,* 9–107.

Vainonen, Nikita. 1997. "Kazhdyi pishet, kak on dyshit." *Zhurnalist* 8: 38–40.

Varichenko, G. V. 1990. "Novaia zhizn' starykh slov." *Russkii iazyk v shkole* 3: 73–76.

Vasil'ev, Vladimir. 1993. "Iazyk nash—vrag vash." *Molodaia gvardiia* 1: 232–42.

"V bor'be za kul'turu rechi uchashchikhsia." 1936. *Russkii iazyk v sovetskoi shkole* 1: 1–40.

"V Gosdumu vnesli zakon o zaprete inostrannykh slov." 2013. *Lenta.ru* (21 February). http://lenta.ru/news/2013/02/21/fine1/ (accessed 5 April 2013).

Vinogradov, Mikhail. 2013. "ONF kak tekhnologiia." *Nezavisimaia* (19 June). http://www.ng.ru/politics/2013-06-19/3_kartblansh.html (accessed 18 July 2013).

Vinokur, G. O. 1923. "Kul'tura iazyka. (Zadachi sovremennogo iazykoznaniia)." *Pechat' i revoliutsiia* 5: 100–111.

———. 1929. *Kul'tura iazyka.* 2nd ed. Moscow: Federatsiia.

———. [1945] 1967. "Iz besed o kul'ture rechi." *Russkaia rech'* 3: 10–14.

"Vladimir Zhirinovskii, kak glavnyi ideolog zakonnogo proekta, predlozhil svoi slovar'." 2013. *Kommersant" FM* (21 February). http://www.kommersant.ru/doc/2132708 (accessed 5 April 2013).

"V mire slov." n. d. *tvmuseum.ru.* http://www.tvmuseum.ru/catalog.asp?ob_no = 6311 (accessed 19 July 2011).

Volin, B. M. 1936. "Bor'ba za gramotnost'—Osnovnaia zadacha shkoly." *Russkii iazyk v sovetskoi shkole* 1: 16–17.

Volkov, Vadim. 1999. "The Concept of *Kul'turnost'*: Notes on the Stalinist Civilizing Process." In *Stalinism: New Directions,* edited by Sheila Fitzpatrick, 210–30. London: Routledge.

Voloshinov, V. N. [1929] 1993. *Marksizm i filosofiia iazyka: Osnovnye problemy sotsiologicheskogo metoda v nauke o iazyke.* Moscow: Labirint.

Voronova, Tat'iana, and Dmitrii Dmitrienko. 2012. "TsB prislal proverku v Viatkabank." *Vedomosti* (14 February). http://www.vedomosti.ru/politics/news/1503650/cb_prislal_proverku_v_vyatkabank (accessed 20 February 2012).

Vorontsova, V. L., and A. I. Sumkina. 1955. "O knigakh po kul'ture rech." *Voprosy kul'tury rechi* 1: 208–20.

Vorotnikov, Iu. L. 2002. "Seminar Soveta po russkomu iazyku pri pravitel'stve Rossiiskoi Federatsii i Mezhdunarodnoi organizatsii frankofonii (Parizh, 1–2 oktiabria 2001 g.)." *Izvestiia RAN.* Seriia literatury i iazyka 3: 73–80.

Vozniuk, L. V. 1986. "Patrioticheskoe vospitanie uchashchikhsia pri rabote nad proizvedeniiami A. P. Gaidara na urokakh russkogo iazyka." *Russkii iazyk v shkole* 6: 10–12.

"V. Putin: 'Priamaia liniia.'" 2007. *Fond "Obshchestvennoe mnenie"* (25 October). http://bd.fom.ru/report/map/projects/dominant/dom0743/d074322 (accessed 5 December 2007).

"V. Putin v priamom efire (elektronnaia focus-gruppa)." 2006. *Fond "Obshchestvennoe mnenie"* (2 November). http://bd/fom.ru/report/map/projects /dominant/dom0643/domt0643_1/d064332 (accessed 12 November 2006).

"V. Putin v priamom teleefire: Otsenki rossiian." 2006. *Vserosiiskii tsentr izucheniia obshchestvennogo mneniia (VTsIOM).* Press release no. 567 (1 November). http://wciom.ru/no_cache/arkhiv/tematicheskii-arkhiv/item/single/3510.html?sHash = 9e64991fa0& print = 1 (accessed 12 November 2006).

"V. Putin v priamom teleefire: Otsenki rossiian." 2007. *VTsIOM.* Press release no. 797 (24 October). http://wciom.ru/novosti/press-vypuski/press-vypusk/single/9020.html?no_cache = 1&cHash = bcb8dbad8d&print = 1 (accessed 18 December 2007).

"Vstrecha s shef-korrespondentami moskovskikh biuro vedushchikh amerikanskikh SMI." 2001. *Prezident Rossii* (10 November). http://archive.kremlin.ru/appears/2001/11/10/0002_type63376type63380type63381_28694.shtml (accessed 29 April 2013).

"Vystuplenie i otvety na voprosy v khode sovmestnoi press-konferentsii s Prezidentom Frantsuzskoi Respubliki Zhakom Shirakom." 2002. *Prezident Rossii* (15 January). http://archive.kremlin.ru/appears/2002/01/15/0002_type63377type63380_28774.shtml (accessed 29 April 2013).

"V zashchitu very i dukha naroda!" 1997. *Literaturnaia Rossiia* 48: 11.

Wiezbiska, Anna. 2001. *Ponimanie kul'tur cherez posredstvo kliuchevykh slov.* Moscow: Iazyki slavianskoi kul'tury.

Williams, Raymond. [1976] 1983. *Keywords: A Vocabulary of Culture and Society.* Rev. ed. New York: Oxford University Press.

Wilson, Andrew. 2005. *Virtual Politics: Faking Democracy in the Post-Soviet World.* New Haven: Yale University Press.

Wood, Elizabeth A. 2005. *Performing Justice: Agitation Trials in Early Soviet Russia.* Ithaca: Cornell University Press.

Woodmansee, Martha, and Mark Osteen, eds. 1999. *The New Economic Criticism: Studies at the Intersection of Literature and Economics.* London: Routledge.

Woolard, Kathryn A. 1998. "Introduction: Language Ideology as a Field of Inquiry." In *Language Ideologies: Practice and Theory,* edited by Bambi B. Schieffelin, Kathryn A. Woolard, and Paul Kroskrity, 3–47. New York: Oxford University Press.

yavleev. 2012. "8 millionov iz biudzheta budet vydeleno na DDOS, vzlom i spam oppozitsionnykh saitov." *yavleev.* 3 February. http://yavleev.livejournal.com/704.html (accessed 21 August 2012).

Yurchak, Alexei. 2006. *Everything Was Forever, Until It Was No More: The Last Soviet Generation.* Princeton: Princeton University Press.

"Zaiavlenie chlenov Soveta v otnoshenii zakonoproekta no. 89417–6 'O vnesenii izmenenii v Federal'nyi zakon "O zashchite detei ot informatsii, prichiniaiushchei vred ikh zdorov'iu i razvitiiu".'" 2012. *Sovet pri Prezidente RF po razvitiiu grazhdanskogo obshchestva i pravam cheloveka.* http://www.president-sovet.ru/council_decision/council_statement/zayavlenie_chlenov_soveta_v_otnoshenii_zakonoproekta_89417_6. php (accessed 10 July 2012).

Zakhvatov, Andrei. 2000. "'Vlast' reshila operetsia na sootechestvennikov," *Russkii zhurnal* (17 November). http://old.russ.ru/politics/partactiv/20001117-pr.html (accessed 9 June 2010).

"Zakon o mitingakh vstupil v silu." 2012. *Lenta.ru* (9 June). http://lenta.ru/news/2012/06/09/inforce/ (accessed 13 July 2012).

"Zashchitu rodnogo slova." 1994. *Moskva* 8: 145–53.

Zassoursky, Ia. N. 2004. *Iskushenie svobodoi: Rossiiskaia zhurnalistika, 1990–2004.* Moscow: Izdatel'stvo Moskovskogo universiteta.

Zelenkov, Aleksandr. 1997. "Retsepty ot *Komsomolki.*" *Komsomol'skaia Pravda* 188 (13 October). http://dlib.eastview.com.lp.hscl.ufl.edu/browse/doc/6686979 (accessed 19 July 2013).

Zhel'vis, Vladimir. 1997. *Pole brani: Skvernoslovie kak sotsial'naia problema.* Moscow: Ladomir.

Zhirnov, Evgenii. 2000. "Pishite, chto khotite, tol'ko ne vrite." *Kommersant"-Vlast'* (13 June).

Zhivov, V. M. 1996. *Iazyk i kul'tura v Rossii XVIII veka.* Moscow: Shkola "Iazyki russkoi kul'tury."

Zhuravleva, Zoia. 1996. "Gorit vo lbu mentalitet." *Literaturnaia gazeta* 23 (6 May): 3.

Zolotusskii, Igor'. 1998. "Russkaia tema: Period romantizma v nashem otechestve slishkom zatianulsia." *Nezavisimaia gazeta,* 16 January.

Zorin, Andrei. 1996. "Legalizatsiia obstsennoi leksiki i ee kul'turnye posledstviia." In Bogomolov, *Anti-mir russkoi kul'tury,* 121–39.

Zvereva, Vera. 2012. *Setevye razgovory: Kul'turnye kommunikatsii v Runete.* Slavica Bergensia 10. Bergen, Norway: Slavica Bergensia.

Zvereva, Vera, and Aleksandrs Berdicevskis. Forthcoming, 2014. "Substandard Varieties or 'The True Story of Olbanian Language.'" In Gorham, Lunde, and Paulsen, *Digital Russia*.

Zykov, Vladimir. 2012. "Zakon o chernykh spiskakh v Seti ne budet rabotat'." *Izvestiia* (11 July). http://izvestia.ru/news/530114 (accessed 16 July 2012).

INDEX